Politics and Governance in Indonesia

How does an authoritarian state reform its police force following a transition to democracy? In 1998, Indonesia, one of the biggest archipelago countries in the world, faced just such a challenge. Policing had long been managed under the jurisdiction of the military, as an instrument of the Suharto regime – and with Suharto abruptly removed from office, this was about to change. Here we see how it changed, and how far these changes were for the better.

Based on direct observations by a scholar who was involved in the last days of the New Order and who saw how the police responded to regime change, this book examines the police, the new regime and how the police became disassociated from the military in Indonesia. Providing a comprehensive historical overview of the position of police in this change of regime, the book focuses on two key areas: the differences between local and national levels, and the politicization associated with decentralization. Arguing that the disassociation of the Indonesian National Police from the military has achieved only limited success, the book contends that there is continued impetus for the establishment of a professional police force and modern and democratic policing, which will entail effective public control of the police.

A pioneering study of the police in Indonesia, examining key issues in the post-Suharto era, this book will be of interest to scholars of Southeast Asian politics and policing and politics in the developing world.

Muradi received his PhD from Flinders University, Australia. He is Senior Lecturer in the Department of Government, Faculty of Political and Social Sciences at the University of Padjadjaran, Jatinangor, Indonesia.

Rethinking Southeast Asia
Edited by Duncan McCargo
University of Leeds, UK

Southeast Asia is a dynamic and rapidly-changing region which continues to defy predictions and challenge formulaic understandings. This series publishes cutting-edge work on the region, providing a venue for books that are readable, topical, interdisciplinary and critical of conventional views. It aims to communicate the energy, contestations and ambiguities that make Southeast Asia both consistently fascinating and sometimes potentially disturbing.

This series comprises two strands:

Titles which address the needs of students and teachers, published in both hardback and paperback. Titles include:

Rethinking Vietnam
Duncan McCargo

Rethinking Southeast Asia is also a forum for innovative new research intended for a more specialist readership, published in hardback only. Titles include:

1 **Politics and the Press in Thailand**
   Media machinations
   Duncan McCargo

2 **Democracy and National Identity in Thailand**
   Michael Kelly Connors

3 **The Politics of NGOs in Indonesia**
   Developing democracy and managing a movement
   Bob S. Hadiwinata

4 **Military Politics and Democratization in Indonesia***
   Jun Honna

5 **Changing Political Economy of Vietnam**
   The case of Ho Chi Minh City
   Martin Gainsborough

6 **Living at the Edge of Thai Society**
The Karen in the Highlands of Northern Thailand
Claudio O. Delang

7 **Thailand Beyond the Crisis**
Peter Warr

8 **Virtual Thailand**
Media and culture politics in Thailand, Malaysia and Singapore
Glen Lewis

9 **Decentralization and *Adat* Revivalism in Indonesia**
The politics of becoming indigenous
Adam D. Tyson

10 **Truth on Trial in Thailand**
Defamation, treason, and lèse-majesté
David Streckfuss

11 **Civil Society in the Philippines**
Theoretical, methodological and policy debates
Gerard Clarke

12 **Politics and Governance in Indonesia**
The police in the era of *reformasi*
Muradi

* Now available in paperback

Politics and Governance in Indonesia
The police in the era of *reformasi*

Muradi

Routledge
Taylor & Francis Group
LONDON AND NEW YORK

First published 2014
by Routledge

2 Park Square, Milton Park, Abingdon, Oxfordshire OX14 4RN
711 Third Avenue, New York, NY 10017

Routledge is an imprint of the Taylor & Francis Group, an informa business

First issued in paperback 2017

Copyright © 2014 Muradi

The right of Muradi to be identified as author of this work has been asserted by him in accordance with sections 77 and 78 of the Copyright, Designs and Patents Act 1988.

All rights reserved. No part of this book may be reprinted or reproduced or utilised in any form or by any electronic, mechanical, or other means, now known or hereafter invented, including photocopying and recording, or in any information storage or retrieval system, without permission in writing from the publishers.

Notice:
Product or corporate names may be trademarks or registered trademarks, and are used only for identification and explanation without intent to infringe.

British Library Cataloguing in Publication Data
A catalogue record for this book is available from the British Library

Library of Congress Cataloging in Publication Data
Muradi, author.
Politics and governance in Indonesia : the police in the era of reformasi / Muradi.
   pages cm. – (Rethinking Southeast Asia ; 12)
   Includes bibliographical references and index.
   1. Police–Indonesia. 2. Police–Political activity–Indonesia. 3. Police corruption–Indonesia. 4. Police professionalization–Indonesia.
5. Indonesia. Kepolisian. 6. Indonesia–Politics and government–1998–
7. Democratization–Indonesia. I. Title.
   HV8254.A2M873 2014
   363.209598–dc23
                                                      2013047749

ISBN: 978-0-415-71371-9 (hbk)
ISBN: 978-0-8153-7472-5 (pbk)

Typeset in Times New Roman
by Wearset Ltd, Boldon, Tyne and Wear

Contents

List of figures   ix
List of tables   x
Preface   xi
Glossary and abbreviations   xiii

Introduction: the transition to democracy and the police – theories and the case of Indonesia   1

PART I
Historical legacies and early *reformasi*   17

1 The police in Sukarno's era: from colonial state to the overthrow of the Guided Democracy state   19

2 Under the thumb: the police during Suharto's New Order and early *reformasi*   35

PART II
***Reformasi* and its effect on the police**   53

3 Politicization of the police: the struggle over control during the Wahid presidency   55

4 Developing a more independent and professional police force   67

PART III
Consolidation, development and corruption 79

5 Resolving the divisive issues of the rival chiefs and the Group of Eight — 81

6 Corruption in the police — 93

PART IV
Local government perspectives 105

7 Cosmetic changes: roles of the police in local areas — 107

8 The budget, local politics and jealousy — 116

9 Politicization — 123

PART V
Local police perspectives 135

10 Internal conflicts and the effect of extortion — 137

11 The police budget and extortion — 147

Conclusion: disassociation and reform – the position and relationships of the police in post-Suharto Indonesia — 158

Bibliography 175
Index 187

Figures

I.1   The level of police independence and professionalism   6
I.2   The models of separation of the police from the military   9
I.3   The degree of political support for separation of the police from the military   9

Tables

I.1	Comparison of models of police roles post-disassociation	10
I.2	Comparison of models of relationships between the police, the government and the military post-disassociation	13
2.1	Changing the Polri paradigm	43
2.2	Chiefs of the Polri, 1945–2008	45
4.1	Ratio between Polri officers and population at the national and selected provincial levels	69
4.2	The Polri budget, 1998–2008	70
4.3	Changes in the Polri post-disassociation, 1999–2009	74
6.1	Characteristics, patterns and models of corruption and extortion practices and abuse of authority in the Polri post-disassociation	95
6.2	Polri business activities post-disassociation	100
10.1	Kickbacks in police recruitment and education in West Java Polda post-disassociation	139
10.2	Kickbacks for promotion and position in West Java Polda post-disassociation	142
11.1	The contributions of the participation schemes to operational Polres budgets in West Java Polda post-disassociation	149
11.2	Tariffs for brokers in six polres in West Java	152
11.3	Prices of fixers of some services in six polres in West Java Polda post-disassociation	153

Preface

This book was conceived due to the lack of comprehensive studies related to the police and politics in post-Suharto Indonesia, and developed over a ten-year period of work in the field of police studies. Based on direct observations by a scholar who was involved in the last days of the New Order and saw how the police responded to regime change, this book examines the police, the new regime, and how the police became disassociated from the military in Indonesia.

A great number of people have assisted my research for this book, both direct and indirectly. The first "Big Three" were scholars who had a great influence on my scholarly and personal development during my PhD study: Jim Schiller, Priyambudi Sulistiyanto and Anton Lucas, all at Flinders University in Adelaide, Australia. Their patience and expertise encouraged me to become a skeptical scholar; they acted as as 'outsiders' overseeing what I was doing in order to make my research more valuable and objective. These three scholars gave so many new angles and critical approaches that made me see the police from a local perspective, as part of a long process of disassociation from the armed forces. Anton Lucas also provided critical input on early drafts of this book and always reminded me that the strength of the book is what happened at the local level. Priyambudi Sulistiyanto also reminded me that continuity between sections of this book should provide a new perspective for the study of policing in post-Suharto Indonesia.

Other scholars, analysts, journalists, and NGO activists have also contributed to this study through both short meetings and long discussions, mostly in Jakarta and Bandung coffee shops or meeting places. Liz Morrell, Malcolm Cook, Roger Wiseman, Rossi Von Der Vorch, Leonard Sebastian, Rohan Gunaratna, Bill Liddle, David Henley, Erwin Schweisshelm, Gerald Heuett, David Jansen and Srisombat Cocprajakchat have shared important information and analyses with me. Other scholars of Indonesia and NGO activists who have shared their knowledge and expertise with me include Andi Widjadjanto, Cornelis Lay, Makmur Keliat, Adrianus Meliala, Neta S. Pane, Monica Tanuhandaru, Mufti Makarim, Beni Sukadis, Bambang Widodo Umar, Zakarias Poerba, Alfons Leomau, Ikrar Nusa Bhakti, Kusnanto Anggoro, J. Kristiadi, Jaleswari Pringgodhani and Eddy Prasetyono. I also would like to thank Budhiana Kartawijaya, Toto Suwarto and their networks, which provided access to databases of local newspaper clippings.

In the police, several generals have devoted considerable time to my research on their institution, most notably General Awaluddin Djamin, General Chaeruddin Ismail, General Timur Pradopo, Commissary General Nanan Sukarna, Commissary General Sutarman, Commissary General Adang Daradjatun, Commissary General E. Winarto, the late Inspector General Wik Jatmika, Inspector General Ronny Lihawa, Inspector General Andi Chaeruddin, Inspector General Farouk Muhammad, Inspector General Paulus Purwoko, Inspector General Tito Karnavian and the late Inspector General Firman Gani. In addition, many local police chiefs, local regents and mayors from regencies and municipalities in West Java province were always prepared to discuss the role of the police and policing problems in their jurisdictions.

I would like to thank Dorothea Schaefter and Jillian Morison at Routledge in England for helping me throughout the process of publishing this book. Their patience and commitment have provided indispensable technical guidance for me. Special thanks are due to Professor Duncan McCargo, the editor of the 'Rethinking Southeast Asia' series, who has provided valuable inputs to make this book more focused and appealing, and to allow readers to understand its arguments better.

At the School of Politics and International Studies of the Flinders Asia Centre, Robin Shepherdson, Tracey Kohl and Michele Lang also helped with various technical and administrative matters associated with my PhD thesis, which formed the basis of this book.

I would also like to express my gratitude to my colleagues in the Department of Government of the Faculty of Social and Political Sciences of Padjadjaran University, Jatinangor, Indonesia, which has provided support and permitted me to proceed to my doctoral programme after completing the master's programme at S. Rajaratnam School of International Studies Nanyang Technological University, Singapore. These include the Dean of the Faculty of Social and Political Sciences of Padjadjaran University, Professor Dr Asep Kartiwa; the Rector of Padjadjaran University, Prof. Dr Ganjar Kurnia; and also the Deputy Rector, Dr Setiawan.

I am also indebted to my parents who always pray for my health and the safety of their children. Only 25 years ago, the idea that I might become a scholar with a higher degree was only a fantasy and bedtime story for me. It has now become true. Finally I would like to express my greatest appreciation to my wife, Alia Maharani, and my children, Bryanna and Alvaro, for their willingness to support my ambitious and unpredictable life. Their love is immeasurable.

Glossary and abbreviations

ABRI	Angkatan Bersenjata Republik Indonesia – Indonesian armed forces
Akpol	Akademi Kepolisian – police academy
AKRI	Angkatan Kepolisian Republik Indonesia – Indonesian police forces
AMS	Angkatan Muda Siliwangi – Siliwangi Young Generation
APBD	anggaran pendapatan belanja daerah – local annual budget
APRA	Angkatan Perang Ratu Adil – Legions of the Just King
Babinkamtibmas	Bintara Pembina Keamanan dan Ketertiban Masyarakat – Indonesian police NCO for security and order at village level
Babinsa	Bintara Pembina Desa – Indonesian military NCO at village level
Bakesbangpol Linmas	Badan Kesatuan Bangsa, Politik, dan Perlindungan Masyarakat – Agency for National Unity, Politics, and Public Safety
BAKIN	Badan Koordinasi Intelijen Negara – State Intelligence Coordinating Board
Bakorstranas	Badan Koordinasi Bantuan Pemantapan Stabilitas dan Ketahanan Nasional – National Stability and Resilience Coordinating Board
Bareskrim	Badan Reserse dan Kriminal – Criminal Investigation Bureau
Bhayangkara	Indonesian term for the Indonesian National Police (INP)
BPI	Badan Pusat Intelijen – Central Intelligence Board/Agency
Brimob	Brigade Mobil – mobile brigade, police paramilitary unit
Bupati	district head – regent
Dekonsentrasi	semi-autonomy
Densus 88 AT	Detasemen Khusus 88 Anti Terror – Anti-Terror Special Detachment 88

Dewan Konstituante	Constitutional Assembly
DKP	Dewan Kehormatan Perwira – Officers' Honour Board
DPR	Dewan Perwakilan Rakyat – national parliament
DPRD	Dewan Perwakilan Rakyat Daerah – district or provincial assembly
Dukop	Dukungan Operasi – Operational Support Fund
Imparsial	Indonesian human rights monitor
Inkopol	Induk Koperasi Polisi – Polri HQ main cooperative
INP	Indonesian National Police – Kepolisian Negara Republik Indonesia
IPW	Indonesian Police Watch
Kamdagri	keamanan dalam negeri – internal or domestic security
Kapolda	kepala kepolisian daerah – head of provincial police
Kodim	Komando Distrik Militer – military district command
Kominda	komunitas intelijen daerah – local intelligence community
Kompolnas	Komisi Kepolisian Nasional – Indonesian National Police Commission
Kontras	Komisi untuk Orang Hilang dan Korban Tindak Kekerasan – Commission for the Disappeared and Victims of Violence
Kopkamtib	Komando Pemulihan Keamanan dan Ketertiban – Command for the Restoration of Security and Order
Koramil	Komando Rayon Militer – sub-district military command
Korem	Komando Resort Militer – military sub-regional command
KPK	Komisi Pemberantasan Korupsi – Corruption Eradication Commission
Lantas	lalulintas – traffic
Markus	makelar kasus – case trader
MPR	Majelis Permusyawaratan Rakyat – People's Consultative Assembly (upper house of Indonesian parliament)
Murba	Musyawarah Rakyat Banyak – Indonesian leftist party established by Tan Malaka
Muspida	musyawarah pimpinan daerah – local leaders' forum
NU	Nahdlatul Ulama – traditional Muslim organization in Indonesia
PAN	Partai Amanat National – National Mandate Party
Parman	partisipasi teman – friendship participation
Parmas	partisipasi masyarakat – public participation
Parmin	partisipasi kriminal – mafia or criminal participation
PBB	Partai Bulan Bintang – Star Moon Crescent Party
PDIP	Partai Demokrasi Indonesia Perjuangan – Indonesian Democratic Party of Struggle

PKB	Partai Kebangkitan Bangsa – National Awakening Party
PKI	Partai Komunis Indonesia – Indonesian Communist Party
PNI	Partai Nasional Indonesia – Indonesian National Party
Polda	kepolisian daerah – provincial police
Polres	kepolisian resort – district or municipality police
Polri	Kepolisian Negara Republik Indonesia – Indonesian National Police
Polsek	kepolisian sektor – precinct or sub-district police
Polwan	polisi wanita – police women
PPP	Partai Persatuan Pembangunan – United Development Party
Propam	Profesi dan Pengamanan – Professional Ethics Division
PSP	Persatuan Sekerja Polisi – Police Workers' Union
PT.	perseroan terbatas – private limited company
PTIK	Perguruan Tinggi Ilmu Kepolisian – police university
P3RI	Persatuan Pegawai Polisi Republik Indonesia – Police Officials' Union of the Republic of Indonesia
Reformasi	reform
Rekonfu	Rencana, Konsolidasi, dan Fungsi – Plan of Consolidation and Function
Renstra	perencanaan strategis – strategic planning
Reskrim	Reserse And Kriminal – criminal investigation unit
RIS	Republik Indonesia Serikat – United States of Indonesia
Satpol PP	Satuan Polisi Pamong Praja – municipal police
SELAPA	Sekolah Lanjutan Perwira – advanced police school
SEPA	Sekolah Perwira – police inspector candidate school
SESPATI	Sekolah Staf dan Perwira Tinggi – school for police staff and higher-ranking commanders
SESPIM	Sekolah Staf dan Pimpinan – school for police staff and chiefs
TNI	Tentara Nasional Indonesia – Indonesian National Army
UUD 1945	Undang-undang Dasar 1945 – Constitution (Basic Laws) of 1945
Wanjakti	Dewan Kepangkatan dan Jabatan Tinggi – Police Promotion Board
Wedana	(Dutch colonial era) district police chief
Yayasan	foundation
YLBHI	Yayasan Lembaga Bantuan Hukum Indonesia – The Indonesian Legal Aid Institute Foundation

Introduction
The transition to democracy and the police – theories and the case of Indonesia

Background

How does an authoritarian state reform its police force following a transition to democracy? In 1998, Indonesia, one of the biggest archipelago countries in the world, faced just such a challenge. Policing had long been managed under the jurisdiction of the military, as an instrument of the Suharto regime – and with Suharto abruptly removed from office, this was about to change. How it changed, and how far these changes were for the better, is the subject of this book.

For over half a century the Indonesian police (Polri: Kepolisian Negara Republik Indonesia) had been cooperating, conflicting, and integrating as a single institution with Indonesia's armed forces (ABRI).[1] Since its disassociation from the military to become a separate security agency in 2002, Polri has been trying to be involved in and deal with concepts of democratic policing and civilian police.[2] The Polri has had problems in its internal culture and with some of its violent approaches in the past, including when it was used as a scapegoat by the military and other political guardians of the New Order regime.

The fall of Suharto's New Order regime, which ruled Indonesia for 32 years, pushed the Polri to come out from that situation. The disassociation of the Polri from the ABRI was a signal for the Polri to become a professional and independent institution. Polri published the 'Blue Book of the Polri' (*Buku Biru Reformasi Polri*), a formal document intended to be used as guidance for its internal reform.[3] The book's content was a product of the Working Group for Polri Reform, made up of middle- and higher-ranking police officers.[4]

Although the Polri's involvement in the Indonesian democratic transition was a good note in Indonesian history, the Polri's proposed roles could not be put into practice at that point, as the Polri was still under the shadow of the military.[5] A working group formed by President Habibie in 1998 initiated the actual Polri reform.[6] This group, led by Agus Wirahadikusumah (army) and Sofyan Jacoeb (police),[7] was mandated to compile a concept for the internal reform of the Polri after its disassociation from the ABRI. Its legal umbrella was a decree of the Majelis Permusyawaratan Rakyat (People's Consultative Assembly or MPR: the upper house of the Indonesian parliament), MPR Decree No. X/MPR/1998, mandating reform in the legal sector by strictly disassociating the roles and functions, and also the authority, of law enforcement actors in order to achieve proportionality, professionalism and integrity.[8]

As a national police force, the Polri was to be an indivisible part of efforts to maintain sovereignty of state in the context of internal security affairs (Keamanan Dalam Negeri, known as Kamdagri),[9] along with maintaining security and public order. The formulation of policy related to the security of regions has a top-down character, although based on local characteristics.[10] The hierarchical structure of the Polri is related to that of the overall national state administrative system, and to that of the previous ABRI and continuing military territorial organization.[11] Starting from the lowest level there are precincts (polsek) located in sub-districts; police offices (polres) located in districts (more rural) or municipalities (urban); sub-regional police offices (polwil) in charge of directing several district or municipality police offices; and provincial police offices (polda) located in the capital of each province.

One consequence of the reform was active steps to strengthen the potency of local personnel with the principle of "local boys for local jobs". This become the Polri's choice to meet requirements of human resources based on capability, comprehending local characteristics, understanding local society, and being accepted by the local public. However, the law at the time did not accommodate the idea of development of local resources for local police leaders. Law No. 2/2002 on the Polri asserts in its Article 5, point 2 that the Polri is a national police.[12] Therefore the policy of "local boys for local jobs" was only legitimated officially several years later in 2005 by Decision of Chief of the Polri, in 2005–2009 Strategic Plan (Renstra) No. Pol. 20/IX/2005, and then renewed by Decree of Chief of the Polri No. Pol. 9/IV/2007, and again by Decree of Chief of the Polri No. Pol. Kep/37/X/2008 on the Polri Transformation Program toward a Professional and Independent Police.[13]

It is important to research the post-Suharto reform of Polri, considering that there are major problems both internal and external continuing to haunt the processes of the Polri as a national police. The internal problems include its institutional culture; the financial security of its personnel; the lack of funding from the state; rivalries; and inadequate support from the leadership, personnel skills and tools of the police officers. The external problems include the Polri's relations with the TNI (Tentara Nasional Indonesia – Indonesian National Army) and local governments, and corruption and illegal income from criminal and immoral activities and institutions such as extortion, prostitution, gambling and drug cartels.

The time frame 1998–2008 is selected here as appropriate for studying the Polri, for three reasons. First, 1998 was the beginning of the opportunity for the Polri to come out from the shadow of the military. When Suharto was ousted from the presidency, the Polri had a chance to follow the political and social changes such as the people's demands to separate the Polri from the ABRI, as part of the *reformasi* (reform) agenda.

Second, the period 1998–2008 is an important time to evaluate the Polri in its first decade as the major state actor in internal security. The aim of disassociating the Polri from the ABRI was to make both institutions more professional in carrying out their specified functions.

Third, the period 1998–2008 provides a sufficient time span to examine how that intended process of decentralization is running. The role of the Polri in internal security relates to the roles of local government; hence, the process of decentralization and the position of the Polri post-disassociation were intended to involve similar processes and be interrelated.

The aim of this book is to discuss how the process of the Polri's disassociation from the ABRI has been working, and the impacts from that process for the Polri and its relationship with the national government, the military and local government. Institutionally, those institutions may have influenced the Polri in different ways. The influences could be happening from the top, through relationship among the leaders, and downwards through interaction among personnel.

This book also investigates patterns of relations between the Polri and the other institutions on two approaches: the process of political influences and the extension of authority in the form of decentralization. The book will also examine the democratization of Indonesian society and the role of the Polri in this, the extent to which the Polri has demonstrated that professionalism is part of the effort to strengthen democratization process. Another issue addressed in this book is the impact that the disassociation of the Polri from the ABRI has had inside the Polri, and how the Polri as a security actor has been using the authorities for the benefit of the institution itself and its personnel, while reforming its own institution.[14]

A local perspective

The research for this book took multiple case-study approaches where unique features of the cases were made available to be scrutinized. The Indonesian province of West Java was selected as the case study site, for three reasons. First, West Java has an important position in geopolitics as a security barometer for the capital of Indonesia, Jakarta. Second, because of its strategic position, many Polri officers hope to be assigned or positioned in regencies and municipality police offices in West Java province. Third, West Java is also adjacent to Central Java and Banten Provinces, and there is busy national economic traffic on the North Java Coast Road around which the police behaviour are active.

This book aims to depict comprehensively how the Polri in the post-Suharto era have faced various problems and attitudes in managing expectations and in the handling of cases, which have affected their public image. There have been complex problems moving towards democratic approaches, paying attention to public rights, and avoiding corrupt activities such as bribery and extortion – notably in six districts and municipalities of West Java Province: Bandung and Cirebon Municipalities, Cirebon, Garut, Tasikmalaya, and Ciamis Districts.

The police, state and society

According to O'Connor, the police are assumed to be 'guard labour' (people paid to enforce the rules on others) to maintain the power of the state and capital owners.[15] He also states that the police profession is part of state and capital owners' interests, and a labour force in security matters, so are positioned as part of the labour class: not the ruling capital-owning class but serving their interests. Modern capitalism has produced two dimensions of division in the police organization: vertical, between subordinates and superiors; and horizontal, between police roles and specializations.[16]

According to Marenin, both are unlocked in issues of police organization, because of their relation to the structure of power and politics or to public pressure.[17] Similarly, Ake, using cases from African countries, depicts the relation between the state and the police, and also society, as assumed power relations between classes.[18]

Hogg and Findlay describe professional police as the police acting clearly in their roles as the collectors, definers, maintainers and disseminators of criminal justice information, and as being able to enhance a specialist or professional position by cordoning off crucial areas of knowledge.[19] One of the characteristic of a professional police force is that it should be independent in its role and function, independence being defined as having individual discretionary ability that is recognized and relied upon.

Edwards stated three factors that make the police in modern society effective in terms of controlling the society: the lawful power of the police; the structure of the police; and the organized nature of the police.[20] The effectiveness of the police in controlling the life of modern society is also affirmed by commitment to individual freedom, effective participation in society by the police, and the principle of no discrimination and no person being above the law. There are at least three sensitive issues for the police:

> Firstly, the police can only enforce the law as it stands, not as the public or they might prefer it to be, and conversely they have the duty to enforce the law as it stands and not ignore inconvenient or unpalatable issues. Secondly, the police must enforce the law using the powers granted them under the law, and as prosecutors or investigators for the prosecution, they must assemble sufficient evidence in a form which is acceptable to the courts. Thirdly, the arbiters of whether the police powers are used correctly and lawfully and whether the evidence is legally acceptable are the judges and magistrates of the courts themselves.
>
> (Edwards, 2005: 18)

Critchley describes the existence of the police related to the process of liberalization in a society with a strong tradition of democracy. The police tend to be instructed by and under control of political authority in the context of democracy. The police give security for society and invite society to be actively involved in protecting their own property and also the environment against threat of crime.[21] Bayley and Travis also depict the police as the most visible manifestation of government authority performing the most obvious, immediate and intrusive tasks to ensure the well-being of individuals and communities alike.[22]

Hills has a different view from that of Bayley and Travis. Hills depicts the police as an integrated part of society, and therefore not in a neutral zone upholding the law or being a prosecutor. There is a dynamic between political influences inside the police, the interests of the ruling government, and the personal ambition of the police officers.[23] In general, the interest of a ruling government in the police is in the form of gaining and maintaining police support, institutionally, for the extension of its power.

Democratic policing

According to Bailey and Dammert, and to Bruce and Nield, democratic policing is defined as a policing in democratic countries where practices must be in accordance to the norms usually held in democratic countries. The police must have top operational priority to serve the needs of individual citizens and private groups; must be accountable to the law rather than the government; must protect human rights, especially those that are required for the sort of unfettered political activity that is the hallmark of democracy; and should be transparent in their activity.[24]

The important dimensions of the differences in position of the police in democratic countries are: centralization or autonomy; specialist versus generalist; internal versus external control; distance between police and power; maximum or minimum discretion; and single versus lateral entries. The variation of democratic policing in democratic countries depends on the characteristic of their people and constitutions.

The process during which an authoritarian regime becomes a democratic one is called a 'democratic transition'. According to Linz and Stepan, the process of democratic transition is complete when sufficient agreement has been reached about political procedures to produce an elected government; when a government comes to power as the direct result of a free and popular vote; when this government de facto has the authority to generate new policies; and when the executive, legislative and judicial power generated by the new democracy does not have to share power with other bodies *de jure*.[25]

In democratic regimes, the position of the police is no longer as a representative of the regime or under the subordination of the military, as it is in authoritarian regimes.[26] In addition, the position of the police is also equivalent to that of the military, so an effort to reposition the police under military control would be relatively closed by control mechanisms and oversight of the parliament and the public directly.[27]

In addition, in a democratic regime interventions and politicization of the police sometimes occurs, with the police and the military invited by the regime to support its power in order to hold on to power as long as possible.[28] An important element of these contexts is that the presence of state actors in security roles, particularly the police, tend to be vulnerable to public pressure to be better at carrying out roles and functions as security agencies.[29] There also may be opportunities in a democratic regime for some police officers to promote their careers in a synergistic situation provided by military or government intervention into the internal dynamics of the police.[30]

In a context of democratic transition, the relationship between the police, the government and the military can vary. Most government efforts to intervene are over three things: the appointment of police leaders; asking for police support to maintain the security of power; and building a balance of power, especially against pressure from the military.[31] Most efforts by the military to intervene in the police are for five reasons: demands from the president to support the police in fighting crime; institutional sentiment; the police being disassociated from the military but not yet consolidated; police officers being better provided for than the military personnel; and the ability of police administrators in operational matters post-disassociation being considered not good enough.[32] Military intervention in the police during democratic transition can be in three forms; through legislation; through political policies; and through military coups.[33]

The police and politics in developing countries

The police in developing countries have varied levels of professionalism and independence in their roles and functions, with the intervention of those in power, the military, and politics being indicators of this. Police independence and professionalism can be divided into three levels (see Figure I.1).

Level 3 is a good position, when the police have low intervention from political power and the military, and police independence and professionalism in upholding the law can be ascertained objectively.

Level 2 is a middle position, where there is intervention from the government and the military but at the same time the police try to be an objective institution when they take in hand cases related to the government or the military.

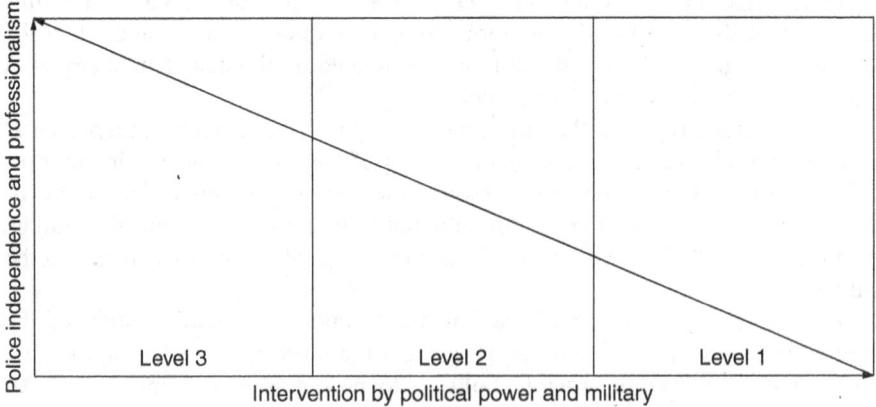

Figure I.1 The level of police independence and professionalism.

Level 1 is the low position of objectivity and professionalism, in which the police are closer to the power of politics and there is a high influence of the military in its decision-making.

This simple scale is provided to highlight how police in developing countries are less independent and professional not just in their organization but in their practices than those in developed and democratic countries. The choice for many police institutions in developing countries, especially those with military or other authoritarian regimes, is the option of following the policy of the political power.[34]

Potholm highlighted that although police in developing countries might be able to cope with refusing and extending themselves away from political influence of the military and the regime, opportunities and actions influenced by both the latter might still be available through discretion and investigation. Potholm also indicated that intervention by political power and the influence of the military also happened during recruitment and promotion.[35]

A problem that emerges from Potholm's argument is that intervention happens through more than simply the political responsibility of the police; there may also be a desire to control and finally subdue police personnel to preserve political or military power. The police in developing countries may be involved in non-legal enforcement duties but also could be in a position to be at the front line for a shaking-up of the regime. Besides, police roles tend to overlap with military roles so that in some states with a poor tradition of democracy having been coopted by a military regime, communist, or authoritarian leaders, the police become part of the military structure.[36]

Applying Potholm's argument, Hills proposed three elementary systems of police structure in African nations and more generally in developing countries: first, a war-born system, with a police structure following the pattern of the organizational system at the moment the police were fighting against colonization; second, a converted system, where the police structure and system is a switchover to a new system, different to the one before, either from conflict or colonization; third, an evolved system, where the police system was formed long before conflict or the independence war. The formation of a police system before conflict gives more opportunity for a political authority to influence and control the police in order to maintain its power.[37]

Hills and Potholm realize that political interference and military intervention in the police in developing countries was a reality and difficult to argue against. It is not surprising the police should accept social and political influences from the environment around the institution. Changes that happen are likely to be pushed by social and political situations.[38] Hills proposed four concepts summarizing the practical problems faced by the police in developing countries: civil order; civil-military relations; governance; and reconstruction.

In terms of civil order, the role and function of the police are as in the international police force, combining the readiness of internal police and the actual environment encountered. While the situation of civil-military relations continues, the police system develops as a combination of civilian and military functions with two roles: maintaining public order and security, and maintaining political stability for the regime. The last concept, reconstruction, applies to the police position in its transition from non-professional and non-civilian police to democratic policing in civilian and professional ways. This context is associated with countries post-conflict, and/or in post-authoritarian regimes, in which the police had been part of the old regime and the military.

Disassociation of the police from the military

Hills depicted the police in developing countries as a critical institution in supporting the democratization process against anarchy and corruption.[39] Tanner, in proposing three phases or stages in the transition to democracy in developing countries, also suggested associated perspectives for testing the police position during each of these stages. First, in the negotiating stage of the transition from authoritarian rule, the police might be viewed as strategic actors, liable to play an ambivalent part in defending the reform movement. Second, during the transition phase itself, the police are seen as an organization undergoing change 'besieged by the dilemmas of changing their behavioural norms, organization and control-oversight mechanisms to accommodate the new system'. And third, in the phase of consolidation, the police and society have to reconcile present and past human abuses.[40]

In the first phase, the police are positioned as an institution, which actively and passively conducts negotiations with the regime. However, in most cases, this negotiation tends to be actively conducted by the military rather than the police.[41] Bayley, in his statement on the police position in a change of politics, asserted that the police formally do not conduct efforts to develop political bargaining with the regime, but remain running the function of taking care of order and security, so that the position of the police does not reside in the effort of developing the institution as its target in politics.[42]

In the second phase, the police try to adapt to the changing situation of politics. One approach is to get use to being observed politically by society and parliament. In most cases, the format of the police tends to follow the existing governmental format: unitary or federal. Usually, the change of police at this phase happens under observation or oversight by parliament and public, rather than altering its institutional format, which would risk disturbing its internal consolidation. This issue is caused by influences from the old regime, by coordination of relationships and functions between the police and local government, and by overlaps with the roles of the military.[43]

In the third phase, the police confess all mistakes in the past, especially in acts of violence against human rights. Tanner asserts that in this phase, reconciliation between the police and society will emerge. Police leaders will allow judicial investigation of human rights abuses to check and judge all personnel who are assumed to have made mistakes and to punish them with what are seen as appropriate penalties.

According to Kalmanowiecki, Hinton and Beltran, the patterns of disassociation of the police from the military follow five models (see Figures I.2 and I.3). First, disassociation of the police from the military confirms the existence of a

Figure I.2 The models of separation of the police from the military.

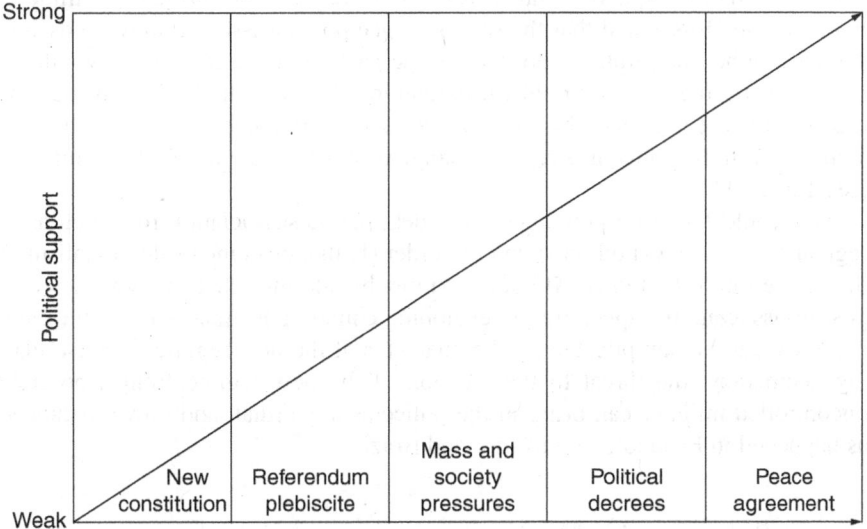

Figure I.3 The degree of political support for separation of the police from the military.

new constitution, where before there was one which did not regulate the composition of the police and the military and more specifically did not regulate how they were to be structured.

The second model is disassociation of the police from the military through a referendum or plebiscite, in which the society's voice is made the basis for the future of a professional and democratic police agency. The cost of implementation of such a separate referendum is not cheap, and it is also a political process that directly involves the community at large. Therefore it can only be done in a state with a size and population that are not too large.

The third model is disassociation of the police from the military because of pressure from the masses and civil society. The crucial element of this model is that it is mass pressure that affects the internal operations of the police.

The fourth model is through political decrees. In some contexts the state performs the separation through a political decision after the fall of an authoritarian regime, by means of a presidential decree, a parliamentary decree or established law.

The fifth model is the disassociation being the result of a peace agreement between the government and rebels or oppositions. The fragility of this model is the bond of the peace agreement and how strong the ties are between the factions or groups in conflict.

Role of the police post-disassociation

Disassociation is characterized by the changing role of the police. However, these changes in role do not necessarily lead to a professional role for the police force, which has expanded into roles that were once performed by military. Potholm and Hills stated that the role of police post-disassociation was possibly similar to what the military had done in the past regime, and that this would be reinforced by the stronger political bargaining power of the police in the new regime. They elaborated this possibility as part of the evolution or the role adjustment of the police in a regime change post-disassociation from the military (see Table I.1).

This could lead to a permanent and ideal post-disassociation role such as in regulatory activities (Potholm), in civil order (Hills), or in the professionalism of the police (author's term). Although it must be admitted that the role of police post-disassociation, especially in developing countries in Asia, Africa and Latin America, can be complicated by the character of the new regime in consolidating democracy, the threat to the creation of the new regime from a possibly uncontrolled military can bring in the police as a guardian and power balancer, as happened in Ecuador, El Salvador and Brazil.[44]

Table I.1 Comparison of models of police roles post-disassociation

Potholm
Regulatory activities – maintenance of law and order – paramilitary – represent regime
Hills
Civil order – governance – civil-military relations – reconstruction
Author
Professionals – power balance – extortion activities – political guardian

The roles of regime representation (Potholm), reconstruction (Hills), or acting as a political guardian (a term used by author) can be seductive and make police leaders feel unable to reject the demands to carry out these roles. An additional but obvious factor that makes police reluctant to be professional is the lure of increased welfare and budgets made available by the new regime, which would not have been experienced in the previous era when the police were still within the military structure.

However, although the terminology used by Potholm, Hills and the author indicate similar stages and roles taken, there is also a recognition that the police role in the post-disassociation era does not necessarily move smoothly along the way to professionalism, but can lead to political irregularities by becoming part of the new regime, or to economic irregularities through deviant practices such as extortion. Such deviations wil have been actually part of the practices of the military during an authoritarian regime and can become more available to the police after disassociation.

Impacts of disassociating the police from the military

Pino and Wiatrowski propose that the factors that influence the process of police reform can be put into four categories: international, national, subnational and individual. Pino and Wiatrowski simply assume that the reality of globalization is an inseparable part of the process that occurs in police organizations, because it directly influences global improvement and also leads to various variants of crime, which requires the handling of a professional police agency.[45] Hinton, Bayley and Marenin argue that the main factor of globalization is the spread of democratization, which many countries in the world have been forced to adopt. As part of the state instrument, the police directly or indirectly also change. One way to do this is to shift to a policing model that is free from the military.

These factors are determined at the national level in relation to the consolidation of democracy in the new regime. This greatly affects how the police emphasize the steps needed for them to be part of the instrument of democracy. In many cases, the lack of consolidation of democracy after the fall of an authoritarian regime actually puts the police in a worse situation than before because it results in political instability, which leads to the police being vulnerable in their internal consolidation in the face of political or regime change.

In some cases, disassociation of roles and functions between the police and the military may not work properly. There may be efforts to draw the police back into being part of the military, with this being done systematically or unsystematically either by the military or the government. Therefore, disassociation of roles and functions between the police and the military must as far as possible be monitored and controlled through public oversight, and will depend on the political foundations that underlie the separation of the police from the military.

According to the five models presented above of the causes of a disassociation of the police from the military, there are many issues that can influence whether or not the disassociations of functions between them are maintained.

From the cases reviewed it appears that there are four such issues: first, the presence or absence of continuing grey areas between the specified roles and functions of the police and the military; second, the placement of police structures post-disassociation; third, the assertiveness of legislation related to the operationalization of roles and functions in the field; and fourth, the pattern of relations between the police, the military, and both central and local governments.

First, in some countries with mature democratic traditions, the separation of functions between the police and the military tends to be assertive, but still involves grey areas as meeting points and separators. One possibility is the existence of paramilitary units that fill these areas.

Second, another possible cause of serious problems post-disassociation is the placement of the police as an institution. There have been at least three models: (1) under direct executive control by the president or the prime minister; (2) under the relevant ministries; and (3) becoming a stand-alone department or ministry. However, generally only the second and third models have been adopted widely, with the national police being either placed under related ministries such as the Ministry of Internal Affairs, Law or Public Security, or else being in a separate Department or Ministry of Police.

Third, post-disassociation there is a need for an umbrella law that is firm and binding to cover the operation of the field. This is because, in some cases, disassociation carries a legacy of conflict that disrupts the effectiveness of the police and military institutions. Each is involved in bad competition, whether related to economic access or simply to keep up the *esprit de corps* of each institution.

The fourth factor is the pattern of relations between the police, the military, and the government, both central and local. In democratic transition countries, the police are usually positioned under the military or the extra-constitutional agency established by the regime. That situation would also have influenced the relationship between the police and local government during a previous authoritarian regime; the police were merely a 'cheerleader' institution and tend to be driven by the military.

Politicization of the police post-disassociation

Cohen and Baker, Reiner, Bayley and Moon define the politicization of the police as the police being intervened in and used by the political regime to its political benefit; this may be characterized by frequent interventions in elections, abuse of power, brutality and suppression of freedom, use of various torture techniques, and/or harsh maltreatment of political suspects, resulting in numerous human rights abuses and torture-related cases of death.[46] Carter and Marenin, Hills, Hunter, and Beltran suggest three models of police politicization post-disassociation: open politicization; closed politicization; and combined politicization.

Open politicization (which will also have happened in the era of an authoritarian regime) involves the ruling government making various efforts to control the police: appointing of the police chief, increasing the police budget, making improvements and introducing modern police equipment, changes that were difficult to achieve when the police were still part of the military.

Closed politicization of the police happens when they are well consolidated and not interested in the offers made by the political regime, since the police have institutional access to the economic network to cover operational needs and welfare.[47] The move to involve the police in power eventually builds up the police's bargaining position against the new regime in power, and even raises a discourse within the new regime on reuniting police into the military structure.[48]

Combined politicization of the police is marked by the new regime playing hard to try to get the police to support the establishing of its political power. This model eventually becomes a picture of the post-disassociation era where the police become one of the institutions that are taken into account by the new regime. This situation is influenced by a continuing strong military position in the new regime, so the police became an alternative political guardian.[49]

Post-disassociation in relationships between the police, government and the military

Relationships between the police, the government and the military post-disassociation in many developing countries have different characteristics. These will depend in part on the power control of the previous regime before a new one replaced it. An interesting thing is that the models of the relationships which develop are directly interrelated, in the sense that relationships between the police and the government will affect those between the police and the military, and vice versa, depending on the circumstances and political conditions in the area (see Table I.2).

Drawing on several writers including Potholm, Kincaid, Hinton, and Beltran, the relationships between police, military and government can be described as four models; professional, quasi-professional, equivalence, and interventionist. The first model, of a professional relationship between the police, the government, and the military, runs on professional corridors, where each institution focuses on its respective field: the police focusing on domestic or internal security, the military on defence, and the government on governance and public service.

The second model, of quasi-professionals relations between the police and government, is defined as being a relatively steady relationship with the two

Table I.2 Comparison of models of relationships between the police, the government and the military post-disassociation

The police's relationship with the government
Professional – quasi-professional – equivalence – interventions
The police's relationship with the military[1]
Professional – equivalence – military's influences – military's controls

Note
1 Model inspired by Welch and Finer's model of military intervention in politics; see Welch (1976).

focusing on their respective fields. However, there is still a desire on the part of the government to control the police for various reasons including maintaining its power and not being disturbed by opposition groups.

The third model, of equivalence, has the police and the government in equal positions. This model is of a transactional relationship, where at any given moment when the police position is strong the government will conduct negotiations, either open or closed, and vice versa. Beltran reports cases where the separation of the police from the military is considered such a mistake that efforts to control the police again are continued until they are successful.

In the fourth model, the relationship that develops between the police and the government is one of intervention, where the government fully controls the police for political advantage. This condition is reinforced by the lack of consolidation of the police post-separation, so that the government can freely control it. In this context, it can be said that this is a major failure of democratization as the new regime in power is doing the same thing as the previous regime in order to maintain its power.

The structure of this book

This book is divided into 11 chapters plus Introduction and Conclusion. A discussion of the background of the book is followed by a presentation of the book's aims and of the theoretical direction of the study. The book discusses important concepts strongly connected to the roles of the police after its disassociation from the military: police and politics; the process and model of disassociation, its pattern and phases; the impact of disassociation; models of relations among the police and other institutions post-disassociation; and patterns of political intervention in the police post-disassociation.

This introduction has suggested how complex and difficult, but also crucial, is the process of disassociating the police from the military as a condition of democratic policing and a part of the democratization process. This book will discuss the arguments of those concepts that appear useful and relevant to the Indonesian case, especially to its local levels.

Part I is divided into two chapters. It generally provides an historical background, but specifically aims to provide information in three areas: about the character of the Indonesian Polri; about military influence inside the Polri; and about other possible historical elements, especially relations between the Polri, the military, and political elites, including the parliament and the government both national and local. This includes several cases related to persons who were close to Suharto's power which the Polri did not solve, instead using someone as a scapegoat. This part of the book also discusses roles and position of the Polri in regime change and the process of disassociation of the Polri from the ABRI. In addition, it explains the characteristics of disassociation of the Polri from the ABRI and presents a new paradigm for the impact of this disassociation.

Parts II and III discuss national perspectives, especially on *reformasi* and its effect on the Polri. Part II includes a discussion of the implementation of the

Introduction 15

'Blue Book' as part of the Polri's effort to develop a more independent and professional force, the politicization of the Polri by the Wahid presidency, and the Polri's response to it. Part III is an account of the efforts to resolve the divisive issues between the Polri chiefs and the Group of Eight, discussing internal consolidation and also constraints on the Polri in the shadow of politicization after Wahid's presidency.

Parts IV and V explore local perspectives, especially relations between the Polri, the military, and local governments. Even though the Polri is a national police, every district police force (Polres) has a different situation and character. This part of the book describes the internal dynamics, funding, and extortion activities by the Polri and relates them to its roles and function. It also describes the process of politicization of the Polres and the response of each institution. This part of the book explains the process of internal conflicts and rivalries, the budget, and corruption. It also discusses the role of third parties positioned as fixers and brokers who pave the way for mutual and beneficial relationships between the Polri at local level and parties with their own interest in the services and roles the Polri can provide to them.

The book's Conclusion summarizes the findings of the preceding chapters and presents a final analysis.

Notes

1 For more about the Polri's roles in Sukarno's era and Suharto's New Order, see Part I.
2 Concepts of democratic and civilian policing and their implementation will be provided in the following paragraphs.
3 For more on the 'Blue Book' of the Polri, see Chapters 2 and 3. See also Mabes Polri (1999a).
4 For more on the working group of the Polri Reform, see Chapters 2 and 3.
5 The Polri's roles in regime change will be discussed in Chapters 2 and 3.
6 The working group was an initiative of President Habibie following public demand for the disassociation of the Polri from the ABRI. See Chapters 2 and 3.
7 Agus Wirahadikusumah was a military major general and Sofjan Jacoeb was a police major general at the time. See Sibarani *et al.* (2001), pp. 23–28; Yunanto *et al.* (2005), pp. 52–53.
8 Kunarto (ed.) (2002).
9 'Kamdagri' was the term used inside Polri to differentiate police and military roles and functions. The term was also adopted by the MPR to issue decrees disassociating the Polri from ABRI – MPR Decrees No. VI/MPR/2000 and No. VII/MPR/2000 – and also by the DPR when it passed its Law of the Polri, Law No. 2/2002.
10 For more discussion of Polri, local government, and *dekonsentrasi* (semi-autonomy) policies, see Parts IV and V.
11 For more comparison of the institutional structures of the Polri, the military, and local government, see Chapters 7 and 8.
12 Article 5, point 2, 'The Polri is a national police, which has integrated roles and functions as shown in point 1'. For detail see Law No. 2/2002.
13 In both decrees, the policy is clearly shown as part of the programme of the Polri; however, the implementation of that policy is not yet clear. For example, see Meliala (2009).
14 A part of this is to investigate the extent to which the widely reported practicing of extortion by its officers is one of the roots of conflict inside the Polri.

15 See O'Connor (1975), p. 304. See also Marenin (1982), p. 380.
16 The modern police force, according to Liang (1992), James and Raine (1998) and Beltran (2009), is an institution that follows and matches societal changes, trying to secure and protect the public and its properties as part of the role and function of the police in modern society.
17 Marenin (1982), pp. 381–383. Compare this with Goldstein (1990), especially Chapter 2.
18 Ake (1981), pp. 123–125. See also Bittner (1997), pp. 67–69.
19 Hogg (1983), pp. 3–21; Findlay (2004), pp. 130–139.
20 Edwards (2005), p. 6.
21 See Critchley (1976); see also Cramer (1964).
22 Bayley (2001), p. 13; Travis (1998), p. 8.
23 Hills (1996), pp. 271–272.
24 Bailey and Dammert (2006), pp. 25–35. Bruce and Nield (2005).
25 Linz and Stepan (1996), p. 3.
26 For more discussion of authoritarian regimes, see Diamond (1999) and Barbara Geddes as quoted in Ulfelder (2005).
27 Beltran (2009). For one documented example see Morris (2010), pp. 218–226.
28 Kincaid and Gamarra (1994).
29 Kincaid (2000), pp. v–58.
30 For example Skolnick (1966); Skogan (2008).
31 Beltran (2009), pp. 15–21; de Fransisco (2006), pp. 94–110.
32 The police in some African and Latin American countries have problems even when they have been disassociated from the military; due to the similarity of conditions to those in military structures, they are used to political bargaining with the new regime to improve their conditions. See Potholm (1969), Marenin (1982), Hills (1996), Kincaid (2000), Hinton (2006), Beltran (2009).
33 Meyer and Atwood (2007); Rodrigues (2006).
34 See Hunter (1998); Silvestri (2000); Loader (1997); Muradi (2007, unpubd), 'A Longing Journey'; Muradi (2007*ii*).
35 Potholm (1969), pp. 153–154. See also Hills (1996), p. 273.
36 See Marenin (1986); Decalo (1973); Alderson (1998), especially Chapters 7 and 8.
37 Hills (1996), p. 287.
38 See for example, Hills (1996), p. 287; also Mueller *et al.* (1960); Wakeman (1988).
39 Hills (1996), p. 272.
40 Tanner (2000), pp. 104–108. See also Bohdan, pp. 319–320.
41 For example see *Dateline* (2009), 'Trouble in Thailand: Riots, Police Crackdown, Corruption Threaten Political Order, Economy', available at: www.dateline.ucdavis.edu/dl_detail.lasso?id=10784 (April 17, 2009).
42 See Bayley (1971). What Bayley says concerns the police in modern democratic society, where roles and functions are already clear. To compare Bayley's statements, see Edwards (2005), pp. 5–9.
43 For example see Marshall (1965), pp. 9–20.
44 See Stepan (1976), pp. 48–52; Seligson (2002); Lobe and Manuel (1987), pp. 1–79.
45 For more discussion, see Nathan and Wiattrowski. Op. cit, p. 13.
46 Cohen and Baker (1991); Bayley (1971); Moon (2004), pp. 128–136.
47 Indonesia's case at the national level will be discussed in Parts II and III and at the local level in Parts IV and V. See Carter and Marenin (1977), Hills (1996), Hunter (1997), and Beltran (2009).
48 See Beltran (2009), pp. 7–11.
49 See Kalmanowiecki (2000), which can be compared with Carter and Marenin (1977).

Part I
Historical legacies and early *reformasi*

1 The police in Sukarno's era
From colonial state to the overthrow of the Guided Democracy state

Civil versus combatant paradigms: police trained by the Dutch and police trained by the Japanese

Indonesia is one of the modern countries that fought for its independence through armed resistance. This is important as it was the basis for the early combatant paradigm of the police as fighters against threats to the nation in a unified cooperation with the military and 'the people'. This paradigm affected the police's role with regard to subsequent regional rebellions and the dual function policy of a combined military and police keeping control over a forcibly unified state, and the use of anti-imperialist justifications in domestic politics and in military and policing policies.

The basic concept and structure of Polri was derived from the models of the Dutch. After the invading Japanese defeated their colonial military in 1942, the Dutch forcibly reclaimed areas of their former colony against fighters for the new Indonesian Republic until they achieved almost complete control again in 1948; they then accepted they could not maintain this and left most of Indonesia for good in 1949.[1]

The Dutch police model closely reflected a modern police organization and structure under a Ministry of Internal Affairs, but with a number of variants in different areas with the local 'native' administration, largely run by the local bupati (regional regent administrators), and the national colonial government's residents both controlling different police forces, their functions and their funding.[2] The Japanese police model represented an emergency policing arrangement, which put police into the military structure. Use of the police was based on effective mobilization when Japan needed to defend its colonies; massive exploitation of the resources of its colony, including unpopular forced labour mobilizations and movements; and the detection and suppression of any potential rebellions.

The foundations for the police system of the Dutch colonial state had been laid in the early nineteenth century with the Regulation of Business Administration of Justice for Regional Courts in Java and the Police Administration on February 11, 1814.[3] The national colonial government, through its central offices and its 'European' regional residents, controlled the centralized mobile, paramilitary field police, the plantation police[4] and the detective and intelligence[5] organizations, while the police chiefs (*wedana*) of its bupati administrators supervised the local police forces (*pangreh praja*).

The Japanese occupation was only three and a half years but had a considerable influence on restructuring the police institution into operating on a military model and being integrated into the structure of the military. The policy of Japan's imperial government was to rapidly integrate the structure of the military and the police forces in its colonized territories in southeast Asia, with Singapore as their headquarters.[6]

The structure of a unified police organization in Japan's occupation era was part of its total mobilization for war against the Allies. This system produced people who served in the police under the Japanese and then later became leaders in the Indonesian military,[7] while some later police leaders had previously been in the military. The police organization under the Japanese was initially run by the Japanese military police (*kempetai*) but was soon taken over by a new centralized civil police department (*keimubu*).[8]

During the Japanese occupation, internal security was in the hands of a variety of organized and semi-organized forces. As well as the *kempetai* and the *keimubu* there were auxiliary police forces, the Japanese military, the PETA (Pembela Tanah Air – Defenders of the Homeland) Japanese auxiliary force, the HEIHO,[9] and other Japanese semi-trained paramilitary groups. There were unclear boundaries between military and police roles and functions, especially in terms of internal security.[10]

Japan surrendered in 1945, and under the terms of the surrender the Japanese administration in Indonesia had to maintain order until the territory was handed over to the Allies. The Japanese-formed Indonesian police had a special place in the preparation and early stages of the struggle for independence against the returning Dutch forces, as they were given responsibility to maintain security and order during the transition process from the Japanese to the Allies. Weapons, including many from sympathetic Japanese units, came through the police to other independence fighters. Many ex-military members, including some of their leaders, disguised themselves and their activities by using police uniforms.[11]

The day after Sukarno and Hatta proclaimed Indonesian independence on August 17, 1945 the new government established constitutional institutions, including the 1945 Basic Laws (UUD 1945) as the State Constitution. Based on the UUD 1945, the police were specified as being part of the executive authority.[12] The day after that, it was decided that the Polri would be included in Ministry of Internal Affairs and would be called the National Police Bureau of the Republic of Indonesia (Djawatan Kepolisian Negara Republik Indonesia), reflecting the Dutch policing model rather than the Japanese model.[13] Three days earlier the first chief of police, R.S. Soekanto Tjokrodiatmodjo, had been appointed.[14]

Allied forces arrived in September 1945 to take over from the Japanese administration, followed by officials of the Netherlands Indies Civil Administration (NICA) led by van der Plas.[15] The Indonesian independence forces resisted this and widespread fighting broke out. The headquarters of the Polri, in the Ministry of Internal Affairs in Jakarta, was occupied by the Allies and NICA.

In February 1946 the Indonesian Republic government decided to transfer its operations out of Jakarta to Yogyakarta. However, the Ministry of Internal Affairs and the Indonesian police moved to Purwokerto in Central Java.[16] About two-thirds of the 20,000 Polri officers in Jakarta left to join the republican police, while a third stayed for a mixture of reasons. It was said that those who stayed were from the Dutch-trained group, while those who left were Japanese-trained.[17] The different decisions became a post-war basis for tensions and conflicts when the two forces were recombined after the abandonment of the Dutch administration and the achievement of full independence under a Republican government in 1950.

In Purwokerto, the new Polri developed its facilities, framework and organizational rules. They established the Security Intelligence Agency, which was the embryo of the Police Security Intelligence Unit (Intelijen Keamanan, known as Intelkam), and a paramilitary police unit, the Mobile Brigade, which later became the Brimob; they prepared for a traffic police (Polantas) and made other improvements.[18] Another important change was the Polri being moved out of the Ministry of Internal Affairs and put directly under the prime minister's office as a clearly national institution. Soekanto recognized that the mechanisms of the ministry made the Polri vulnerable to similar and other efforts, and he wanted the Polri to have a professional independence from local politics in carrying out its roles in public security and order.[19]

Responding to Soekanto's proposals to the prime minister, Sutan Sjahrir, the government issued Decree No. 11/SD/1946 which came into force on July 1, 1946, stipulating that the Polri had become an independent institution directly under the prime minister's office.[20] This effectively changed the Polri into a centralized national police force, covering the entire territory of the Republican state but controlled from the central government, with the local operations of the Polri being separated from the security section in the regional governor's office and becoming a local police agency (*penilik kepolisian daerah*), headed by a police commissioner responsible to the Polri headquarters.[21]

After the surrender of the Japanese, several local organizations had been established by, among others, ex-police to maintain security and order in their areas.[22] They wanted to integrate themselves as a national organization, and on May 12, 1946 had successfully merged into the Indonesian Police Officers' Union (P3RI – Persatuan Pegawai Polisi Republik Indonesia). The organizations were now dissolved and their members were taken into the Polri, while the P3RI became part of the Polri structure.[23]

One of the urgent topics for discussion between Soekanto, President Soekarno and vice-President Hatta was the loyalty of the Polri paramilitary units, the Brimob led by Major General R.P. Sudarsono. In mid-1946, there had been an attempted uprising by a radical faction of the independence movement, the Struggle Union (PP)[24] led by the radical communist Tan Malaka.[25] The attempts had failed, as most Brimob remained loyal to their commanders, Soekanto, and supported the Sukarno-Hatta team and Prime Minister Sjahir.

In September 1946 the government had issued Decree No. 49 from its State Defence Council (DPN, Dewan Pertananan Negara). This DPN decree stipulated that in the interest of supporting national defence, the Polri would become a military unit, with all things related to the development of the Polri becoming the responsibility of the Ministry of Defence and with the Polri being transferred from the prime minister's office for more effective coordination.[26]

On July 21, 1947, the Dutch launched what they called the First Police Action, which many Indonesian nationalists call the First Military Aggression. This Dutch action forced the rapid implementation of the September 1946 DPN Decree No. 49 through the August 1, 1947 DPN Decree No. 112. As the Dutch military occupied Purwokerto, the Ministry of Internal Affairs moved to Yogyakarta while Deputy Chief Soemarto moved the Polri headquarters to the nearby area of Candi Wulan and then, in December 1947, to Yogyakarta. This was also the time of the change of government from Sjahrir's cabinet to that of Amir Sjarifuddin. As Soekanto had been very close to Sjahir with the Polri having direct involvement in formulation of policies, the change of government reduced the Polri's direct influence in politics.[27]

The Amir Sjarifuddin cabinet formulated a separate ministry for police, so that the accountability process could be implemented in accordance with the mechanisms of the parliamentary system. The cabinet also brought in the idea of a ministry of security affairs that would include the Polri and attorney general under the same roof. However, the Amir cabinet formed only a ministry of police affairs and appointed Mr Hindromartono as its first minister.[28]

This concept of ministry of security Affairs was never even started, because the Amir cabinet was trapped in political chaos and replaced by an emergency cabinet.[29] The fall of the Amir cabinet was followed by a political move by the Brimob leader, Mr Hindromartono, a communist sympathizer and a supporter of radical left-wing parties.[30] He triggered the uprising by supporters of the Indonesian Communist Party (Partai Komunis Indonesia – PKI) and the Socialist Party in the East Java town of Madiun, where an 'Indonesian Soviet Republic' was declared. This rebellion, later known as 'the 1948 Madiun Affairs', included the involvement of some members of the military and the police, but was defeated by the Republican government within a few weeks.

The Dutch launched the second attack on Republic territory. The second wave of Dutch attacks put Yogyakarta in Dutch hands. The Polri leaders followed the pattern of the independence struggle, being controlled by military leaders under the deputy chief of the Polri, Soemarto, until the Dutch in Yogyakarta captured him with the other Republican leaders. The Polri chief, Soekanto, was arrested after breaking off in the middle of his tour of foreign countries seeking support and assistance to build and develop the Polri.

As Yogyakarta had been occupied and the chief and acting chief of the Polri captured, Sosro Danoekoesoemo took over temporary leadership, supported by head of the Yogyakarta Special Region Police, Djen Muhammad Soerjopranoto, and moved the Polri headquarters to Sleman, just outside Yogyakarta. From there, they coordinated all Polri offices in Java and issued a confirmation of the earlier decision to prohibit Polri officers from cooperating with the Dutch, even if any such cooperation was regarded as an individual rather than an institutional matter.[31]

With the arrest of leaders of the republic in Yogyakarta, an Emergency State of the Republic of Indonesia (Pemerintahan Darurat Republik Indonesia) was set up in West Sumatra, headed by Mr Sjafrudin Prawiranegara. This affirmed the authority of the Polri, after receiving a mandate from the captive Hatta cabinet, and appointed Omar Sahid as Polri chief.[32] In another response to the arrests of most of the state leaders, General A.H. Nasution, military commander of Java, formed a military government in Java with himself as leader and the Polri chief as a deputy, along with the attorney general and the commander of the military police.[33] This government operated through a system of military district commands, which included the Polri.[34]

The United Nations called for a ceasefire in December 1948, and then in January 1949 called for the reinstatement of the Republic government over the whole of Indonesia; in mid-July 1949 Mr Sjafrudin Prawiranegara passed his temporary mandate as president back to Sukarno. Based on the agreement, the Dutch army had to retreat from Yogyakarta and was obliged to supply police uniforms, military armaments, and equipment.[35]

A month before the Dutch left Yogyakarta, the Polri made records of all police officers and opened new applications to replace officers killed in the war.[36] Temporarily, the Polri was put under Sultan Hamengkubuwono IX as coordinating minister for security affairs, while Soekanto was deputy coordinating minister as well as Polri chief. While still based in Yogyakarta, the Polri opened a branch office in Jakarta.[37] The task of this branch office was to improve the relationship among the police forces of different components of the RIS (Republik Indonesia Serikat – United States of Indonesia) and to provide assistance to police officials in the regions.

Sukarno became the president of the RIS. For a few weeks, the position of the chief of the RIS police was still held by the chief of the Dutch General Police, G. van Nes, but on January 19, 1950 the Polri chief took over that position. He was given the authority by RIS Presidential Decree No. 22/1950 to implement both operational and administrative control.[38] However, the equipment for police remained under the equipment office of the Ministry of Internal Affairs.

The integration of the various police forces of the RIS faced major problems. One was the sentiment between officers who were considered to have cooperated with the Dutch and those who had fought for the Republic. Issues of having been previously trained and worked under the Dutch or the Japanese were mixed in with this. These issues and tensions were reduced under the Dutch-trained and Republic-supporting Police Chief Soekanto but continued for the next decade.

Another problem was the division between the roles of the Polri and the regional police forces of the federated states of the RIS. A national-level Police Commission was set up, chaired by the prime minister with relevant ministers and police heads as members. It established a Working Group of the RIS Police Chief, representatives of various state police forces, and an academic police expert, Prof. Djoko Sutono.

Taken hostage by the political situation

The roles of the Polri during the Parliamentary Era, between 1950 and 1959, did not undergo significant changes compared with the previous period of the struggle for independence. The pattern of the relationship between national police and local government began to become clearer, but not at all completely or consistently. Formally, local government had no authority to control the national police but could only coordinate practically with them.

In the newly flourishing parliamentary democracy the potential voting power of the police, their dependants and their sympathizers was appealed to by some political parties in attempts to attract their votes in the first general election in 1955 by promoting policies which appeared to benefit the police.[39] The agenda of discussing the position of the Polri was marginalized by the larger political agenda and by the security situation, which disrupted the stability of Indonesia due to rebellions and separatist movements.[40]

Based on Presidential Decree No. RIS. 22/1950, issued during the short-lived period of the RIS, the Polri was under the prime minister's office, with administrative support and supervision from the Ministry of Internal Affairs. However, on October 3, 1950, Prime Minister M. Natsir issued Decree No. 6/PM/1950. This transferred the political accountability of the Polri to the deputy prime minister, Sultan Hamengkubuwono IX, but only in an intermediary role of the attorney general to the deputy prime minister, with final political accountability of the Polri to the parliament in the hands of the prime minister, while administrative supervision remained in the Ministry of Internal Affairs.

Another change followed a few months later. Natsir was replaced by Sukiman Wirjosandjojo as prime minister, and issued a decree putting the Polri directly under the prime minister's office again. In the swirling national politics of the time the Sukiman cabinet lasted less than a year and was replaced by the Wilopo cabinet. Wilopo also stated that there would be a police law, which would define the role and function of the Polri in preventive and repressive activities with the use of violent or non-violent measures, while the Polri chief and representatives of the Ministry of Internal Affairs were made his advisors on public security. The decree stipulated formal relationships between the Polri and local police:

1. The head of provincial police was under the tactical leadership of the governor, while in technical administrative affairs, the head of the provincial police would report to the Polri headquarters.
2. The head of sub-regional (*keresidenan*) police or head of district (*kabupaten* or *kota*) police was under the tactical leadership of the head of the *keresidenan*, the bupati (mayor), while in technical administrative affairs he would report directly to the head of the provincial police.

The chief of the Polri immediately set up a structure for provincial and local police, and established provincial police offices, including in Jakarta.[41]

After conflicts with President Sukarno and shifts between and within party alliances, Wilopo lost his party's support and was replaced by Ali Sastroamidjojo.

Unexpectedly, the minister of justice, Mr Djodi Gondokusumo, proposed a radical plan to split the Polri into three departments: repressive police, preventive police, and paramilitary police.[42] This proposal had never been discussed with the Polri or P3RI. The Polri and the P3RI asked for the formation of a special committee to discuss the status of police comprehensively before it was followed up by the cabinet.[43]

A state committee under the deputy prime minister was set up to consider the matter and make recommendations. It could not work optimally because of the general election in 1955, but it did produce useful recommendations. One was a confirmation of the essence of the Polri as a national police, as well as a mechanism of political and administrative work accountability for the Polri. This followed up recommendations of the committee about the need for legislation and coordination between law enforcement agencies and submitted a draft bill for the coordination between the Polri, the Ministry of Justice Affairs, and the attorney general to the parliament for discussion in October 1956.

The status of the Polri was not a high priority for cabinets at this time. The elected parliament and constitutional assembly in 1955 focused on constitutional issues,[44] while the second Ali Sastroamidjojo cabinet was also preoccupied with unrest and rebellion in several regions. He lost the support from coalition partners and resigned within a year. President Sukarno appointed Soewirjo to form a cabinet, but he failed to build a sufficient coalition with other parties. The stability and unity of the republic continued to be threatened by a series of rebellions against the central government and its policies, including the Darul Islam/ Tentara Islam Indonesia (Islamic State/Indonesian Islamic Army, DI/TII) in West Java, Aceh, and South Sulawesi;[45] the Angkatan Perang Ratu Adil (APRA – 'Legions of the Just King') in Bandung,[46] South Maluku Republic (RMS);[47] the Andi Azis uprisings;[48] the Permesta Pemerintahan Revolusioner Republik Indonesia/Perjuangan Semesta (Revolutionary Government of the Republic of Indonesia/Universal Struggle); and other cases of sabotage and assassination attempts against President Sukarno. The Polri, particularly through its Brimob units, was actively involved in the suppression of these threats to the authority of the central government.[49] It also managed to make some further improvements in its organization and capabilities.[50]

In the 1950–1959 period of parliamentary democracy, the relationship between the Polri and local leaders referred to the policies created at the central level, which made the Polri politically accountable to the local leaders and administratively directly under the Polri headquarters.[51] During this period, the relationship between the Polri and local government was in line with policy at the national level, although at certain times even the Ministry of Internal Affairs, which held the overall line authority over local governments, had authority only in coaching and operational matters, while political police operations were directly responsible to the prime minister.

Nowhere to run: Sukarno, communism and the military

During the 1959–1965 Guided Democracy era, politicization of the Polri was strong and internal conflicts emerged. These included the relations between the formerly Dutch- and Japanese-trained senior police; the intervention of Sukarno, the military, and political parties; and the PKI's attempts to control the Polri leader selection process and important police units. Politicization was also associated with individual vertical mobility, where Polri officers and factions tried to involve external elements as part of their political bargaining power to improve their own careers.

Almost immediately, the increased concentration of power in the president had what many in the Polri saw as a benefit. The Polri chief became the deputy minister, although not in the new primary cabinet,[52] and the national police now reported directly to the president. The newly titled Deputy Minister of Police held a conference on October 19–20, 1959, attended by the police commissioners (provincial police heads), which issued a police manifesto declaring the support of the police for the continuing revolutionary principles of Guided Democracy[53] and set up a 'Committee of Ten' to plan for the implementation of the manifesto.[54]

The task of the Committee of Ten was to discuss five main issues: the status of the Polri; security policies; promotion and dismissal in the Polri; the Polri education system; and supervision against corruption.[55] The discussion went well until a problem appeared when the committee proposed three of its members; Soeleiman Effendi, Djen Moh. Soerjopranoto and Soekarno Djojonegoro, be appointed to important positions within the Polri. Opposing this, Soekanto proposed a different three: Soekarno Djojonegoro, M. Jasin and Saleh Sastranegara. There were three significant motives – professional, personal and political – underlying this disagreement. First, several members of the committee wanted fresh leadership, including a replacement of those who had trained under the Dutch and had been holding the most senior positions for many years.[56] Second, there were older officers who had personal ambitions to replace Soekanto as chief of the Polri.[57] Third, several members of the committee were driven by PKI and PNI (Partai Nasional Indonesia – Indonesian National Party), who did not like Soekanto due to his being close to the elite of the PSI (Partai Sosialis Indonesia – Indonesian Socialist Party) such as Sjahrir.

Soekanto, as Polri chief, rejected the recommendation of the Committee of Ten, but the powerful Jakarta police commissariat responded by sending a joint statement to him and the committee demanding the implementation of all the committee's recommendations as soon as possible. Soekanto ignored the letter; then seven members of the Jakarta police commissariat, including the two on the Committee of Ten,[58] met Minister of Defence and Security Affairs, Lieutenant General Nasution, on December 11, 1959 and proposed that Soekanto be replaced. Nasution suggested that the matter be settled within the Polri. Seven officers decided to go to the presidential palace to meet Sukarno directly. Soetjipto Danoekoesoemo, the Brimob commander of the Central Java police commissariat, urged this decision.[59]

The president responded the complainants' visit by calling in Soekanto, who was accompanied by M. Jasin and Soebroto Brotodirdjo, and telling him not to take any steps against the seven. However, Soekanto considered they had breached organizational discipline, violated the hierarchical ethic among officers and committed abuses against their honour codes. He delivered a public speech on the state-owned radio station about this and its unwanted involvement of the Polri in political conflict.[60]

Sukarno reacted strongly to what he saw as a violation of his order and temporarily dismissed Soekanto as deputy minister of police/chief of the Polri, appointing Chief Commissioner Soekarno Djojonegoro in his place. Soekanto did not respond to this, believing that what was happening was only a part of the political dynamics.

In this increased politicization of the Polri there was a succession of changes to the title of its chief, from Deputy Minister of Police/Polri Chief to Minister of Police/Polri Chief to Minister/Polri Chief of Staff, then to Minister/Polri Commander, with Polri renamed as the Indonesian Police Force (AKRI), matching the name of the Indonesian armed forces (ABRI). These changes reflected the succession of government, presidential and parliamentary decrees, resolutions and acts which increasingly militarized the police.[61] The militarization of the Polri and its integration into being a branch of the ABRI ended the debating about the Polri position, which was now under the umbrella of the Ministry of Defence and Security with the other state security institutions.

Soekarno Djojonegoro led the Polri for four years (December 1959 to December 1963), and little internal conflict emerged. However, there were more obvious party political interests and manoeuvres. Police Brigadier General Soetarto was one of those manoeuvring. He had been a supporter of the PKI since his early career as police officer in Central Java.[62] He maintained close relations with the PKI, and became a contact in the Polri in order to control the dynamic steps of the Polri in accordance with PKI policy. Under Soekarno Djojonegoro he was appointed as deputy chief of Polri operations.

PKI sympathizers were not satisfied with the policies made by Soekarno Djojonegoro, especially his anti-communist policy and the placement of what they considered 'counter-revolutionary' officers in strategic positions – and so they sought support from Soebandrio and the elite circles around President Sukarno to replace him. President Sukarno also heard about this, and by the end of 1963 he had formed a group to find nominations for a new minister/commander of the Polri.

The team finally recommended Adjutant Chief Commisioner Soetjipto Danoekoesoemo, Commander of the Mobile Brigade, a young officer trained by the Japanese and promoted up three levels.[63] It was believed that if promoted, he could answer the president and control the police effectively. President Sukarno needed the Polri under his control in order to use it as a revolutionary guard to protect his regime and all his policies.

Soetjipto Danoekoesoemo realized that his appointment was part of a political scenario, so that President Sukarno's men including Chaerul Saleh, Dr Soebandrio, and Soetarto could control the Polri. Soetjipto Danoekoesoemo not only had to deal with PKI sympathizers inside Polri, but also faced opposition from senior Polri officers who thought he should not have been appointed without the consent of his superiors. These two groups found a common interest against him, and there was an incoherent accusation, including from Soebandrio, that he was both a 'CIA goon' and part of a 'Murba cadre' (Murba being the Musyawarah Rakyat Banyak – Indonesian Leftist Party – established by Tan Malaka).[64]

Finally, after many efforts by senior police officers and PKI supporters, he was replaced with Soetjipto Joedodihardjo in May 1965. The inauguration of Brigadier General Police Soetjipto Joedodihardjo as minister/commander of the Polri was regarded as a victory for the Soetarto group. Soetarto himself was still deputy head of the BPI (Badan Pusat Intelijen – Central Intelligence Board/ Agency), which strategically made him able to control the Polri completely in almost all provinces and at all levels.[65] The policies made by Soetjipto Joedodihardjo could be seen from two aspects: political gratitude and administrative aspects of leadership. From the first aspect, Soetjipto had once been shoved aside and replaced by Soetarto as deputy chief of the BPI and appointed as head of the civic defence unit (*pertahanan sipil*) of Indonesia during the short Soetjipto Danoekoesoemo period; he was then temporarily retired along with Djen Moh. Soerjopranoto, the former deputy minister/chief of the Polri in Soekarno Djojonegoro's period. Soetarto's group, communicating via Dr Soebandrio to President Sukarno, raised Soetjipto Joedodihardjo's name again.[66]

However, he inherited relatively acute internal conflicts. Competing groupings inside the Polri put him in a dilemma. Each group tried to gain influence in every policy made by Soetjipto and tried to prevent policies proposed by other group. Soetjipto Joedodihardjo made some structural adjustments as part of his efforts to accommodate both groups in the new structure.[67]

Another development during Soetjipto Joedodihardjo's era was the founding of the police academy (Akpol), like the military one, to provide early education for police cadets. This establishment of Akpol was also in line with the Struggle Programme of the Polri (Program Perjuangan AKRI), declared by Soetjipto Joedodihardjo, demonstrating police determination to support programmes created by President Sukarno. The public declaration of this Struggle Programme emphasized the political position of the Polri under the leadership of Soetjipto Joedodihardjo, which had been influenced by its pro-PKI factions, as Soekarno's doctrine of 'Nasionalis, Agama dan Komunisn' (NASAKOM: Nationalism, Religion and Communism) declared it should be. When the September 1965 Movement (G 30/S PKI) broke out, the names of several high officers of the Polri, including Soetjipto Joedodihardjo himself, were included in the list of those named as being on the 'Indonesian Revolution Council' (Dewan Revolusi Indonesia, DRI*)* which was publicly announced by Colonel Untung, the leader of the very short-lived September 1965 Movement.[68]

After the quick suppression of the movement, the political situation gave an opportunity to clear the Polri of its communist faction. The police's determination to work together with the military concentrated on involving the Polri in crushing the communist movement across Indonesia to implement and protect the state ideology of Pancasila.[69] Almost a year later, Soetjipto, as minister/ commander of the Polri, issued a decree[70] to make internal improvements to deal with the BPI and communist issues in the Polri itself.[71] Two high-ranking officers, 35 middle-ranking officers, 198 administrative employees, and 41 NCOs were found to have been involved in the September 1965 Movement. Police Brigadier General Soetarto was one of two high-ranking officers.[72]

However, steps taken by Soetjipto Joedodihardjo were considered slow and brought accusations against him. He was accused of being too close to Soetarto and of trying to halt the investigation process.[73] Other groups considered that all inspections, detentions and investigation processes involving other institutions were serious interventions in the independence of the Polri. The groups demanded a change of leadership in the Polri as part of the political momentum to build a new Polri in the wake of the September 1965 movement. However, there were different responses from other institutions, especially from the army and Major General Suharto, who were effectively in charge of the government.[74] They supported Soetjipto's policy on the process of investigation and arrests, as a process of conflict resolution. Against the first accusation, it was officially confirmed that Soetjipto Joedodihardjo was relatively 'clean' from the influence of the communists. Against the second one, the issue of interferences from other institutions was considered to be a decoy, because from the beginning the Polri had made an agreement with the army and navy[75] to clear out the influence of communists in their organizations.[76]

The period of Guided Democracy was an important period for the Polri because of three crucial issues: the increasing militarization of the Polri; internal conflict as a result of political intervention; and the relationship between the Polri and local governments. The Guided Democracy period marked the integration of police into the military structure, operationally, politically and administratively, with it being taken into the Ministry of Security and Defence Affairs which had the ABRI commander as its minister.[77]

Meanwhile, internal conflicts in the Polri, arising from dissatisfaction and poor career mechanisms, also brought in external parties with the manoeuvring of PKI sympathizers and the political elites of President Sukarno's circles, and with interventions caused by various interests of other political parties in the parliamentary democracy period. These manoeuvrings and interventions were pursued by a dominant pro-communist group of police officers capable of controlling the internal dynamics of the Polri, until the fall of President Sukarno and the 'Old Order' regime.

This chapter has examined the Polri from its first formal establishment in 1945 until the fall of the Sukarno regime in 1965, and its influences from the previous Dutch and Japanese models of policing. Reviewing this period is important in understanding the Polri during the New Order and post-Suharto. The complexities and problems facing its historical relations with the military, although in some ways similar to those in other developing countries, have been part of the uniqueness of this nation-state born in the revolution.

This chapter has described how those dynamics included the rise of internal conflict between the Dutch-trained and the Japanese-trained in policing, and discussed the roles of the Polri in other dynamics of Indonesian politics involving relationships between the Polri, the military and the government, including the form and rise of internal conflicts and attitudes of the Polri in responding to the changes and dynamics of national politics.

Meanwhile, this chapter has shown that the role of the Polri as part of the military structure had its origins in the Indonesian struggle for independence. However, the strengthening of internal conflict during the period until the fall of the liberal parliamentary democracy, followed by the strong political intervention in the Guided Democracy period, made the Polri an institution with relatively little political bargaining power against the government, political parties or the military. This situation made the Polri tend to be subordinate to the military and representative of the regime, and caused it to oscillate in the conflicts that occurred among the political elite over national politics and the military.

Notes

1 Dutch control and policing continued in the western half of New Guinea until 1962, when it became part of Indonesia.
2 More discussion of the Dutch colonial structure and the position of the police will be given in following paragraphs.
3 See Oudang (1952), pp. 1–4, and Soeriatmadja (1971), pp. 65–87.
4 For more discussion on the plantation police, see Peluso (1992).
5 The General Investigation Bureau (Algemeene Recherche Dienst) was the successor of the Political Intelligence Bureau (Politieke Inlichtingendienst, PID), responsible for providing political intelligence to the colonial authorities. Cribb (1992), pp. 375–376. See also Jenkins (2009), p. 11. Some Indonesian writers have translated the term PID as the 'Police Political Intelligence Unit' of the Dutch colonial government; see Zachrie and Wiwanto (eds) (2010), especially Chapter 1.
6 For further explanation, see Tanumidjaja (1971), pp. 1–3; Anderson (1972); Sundhaussen (1982); Nasution (1982), pp. 120–123.
7 Two examples are Soerjadi Soerjadharma, the first chief of staff of the Indonesian Air Force (TNI AU), and President Suharto. For Soerjadharma see Nasution (1982), pp. 123, 125. For Suharto see Elson (2001) and Jenkins (2009), pp. 9–11.
8 Java was under the military administration of the 16th Army. Kalimantan and Eastern Indonesia were under the administration of the 2nd Fleet of the Navy, and Sumatra was under the 25th Army.
9 A small organization of auxiliary units was formed from late 1942, primarily used for guarding duties. Sundhaussen (1982), p. 3.
10 One consequence after the Japanese surrender was the rapid establishment of many paramilitary groups named after the region where they were set up. See Jones et al. (2004); Wenas (2006).
11 Yamamoto, a Japanese military commander, knew this, but he did not tell the Allied commanders. See Sundhaussen (1982), p. 7. These military leaders included A.H. Nasution, T.B. Simatupang and Kemal Idris. For more about them see Nasution (1956); Crouch (1978), pp. 24–32; Anwar et al. (1997).
12 Soeriatmadja (1971), pp. 100–103.
13 The transition of policing in the early Republic came about because several of the leaders of the police had previously been active as police officers or Dutch colonial

government as *wedana* (heads of local police), including Soekanto, Soemarto, Soekarno Djojonegoro, and others. See Soeriatmadja (1971), pp. 22–29; Jenkins (2009), pp. 83–86.

14 As cited in Tanumidjaja (1971), pp. 3–4:

> In exercising police tasks, judicial leadership is in the hands of the Attorney General. All things related to instructions from the higher level have to be submitted to the chief of the Polri, His Excellency Raden Said Soekanto Tjokrodiatmodjo, with address: Department of Internal Affairs, Rijswijk No. 7. This Edict should be noted by all civil servants and other concerned parties.

See also Turan *et al.* (2000), p. 45.

15 Anderson (1972); Sundhaussen (1982), p. 10.
16 Intended to avoid the vulnerability of the threatened Republican government having all its institutions in one city.
17 Wiradihardja (1971), pp. 12–15.
18 For these and other developments during Sekango's time in office see Hadiman (1998), pp. 24–35.
19 Turan *et al.* (2000), p. 56.
20 In March 1950, the Ministry of Internal Affairs extended the roles and functions of the Pamong Praja as Municipal Police (Satuan Polisi Pamong Praja: Satpol PP). As security officers for local government after Indonesian Independence, the Pamong Praja had been given only limited roles and functions. See *Berita Indonesia* (November 3, 1951), 'Kepolisian Negara di Bawah PM'; Sato (1996).
21 See Oudang (1952), pp. 34–39.
22 These included the Police Youth Movement of the Republic of Indonesia (Angkatan Muda Polisi Republik Indonesia) in Jakarta; the Indonesian Police Youth (Pemuda Polisi Republik Indonesia) in Kediri, East Java; the Police Special Vanguard (Barisan Polisi Istimewa) in Solo, Central Java; the Union of Police Workers (Persatuan Sekerja Polisi) in Purwokerto, Central Java; and the Labor Association of the Indonesian Police (Ikatan Buruh Polisi Republik Indonesia) in Bojonegoro, East Java.
23 The P3RI became representative of the Polri in playing an active role in social and political affairs, participating in the 1955 elections and assigning the Polri representatives in the Constitutional Assembly (Dewan Konstituante). For more on P3RI, see Mabes Polri (1999b), pp. 52–58.
24 For more information about the PP, see Anderson (1972); Jamin (1946).
25 For more discussion of Tan Malaka, see Jamin (1946); Poeze (1988); Poeze (1999); Poeze (2008).
26 For more on this decree about the Polri becoming part of the military force, see Hadiman and Suparmin (1985), pp. 237–238, Oudang (1952), pp. 66–69, and Soeriatmadja (1971), pp. 78–83.
27 Soekanto had a close relationship with Sjahrir and other members of the Socialist Party. This relationship with Sjahrir was later used by the Communist Party in pushing him out from his position as Polri chief in 1959. See Turan *et al.* (2000), pp. 163–173; *Pikiran Rakyat* (July 1, 1957), 'Polisi Soekanto di Daerah-daerah: Saya Tak Lihat ada Separatis'.
28 'Mr' is the title of someone with a legal qualification. More information on Mr Hindromartono is in Gunseikanbu (1943), p. 10.
29 The position of the Polri was effectively maintained under this emergency cabinet, which answered directly to President Sukarno who appointed Vice-President Hatta as Prime Minister. This government's Decree No. 1/1948 stipulated that for the period of the emergency cabinet, the Polri would be directly under the team of the president and vice-president, as head of state and head of government respectively.
30 Anderson (1972), pp. 299 and 422. See also Hadiman and Suparmin (1985), pp. 340–341. For more information on Hindromartono, see Gunseikanbu (1943), p. 10.

32 *Historical legacies and early* reformasi

31 For more explanation on the Polri's policies of coordination across Java see Hadiman and Suparmin (1985), pp. 385–386.
32 Hadiman and Suparmin (1985), p. 384.
33 On May 15, 1949, the Government integrated the Polri and the military police into the Government Military Police (PPM). Since the Polri was in the military government, almost every structure of the Military District Command had a crime investigation section and detectives as well as other common police structures. However, while the heads of the Military District Command were military personnel, the positions associated with police tasks were still held by police officers or military police officers as members of the overall PPM. Administratively and organizationally, the Polri was a separate department, with its presence in the PPM being only for field operations.
34 Hadiman and Suparmin (1985), pp. 420–425.
35 The Agreement also stated that all political prisoners arrested by the Dutch when they had attacked Yogyakarta and Indonesian territories in their Second Police Action had to be released. Reid (1974).
36 There was no official documentation of how many Polri members were killed during 1945–1949, but according to M. Jasin, thousands were killed across Indonesia. See Zachrie and Wiwanto (eds) (2010), pp. 93–130.
37 For more discussion on the RIS, see Reid (1974).
38 Not only administrative control, as had been planned by Van Nes.
39 The political parties were interested in getting support from the Polri personnel and their families. There were more than 40,000 personnel, which would give parties a significant number of supporters from the Polri. See Feith (1957); Lev (2009), pp. 193–201; and Suryadinata (2002), pp. 19–34.
40 As the state security actors, the Polri and the TNI were involved in fighting rebellions and separatist movements. See Soeriatmadja (1971); Tanumidjaja (1971); Wiradihardja (1971); and Hadiman and Suparmin (1985).
41 Based on Chief of the Polri Decree No. 5/IV/Sek/1952 dated January 7, 1952, the Decree of Minister of Internal Affairs No. Pol. 4/2/28/Mm dated March 13, 1952 and the Decree of the Prime Minister No. Pol. 25922/1952 dated July 31, 1952. The structure included: The Police of Jakarta; The Police of West Java Province; The Police of Central Java Province; The Police of East Java Province; The Police of North Sumatra Province; The Police of Central Sumatra Province; The Police of South Sumatera Province; The Police of Kalimantan Province; The Police of Sulawesi Province; The Police of Nusa Tenggara Province; The Police of Maluku Province. The function and structure of Departments were: Secretariat; Civil Affairs; Finance; Equipment; Regional Inspection; Mobile Brigade (Brimob); State Safety Supervision; Crime Investigation; Maritime Police; Education and Inspection. The organizational structure of the provincial police suited the needs of each province, but followed the organizational structure at the central level. The institutional structure of the Polri was then: National Police Headquarters; Provincial Police; Municipality Police; Sub-Regional Police; District Police; Precinct Police; Local Area Police; Sub-District Police; Police Post.
42 Tanumidjaja (1971), pp. 115–120. Turan *et al.* (2000), pp. 157–161.
43 The State Committee formed was led by Mr Wongsonegoro, deputy prime minister, with members: Police Commissioner Waluyo Soegondo as secretary, Djanuismadi as the representative from the Ministry of Internal Affairs, Mr Soedrajat and Mr Senoadjie as representatives from the Ministry of Justice Affairs, and Mr Memet Tanumidjaja as representative from the P3RI. The members of the committees were non-partisan, except Wongsonegoro who was a PNI member.
44 In particular, Indonesia was building a new constitution through the Constitutional Assembly and Parliament. Officers of the Polri who became Members of Parliament and of the Constitutional Assembly were Mr Mohammad Basah and Memet Tanumidjaja for the Parliament, and Soekarno Djojonegoro, A. Bastari, and Moedjoko for the Constitutional Assembly.

45 The DI/TII uprisings were led by Kartosuwiryo and followed by several regions in Aceh and South Sulawesi because they were dissatisfied with central government policies. See Ramage (1995), pp. 21–35.
46 Westerling, an ex-captain of the Dutch army, led the APRA rebellion to create an unstable political situation after the transfer of sovereignty of Indonesia from the Netherlands. See Wilson (1989).
47 The RMS uprising was a self-proclaimed republic in the Maluku Islands in April 1950 led by Dr Soumokil. See Wilson (2008), pp. 32–35.
48 Andi Aziz, a former captain of the Koninklijk Nederlands Indisch Leger (the Royal Netherlands East Indies Army) in the State of Eastern Indonesia was unsatisfied with the process of re-integration of that state into the RIS and then the NKRI (Negara Kesatuan Republik Indonesia – Unitary State of the Republic of Indonesia), and demanded all personnel under his command be accepted as personnel in the RIS Army. See Feith (1957), pp. 65–68.
49 Kahin (1999), pp. 446–450; Djojoadisurjo (1978), pp. 127–129; Hadiman and Suparmin (1985).
50 Including establishing the Air and Maritime Police, the Pioneer Police, Police Women's and Railway Train Police Units, joining Interpol, and forming the National Central Bureau (NCB) as the branch of the Interpol in Indonesia.
51 Even though that relationship was referred to only in a Prime Ministerial Decree, not in laws or higher legal forms such as Presidential Decrees. In Law No. 22/1948 and Law No. 1/1957 on local government there were no explanations about local authorities on police matters. This mean that policies of local leaders in relation to police were to follow those set at the national level.
52 Primary Cabinet Members were ministers who has power to make policy and decisions. The Polri chief and the TNI, attorney general, and supreme court were cabinet members, but not as primary cabinet members. See Simanjuntak (2003), pp. 199–207; Lev (2009), pp. 193–201.
53 Hadiman (1998), pp. 90–91.
54 The Committee of Ten consisted of: Chief Commissioner Djen Moh. Soerjopranoto, Head of the Jakarta Police Commissariat; Chief Commissioner Soeleiman Effendi, Head of the Crime Investigation Unit of the Polri; Chief Commissioner Soekarno Djojonegoro, Head of the East Java Police Commissariat; Chief Commissioner Sadikun, Head of the Riau Police Commissariat; Chief Commissioner Sarwono Tjokrodiningrat, from Inspection Section, Headquarters of the Polri; Adjutant Chief Commissioner Mr Drs Soebroto, Secretary of the Polri; Adjutant Chief Commissioner Soetarto, Head of Supervision, Central Java Police Commissariat; Commissioner AR Djajalaksana, Head of the Crime Investigation Unit, Central Java Police Commissariat; Commissioner Moedjoko Koesoemodihardjo, from the Dinas Pengawasan Keamanan Negara (State Security Intelligence Service) Section, Headquarters of the Polri; Commissioner Soetjipto Danoekoesoemo, Commander of Brimob, Central Java Police Commissariat. See Zachrie and Wiwanto (eds) (2010), pp. 209–213.
55 The corruption in the Polri happened almost from its establishment; however, the motive for corruption in the Polri then was not the same as in the current era. For example, see Djamin (1995), pp. 80–89.
56 This interest came from Polri officers who graduated from the Japanese Police School, such as Soetjipto Danoekoesoemo, A.R. Djajalaksana and Moedjoko Koesoemodihardjo; they claimed support from other Japanese-trained officers.
57 This interest came from senior officers such as Soekarno Djojonegoro and Djen Moch. Soerjopranoto who, with Sosro Danoekoesoemo, had previously taken over the leadership of the Polri when the Dutch in the Second Police Action had arrested Soekanto and Soemarto.
58 The two were Soetarto and Soetjipto Danoekoesoemo, while the other five were Chief Commissioner Enoch Danoebrata, and Commissioners Soemeru, Soeparto, Drs

Soekandar and Poerwata. Only Soetarto and Soetjipto Danoekoesoemo were directly involved with this conflict; the others just followed because they had information that the committee had supported Sukarno, so they joined that group. Djamin (1995), pp. 80–89. Zachrie and Wiwanto (eds) (2010), p. 213.
59 Hendrowinoto *et al.* (2007a), p. 68.
60 For more about this speech, see Turan *et al.* (2000), p. 167.
61 Government Decree (Peraturan Pemerintah, PP) No. 10/1959 on the militarization of the Polri by integrating it into the ABRI, and PP No. 57/1959 on changes in the organizational structure of the Polri, which modified the former Presidential Decree No. 21/1960; MPRS (Majelis Permusyawaratan Rakyat Sementara – Temporary People's Consultative Assembly, the first title of the Parliament in the Guided Democracy period) Resolution No. II/MPRS/1960; DPR GR (Dewan Perwakilan Rakyat Gotong Royong – Mutual Aid National Parliament, the later title) Act No. 13/1961; Presidential Decree No. 225/Plt/1962; Presidential Decree No. 134/1962, dated April 12, 1962; and Presidential Decree No. 15/19.
62 For example, *Pelopor Baru* (September 7, 1966), 'AKRI Waspada Thd Subversi Komunis'.
63 There were many senior police officers with higher rank and experiences considered better qualified to be Minister/Commander of the Polri. These included Soetjipto Joedodihardjo, who had been replaced as a deputy head of the BPI (Badan Pusat Intelijen – Central Intelligence Board/Agency) the year before by Soetarto.
64 *Merdeka* (October 5, 1964), 'Kita Tidak Gentar Menghadapi Ancaman'. See also *Sinar Harapan* (December 31, 1964), 'Rapatkan Barisan di Bawah Bendera Revolusi'.
65 For example see *Angkatan Bersenjata* (July 2, 1965), 'AKRI Berjuang Untuk Amankan Revolusi'; and *Angkatan Bersenjata* (September 7, 1965), 'AKRI adalah A.K. Revolusi Indonesia dan A.K. Ampera'. Beside Soetarto, there were other PKI sympathizers in charge in the BPI who wanted to use the momentum to replace Soetjipto Joedodihardjo as chief of the INP (Indonesian National Police) after the PKI failure. See *Pelopor Baru* (January 18, 1967), 'Men/Pangak Belum Punya Fakta-fakta Nyata Tentang Gerpol/PKI'. See also Wiwoho and Chaeruddin (1990).
66 *Berita Indonesia* (May 10, 1965), 'Brigjen Polisi Soetjipto Joedodihardjo Diangkat Sebagai Men/Pangak'.
67 *Sinar Harapan* (June 3, 1965), 'AKRI Harus Utuh, Efektif & Penuh Data Improvisasi'.
68 *Berita Indonesia* (March 7, 1967), 'Men/Pangak Soetjipto Joedodihardjo Kepercayaan Kepada Pak Harto Kehormatan Bagi ABRI'.
69 *Berita Yudha* (July 16, 1966), 'Pancasila Tidak Boleh Jadi Monopoli Golongan'. See also *Kompas* (August 27, 1966), 'Sikap AKRI Sudah Jelas'.
70 Decree No. Pol. 34/SK/MK/66 on April 5, 1966 on the formation of clearance teams.
71 *Kompas* (July 29, 1966), 'Oditur-oditur AKRI Diambil Sumpahnya'.
72 The other was Police Brigadier General Soemarsono, Former Head of the East Java Police Commissariat.
73 Police Brigadier General H. Soejono and Chief Commissioner Drs Boegi Supeno led the investigation. See *Pelopor Baru* (December 8, 1966), 'Roda peradilan Dalam AKRI Diharapkan Dapat Berputar Cepat'; *Pelopor Baru* (June 8, 1967), 'Polisi-polisi Yang Diadili'.
74 *Angkatan Bersenjata* (August 4, 1966), 'Penyelesaian Intern AKRI Perlukan Kecepatan Berpikir dan Tindakan Tegas'.
75 The Air Force was not included as there were concerns that some of its senior members had at least sympathized with the September 1965 Movement, and several of its officers had been directly involved in it.
76 *Pelopor Baru* (November 14, 1966), 'AKRI Pegang Teguh Pernyataan Bersama ABRI 5 Mei'.
77 For more discussion of Sukarno's relations with the security agencies during the Guided Democracy period, see Ledge (2003); Lev (2009), pp. 267–275.

2 Under the thumb

The police during Suharto's New Order and early *reformasi*

> The Police during Suharto's New Order era was a law enforcement agency with tied hands and feet.
>
> (Adrianus Meliala, 2009)

Corruption, intervention and independence

Major General Suharto succeeded Sukarno as acting president in 1967 and became president in 1968, and the New Order regime was established and consolidated. Post-Sukarno, the Polri took part in the consolidation and was 'cleansed' from the influence of communist elements. As part of the military regime the Polri became a watchdog of the regime to secure all the policies of the New Order, which relied on political stability, national security and prohibitions of various activities thought to be against its interests in economic development (Bienen 1968: 37–40; Ulfeder 2005: 310–312).

Hoegeng Iman Santoso's term (1968–1971)

President Suharto replaced Soetjipto Joedodihardjo as police minister/Polri chief with Police Commissioner General Hoegeng Iman Santoso, with Police Inspector General Tengku Abdulaziz as his deputy.[1]

During Hoegeng's three-year leadership of the Polri, internal conflicts were lessened, with some of the non-communist officers who had been involved restored but to non-strategic positions.[2] Hoegeng also successfully resolved a small revolt against their non-indigenous officers by local police in the newly annexed Papua territory over corruption issues.[3]

His persistence against corruption led to conflict with the military and political elites around Suharto.[4] His popularity with the general public became increasingly strong and, perhaps, of concern to Suharto.[5] He fell from presidential favour by publicly stating and promoting the idea that in the future, the Polri would return to its original role and function as a state apparatus for maintaining a situation conducive to supporting internal security (*kamdagri*) and public security and order, so that it was not appropriate for the Polri to remain in the same organization under the Ministry of Security and Defence Affairs and the ABRI.

Mohammad Hasan's term (1971–1974)

Mohammad Hasan was expected to continue the momentum of the Polri in its role of maintaining the security and economic stability of Suharto and the New Order regime.[6] While Hasan was Polri chief[7] the government started its first Five-Year Development Plan (Pelita – Pembangunan Lima Tahun), which was considered to be the the New Order regime's most important and prestigious showcase programme to improve the Indonesian economy.[8]

However, this was also an era of political consolidation for the New Order, and the Polri was involved in political cases: a Russian diplomat in Indonesia who was allegedly defecting to the United States;[9] the birth of the Petition 13 Group (Kelompok Petisi 13) as a political response from the public to the poor performance of the Polri;[10] the minister of internal affairs[11] at the time, Basuki Rachmat, ordering the heads of local police, who were subordinate to the chief of the INP (Indonesian National Police – Kepolisian Negara Republik Indonesia), to report on the local security situations to provincial governors or district bupatis and insisting that the reports were related to their responsibility to assist local government in securing its territory;[12] the first general election in the New Order era in 1971 and the general session in 1973; and the Affair of January 15, 1974 (Malapetaka 15 Januari, known as Malari), which interrupted for the moment that political consolidation.[13]

The role of the Polri in these political events did not appear strong, especially in the Malari riots where various factions of the military were involved. Kopkamtib (Komando Pemulihan Keamanan dan Ketertiban – Command for the Restoration of Security and Order)[14] took over the situation, leaving the Polri to take only a back-up role.[15] Polri also restructured their territorial organization to match the territorial military command in the TNI AD (Indonesian Army Land Forces) territorial structure.[16] These situations certainly built strong inducements for the Polri in all its policies and operations.[17]

Widodo Budidarmo's term (1974–1978)

Police Major General Widodo Budidarmo had previously been head of the Jakarta Metro Polda. Although he was one of the two[18] recommended by the Polri's Wanjakti (Dewan Kepangkatan dan Jabatan Tinggi – Police Promotion Board), his performance as Polri chief was widely considered to be poor. The deputy commander of the ABRI and commander of Kopkamtib, Admiral Sudomo,[19] even stated explicitly that the Widodo era was the worst phase in the history of the Polri.[20] The only Polri activity to be appreciated was its supporting role as part of the ABRI in the integration of East Timor into Indonesia.[21]

The Polri was more widely complained about for its increasing corruption and extortion[22] – as reflected in the use of the term 'prit Jigo' (stop, bribe, and go) to describe the method used to solve traffic violations – and illegal racketeering,[23] which increased in the Widodo era.[24] Moreover, the increase in corruption had involved middle- and high-ranking officers in Widodo's Headquarters, with the commercialization of titles and jobs in the Polri from the headquarters down to Polda and Polres.[25] One of the Polri headquarters' corruption cases reportedly involved Rp.6.4 billion, a very large amount of money at the time.[26] This incident made President Suharto decide to immediately replace Widodo with a more competent police officer to rule the institution.[27]

Awaloedin Djamin's term (1978–1982)

The internal situation of the Polri was considered so bad that the Ministry of Security and Defence Affairs and the ABRI headquarters did not look for recommendations from the Polri's Wanjakti and went outside Polri headquarters to find recommendations to replace Widodo. They found Awaloedin Djamin, a police lieutenant general with a doctoral degree who had served as ambassador to West Germany.[28]

Djamin acknowledged the poor image of the Polri, but he argued that it the Polri was not solely to blame. The number of police officers was too low compare to the population and the scope of their work.[29] Djamin also assumed that the low operational budget was the biggest reason behind the poor performance of the Polri;[30] in addition, the educational process needed to be reviewed as it was producing only low capabilities among the Polri officers.[31]

Djamin resolved cases involving Widodo's deputy and other police officers.[32] Another problem was that Polri had unclear boundaries; this had contributed to the decline of its public image as it was widely seen as similar to the military, given that its pattern of law enforcement adopted military approaches.[33] Djamin attempted to increase the number of police relative to population with a strategic plan for the Polri;[34] he also promoted the teaching of measured and focused policing based on stringent selection and publication of manuals for Polri officers and personnel.[35]

Other positive steps related to the roles and functions of the Polri in the field were improving community participation by establishing self-organized Registered Security Guards (Satuan Pengamanan – Satpam), especially in business sectors.[36] To improve security in rural communities, Djamin intensified the Neighbourhoods Security System (Siskamling) programme, which was based on initiatives by local communities to protect and secure their own area themselves.[37] These were coordinated by the Polri through the local Babinkamtibmas (Polri NCO for Security and Order at Village Level).[38]

Another Djamin policy related to the budget for the Polri. The government raised its allocation from Rp.4 billion to Rp.6.5 billion in 1981.[39] In addition, during Djamin's period in office, the Book of the Indonesian Code of Criminal Procedure (KUHAP: Kitab Undang-undang Hukum Acara Pidana) was completed and promulgated in 1981. This new code confirmed that the investigators in criminal cases would be Polri officers.[40]

Anton Soedjarwo's term (1982–1986)

Polri chief Anton Soedjarwo demonstrated further consolidation and subordination of the Polri into ABRI. Before and during his period as Polri chief, Soedjarwo's framework policy was known as the Plan of Consolidation and Function (Rekonfu: Rencana, Konsolidasi, dan Fungsi).[41] This operational-practical approach gave the impression that Anton Soedjarwo used military training patterns. Anton Soedjarwo also developed, revised and applied the Police Code of Ethics, which was a barometer for police performance in support of the New Order regime.

Under Soedjarwo the Polri were noticeably co-opted into the violent practices of ABRI, with two obvious examples being the Tanjung Priok tragedy in September 1984[42] and the Petrus Affair (*penembak misterius* – mysterious shootings).[43] The intervention made by ABRI was large and brutal, with the Polri considered to be acting as a tool of ABRI and Kopkamtib. It was no surprise, then, that there was a tendency to include the Polri in the blame for the tragedy, although the Jakarta military command carried out the main operation.

The Petrus Affair was a 'state crime' where thousands of alleged criminals were killed and left lying in the streets.[44] This happened mainly in areas of increased crime such as North and South Sumatra, Jakarta, West Java and East Java. The policy came from the Kopkamtib, and used various security institutions, especially the Territorial Army Commands and some local police, as executioners. This state-organized team terrorized criminals, alleged criminals, and anti-government activists, spreading fear of death on the street, which made criminals turn themselves in as they felt safer in prison.

Moch. Sanoesi's term (1986–1991)

Anton Soedjarwo was replaced by Lieutenant General Moch. Sanoesi, the first of the high-ranking police officers who had not been a combatant in the 1945–1949 War of Independence. He did not faced political problems, as the New Order was well consolidated; in 1988 Suharto's fifth re-election was organized easily, and Suharto felt that the internal security and order situation no longer needed the powerful military-oriented Kopkamtib and replaced it with the civil-oriented Bakorstranas.[45] Resources allocated to the police were still limited, and Sanoesi established a programme called Dynamic Optimization (Optimasi dan Dinamisasi, known as Opdin) to make the best use of them.[46]

During Sanoesi's term the Polri was relatively free from ABRI's intervention in its operational context, except on sensitive issues related to politics and state affairs. Sanoesi's most recognized achievement was in fighting crime, especially combating smugglers along the Straits of Malacca, including those impersonating members of the separatist Free Aceh Movement (Gerakan Aceh Merdeka) in order to smuggle weapon and drugs.[47]

Kunarto's term (1991–1993)

President Suharto appointed Police Lieutenant General Kunarto as the next Polri chief.[48] His main strategy was summed up in the slogan 'Best Service Through Togetherness', intended to build internal solidarity among police to focus on the roles and functions of police professionalism.[49] Kunarto believed that in the future the Polri as an institution should be separated from the military, because of its different culture and approaches, and that there should no longer be intervention and overlapping with the military and the government based on the political and economic interests of the Polri.[50] He was prepared to refuse what he considered unacceptable government pressures.[51] During Kunarto's time in office the 1992 general election was successfully organized with the police providing security.

Kunarto led the Polri for only two years, because he was asked by the commander of the ABRI at the time, Tri Sutrisno, if he would agree to be replaced since the chiefs of all the three other branches in the ABRI were going to change and ABRI wanted stability and consistency in the changeovers.[52]

Banurusman Astrosemitro's term (1993–1996)

Police Major-General Banurusman Astrosemitro was strongly recommended by Kunarto as his replacement and was approved by ABRI headquarters and Suharto, having demonstrated his ability to maintain security during the 1992 Non-Aligned Summit in Jakarta.[53] In Banurusman's three years in office, the Polri faced three big cases: a murder case involving an Indonesian in the United States;[54] implementation of a new traffic law;[55] and the murder of Marsinah, a labour activist at the Catur Putra Surya company (CPS) in Sidoarjo, East Java, in 1993.[56] The Polri solved the first two problems well, but were not successful in handling the case of Marsinah. There was great political pressure, and it was alleged that personnel of the Kodim (Komando Distrik Militer – Military District Command) and Koramil (Komando Rayon Militer – Sub-district Military Command) were involved in the murder, so the Polri preferred not to disclose the proceedings of this case to the public.[57]

Banurusman recognized that the Polri was still controlled within the hierarchical confines of the ABRI command and by the intervention of other branches, particularly the army, with almost no resistance from the Polri. The Polri in the Banurusman era tried to avoid handling political cases, putting its limited resources into acting against perpetrators of crime who attacked not only the community but also the officers of the Polri.[58]

Dibyo Widodo's term (1996–1998) and the fall of Suharto

Political tension began to heat up in 1996 because of people's dissatisfactions with the government and because of the upcoming general election. Feisal Tandjung, commander of ABRI at the time, replaced Banurusman with Police

Lieutenant General Dibyo Widodo to prepare security measurements for the upcoming election. Dibyo took quick steps in this by improving the Polri's internal structure,[59] establishing a Fast Response Unit (URC: Unit Reaksi Cepat), and increasing the number of companies in the Brimob from 49 to 56. The government also replaced the current law on the police with a new one.[60]

The first test of Dibyo's leadership was the July 27, 1996 affair.[61] The internal conflict within the Indonesian Democratic Party (PDI) between Megawati Sukarnoputri and government-backed Soerjadi factions eventually turned into a conflict between the people and government, with the Polri and the military involved. Although security for the 1997 general election was generally adequate, the number of conflicts and chaos due to the government policy of taking one side in a party before an election became a trigger of growing discontent.

Eventually, on May 12, 1998, security officers allegedly shot four Trisakti University students in a public protest rally in the middle of Jakarta. The incident, later known as the Trisakti Case, triggered widespread rioting, mainly against the New Order but in some areas based on anti-Chinese feelings and religious and ethnic issues. This situation rapidly went beyond the control capabilities of the Polri; the security of the capital and of a number of other strategic cities including Medan, Bandung, Surabaya, Yogyakarta and Makassar was taken over by ABRI, with the Polri only supporting the other ABRI branches, especially the army.[62]

To help protect the image of the Polri, Dibyo Widodo set up a Polri team to investigate the Trisakti tragedy, to reduce the danger of the Polri being set up as a scapegoat. He also involved civil society by asking Adnan Buyung Nasution to be attorney for the Polri's officers and personnel. This was considered too much for ABRI Headquarters. On June 28, General Wiranto, the Minister for Security and Defence and commander of ABRI, asked President Habibie to replace Dibyo Widido with Roesmanhadi, a member of Wiranto's own expert staff.

The roles and position of the Polri in regime change

After Suharto resigned, the regime was in the hands of Habibie but was mainly dependent on the decisions made within ABRI. As major civil disorder – including demonstrations, rioting, and inter-ethnic, inter-religious and separatist violence – flared up and spread across Indonesia,[63] all the elements of ABRI were needed to restore security and order. This meant the Polri was acting to support the regime, and there were no reported cases of police officers or personnel refusing orders or try to bring the police down. Although there were many incidents of violence by ABRI, such as the November 11–13, 1998 Semanggi I and the September 24, 1999 Semanggi II Cases in Jakarta, the Polri was no longer trapped as a scapegoat and the military was seen as the actual perpetrators of the violence.[64]

There are at least five possibilities for a police force during a regime change: supporting the ruling regime; supporting political change; being neutral; supporting strong leaders who take over the situation; and initiating the constitutional change of the regime. There are in fact other possibilities, including mixtures of these five.

There was not really any likelihood that the Polri would take any action conflicting with ABRI. There was a combination of reasons for this. The Polri was subordinate and relatively powerless in relation to ABRI. The appointment of 'Wiranto's man' Roesmanhadi as the Polri chief gave ABRI direct personal access to authority and information about the dynamics of ideas and activities within Polri. The Polri therefore followed the ABRI lead in supporting the ruling regime while it made political changes towards a democratic system.

The disassociation of the Polri from ABRI

A major element of dismantling the New Order regime was the disassociation of the Polri from ABRI. This has been described by Indonesian police academics[65] as having been desirable for several reasons. However, when the changes were made in the early years of post-Suharto *reformasi*, they were not due to active pressures from the Polri itself but were forced on it by ABRI decisions, supported by the public.[66]

Four things affected the Polri during the regime change: internal dynamics in the ABRI;[67] policies related to the change of national leader;[68] national-level leaders who voiced the need to change the national leader;[69] and public demands for a change of national leader and implementation of government free of 'korupsi, kolusi dan nepotisme' (KKN – corruption, collusion and nepotism).[70] These issues made the Polri recognize that they should seek independence and professionalism, and should no longer be dictated to or controlled by the ABRI.[71]

In fact, there had been several discussions within ABRI about disassociation ever since the late 1980s[72] when the Ministry of Security and Defence Affairs Working Group had recommended that the Polri remain within the ministry but be disassociated from the ABRI. This proposal from the Ministry of Security and Defence Affairs was submitted to the National Resilience Institute (Lemhanas),[73] which formed another working group to consider the recommendations. After three years, the Lemhanas working group made its report, which essentially agreed with the conclusions of the ministry working group.

Sofjan Jacoeb, head of Jakarta Metro Polda, then suggested that Polri chief Banurusman ask universities to promote the disassociation of the police from ABRI. This produced supportive ideas, opposing arguments, and publicity, which brought the issue into public discourse. The members of the national parliament's committee discussed the issue in the context of defence and security, considering the possibility of full autonomy of the Polri from the ABRI.[74]

After Suharto's resignation, Dibyo Widodo's policy to set up a Polri team to investigate the shootings of the Trisakti tragedy as well as a Reform Team[75] raised support from the public, universities, and members of parliament for the disassociation of the Polri from the ABRI. However, the replacement of Widodo with Roesmanhadi halted this momentum, although the Reform Team's report[76] and suggestions for changes was presented to the leaders of ABRI on October 1, just one month before the special session of parliament in November 1998.

Nevertheless, greater pressure for changes was coming from ABRI. This was partly to improve its image, partly in response to public and parliamentary demands and its leaders' convictions about the need for ABRI to carry out reforms and move into a new role as a professional military organization without the dual role. The recommendations, as presented to Wiranto as commander of ABRI and Minister of Security and Defence Affairs, was 'moving back to barracks', where ABRI should be focused as professional military with three branches (army, navy and air force); its command structure should be simplified; and the Polri, with its different role and function, should be disassociated from ABRI.

There was much support for this but also public disagreement from members and retired members of ABRI,[77] and from the public, who distrusted the Polri and its military-like tendency to brutality, while Roesmanhadi took only a cautious position. The opposition used four main arguments: first, the Polri was not ready or was too weak;[78] second, there were historical, political, and emotional reasons for not disassociating;[79] third, the moment of proposed disassociation was considered not a good time for it;[80] fourth, the army, particularly its territorial units, would lose legitimacy and justification when performing extra-legal territorial activities.[81]

Minister and commander Wiranto, with the agreement of important senior ABRI officers, made the historic decision to recommend to President Habibie that the disassociation should be carried out in six months, on April 1, 1999, announcing this on the fifty-third anniversary of ABRI.[82] The Polri accepted the disassociation, sent members for a joint ABRI/Polri committee in the Ministry of Security and Defence Affairs, and set up internal groups to work out the practical details. It also followed Wiranto's suggestion that its Reform Team continue, with the result that a 'Blue Book' appeared in July 1999 and was used subsequently as a guide for reforms in the Polri.[83] Less than two years later, on 1 July 2000, in the era of President Abdurrahman Wahid, the Polri, disassociated from ABRI, came directly under the supervision of the President's office.[84]

A new INP paradigm and its impact on the disassociation of the Polri from ABRI

The Polri's disassociation from the ABRI also marked a change in paradigm from police as fighters for independence to professional police dealing with internal security affair (Kamdagri). The Polri, post-disassociation from the ABRI, had to follow the 'Blue Book' as guidance to become an independent and professional police force, ridding the Polri institution from all military culture.

The Polri paradigm as a professional police force had been built along with the development of the Polri organization since its formulation and then after detaching from the Ministry of Home Affairs in 1946. Changes in this policing paradigm occurred in 1959 in the regime of Sukarno's Guided Democracy (see Table 2.1). There was a changing awareness between the Polri and ABRI that they had

Table 2.1 Changing the Polri paradigm

Era and chief	Self-perception	Basic idea	Roles
Sukarno era			
Soekanto[1]	Combatant police	The Polri is part of the people	Internal security and fighter function
Soekarno Djojonegoro[2]	Combatant police	The Military and the police have similar roles and functions	Integration with the military
Soetjipto Joedodihardjo[3]	Combatant police	Integration of the Polri with the people to support the revolution (Struggle Program of Takari)	Mixed roles and functions between internal security, defence, and regime protection
Suharto Era			
Hugeng Iman Santoso[4]	Combatant police	Dual function of ABRI (Base on *Cadek II*)	Part of ABRI, the Polri has a security and defence role, involved in socio-political affairs
Awaloeddin Djamin[5]	Combatant and professional police	Integration of roles between ABRI, the Polri and the people	Internal security and defence role to support ABRI and protect the regime
Post-Suharto era			
Roesmanhadi[6]	Independent professional police	Disassociation from ABRI	The Polri has only internal security role; different roles and functions from the military
Da'i Bachtiar[7]	Independent professional police	Addition of anti-terror police	The Polri becomes the main agency in counter-terrorism in Indonesia
Sutanto[8]	Independent professional police and public policing	Community policing; integrating the police role with the public	The Polri encourage the public to solve security problems, to protect and secure life and properties

Notes
1 Mabes Polri (1987).
2 Mabes Polri (1959).
3 Mabes Polri (1965).
4 Departemen Pertahanan dan Keamanan (1966); Rinakit (2005), p. 103.
5 Djamin (2001a).
6 Mabes Polri (1965).
7 See Chief of the Polri Decree, Skep Kapolri No. Pol.: Skep/30/VI/2002 on the establishment of the INP 88 Special Anti-Terror Detachment (Densus 88 AT). See also Anti-Terror Law No. 15/2003.
8 See Chief of the Polri, SKep Kapolri No. Pol.: Skep/737/X/2005 on the implementation of community policing.

similar roles and functions based on experiences in the past and future challenges. The change in paradigm had occurred again as Soetjpto Joedodihardjo led the Polri with strong support from President Sukarno and the Central Intelligence Agency (BPI) led by Deputy Prime Minister Soebandrio and his deputy, Police Brigadier General Soetarto. Soetarto directed the paradigm change, marked by the publication of the Takari Struggle Programme (Program Perjuangan Tahun Berdikari), which was a manifesto of government programmes related to anti-neocolonialism policy.

This programme had been abruptly revised in line with the fall of Sukarno's 'Old Order' regime from power in 1965; it was affirmed by the ABRI seminar that was conducted in November 1966 related to the future role of the police, which generated the ABRI doctrine, *Catur Dharma Eka Karma*,[85] and then by the Army Staff College (SESKOAD) Seminar in 1967, to make clear that the doctrine was to be a joint one for all three armed forces and the Polri.

The paradigm had been implemented during Hoegeng Iman Santoso's era as chief of the Polri (1968–1971). He was not comfortable with this paradigm, since it gave many opportunities for intervention from ABRI. However, Hoegeng was powerless to resist the doctrine. In the era of Awaluddin Djamin (1978–1982), the word 'professional' was added to the Polri self-perception to support both the remaining doctrine of Polri as independence fighters and also their characterization as being professional personnel. Awaluddin Djamin took various measures to organize and clean up the Polri against deviant practices.

The new paradigm of Polri post-disassociation was implemented during Da'i Bachtiar's term (2001–2005). Bachtiar made giant steps towards realizing the Polri's new paradigm of being an independent and professional police force, lobbying and pushing the DPR and the president to issue a new police act, Law No. 2/2002 on the Polri, and taking over the role of counter-terrorism from the military.[86] During Sutanto's term as chief of the Polri (2005–2008), the self-perception added public policing to support and extend the paradigm of Polri as independent and professional. The implementation of public policing had consequences for the role of the Polri of integrating it more with the public, while encouraging the public to solve its own security problems, protecting and securing itself and its properties.[87]

The change of police paradigm in the organization also affected the recruitment pattern for the Polri leaders (see Table 2.2). The Brimob and the criminal investigation unit (Reskrim: Reserse and Kriminal) were dominant in providing 16 of the 19 leaders for the Polri during the period between 1945 and 2008. The confirmation of the Polri paradigm in police history as combatant police was indicated by the high representation (eight out of 19) of chiefs of the Polri coming from the Brimob.

Nevertheless, there have been an equal number who came up through Reskrim and significantly it appears that there has been a clear shift away from Brimob backgrounds to Reskrim ones, including five of the six chiefs from 1998 to 2008. This could be an indication of the paradigm change from more 'combatant' to more 'professional'.

Table 2.2 Chiefs of the Polri, 1945–2008

Name	Period	Unit	Graduated
R.S. Soekanto	1945–1959	Reskrim	Aspirant Commisaris van Politie[1]
R. Soekarno Djojonegoro[2]	1959–1964	Brimob	Ambtenaar Ilandesche Bestuurdients[3]
R. Soetjipto Danoekoesoemo	1964–1965	Brimob	Koto Kaisatsu Gakko[4]
Soetjipto Joedodihardjo	1965–1968	Brimob	Ambtenaar Ilandesche Bestuurdients
Hugeng Iman Santoso[5]	1968–1971	Reskrim	PTIK Class of 1952
Mohamad Hasan[6]	1971–1974	Lantas	PTIK Class of 1957
Widodo Budidarmo	1974–1978	Polair	PTIK Class of 1955
Awaluddin Djamin	1978–1982	Reskrim	PTIK Class of 1955
Anton Sudjarwo	1982–1986	Brimob	SPN[7]
Moch Sanoesi	1986–1991	Intelkam[8]	PTIK Class of 1962
Kunarto	1991–1993	Brimob	PTIK Class of 1965
Banurusman Astrosemitro	1993–1996	Brimob	Akpol Class of 1965
Dibyo Widodo	1996–1998	Brimob	Akpol Class of 1968
Roesmanhadi	1998–2000	Reskrim	Akpol Class of 1969
Rusdihardjo	2000	Reskrim	Akpol Class of 1969
S. Bimantoro	2000–2001	Brimob	Akpol Class of 1970
Chaeruddin Ismail[9]	2001	Reskrim	Akpol Class of 1971
Da'i Bachtiar	2001–2005	Reskrim	Akpol Class of 1972
Sutanto	2005–2008	Reskrim	Akpol Class of 1973

Sources: Djamin (2006); Hendrowinoto (2007); Mabes Polri (2008); Muradi (2009); PTIK (2010).

Notes
1 An Aspirant Commisaris van Politie was a graduate of the Higher Officer Police Academy in Dutch Colonial Indonesia; Soekanto was one of those who graduated from that Academy.
2 During the Dutch occupation, Soekarno Djojonegoro was a police *wedana*. When the Japanese took over Indonesia from the Netherlands, he joined the Department of Police and was as an officer in the Tokubetsu Keisatsu Tai, a police paramilitary unit in the Japanese colonial system.
3 An Ambtenaar Inlandesche Bestuurdients (Pangreh Praja in Indonesian) was a native public servant in the Dutch colonial system, including those who served as a *wedana* or in its lower ranks.
4 The Koto Kaisatsu Gakko was a police academy for higher-ranking police officers in Sukabumi, West Java, during the Japanese occupation.
5 Hoegeng was trained in three police schools: to become a Hoofd Agent Politie (Chief Police Agent) in the school for lower ranks in the last years of the Dutch occupation; at the Futsuka Kaisatsu Gakko, the second level of police academy, during the Japanese occupation; and at the PTIK during the first years of Independence, graduating in 1952.
6 M. Hasan was trained in two institutions: at the Secondary Training School for Native Officials (Middlebare Opleiding School voor Inlandsche Ambtenaren, Mosvia) under the Dutch; and the PTIK from 1952 to 1957. See *Kompas* (September 15, 1971), 'Mohamad Hasan, Kapolri yag Baru'; *Kompas* (October 4, 1971), 'Menteri Pertahanan dan Keamanan Soeharto: Pergantian Pejabat Tak Ada Hubungannya Dengan Suka atau Tidak Suka'.
7 The State School for Police (Sekolah Polisi Negara) was a conversion from the Japanese-era Koto Kaisatsu Gakko, and subsequently became the Police Academy in 1965. Anton Soedjarwo was the only one of the chiefs of the Polri who did not have an academic degree.
8 As a Polri officer, Sanusi had never had an appointment to a special unit such as the Reskrim Unit or the Brimob Unit. One of his staff when he was chief of the Polri told me that Sanusi was a good general of the PTIK, but then didn't respond when I showed him some evidence that Sanusi had a close relationship with BAKIN and ABRI headquarters. It is known that during that time, if you got close to ABRI and BAKIN headquarters this would take you to a higher and more strategic position in any institution.
9 Chaeruddin Ismail was made acting chief of the Polri when President Wahid tried to replace Bimantoro as chief of the Polri. See more in Chapter 3.

This was caused by three factors. The first was the strong political and military intervention in the process of selecting the chief of Polri after the Polri permanently joined with the ABRI. Political intervention from political parties and governments was strong in the Guided Democracy era up to the fall of Sukarno, although the Polri had joined the ABRI.[88] By contrast, the control was strong over Polri during the fall of Suharto's New Order, showing how the headquarters of ABRI systematically controlled internal dynamics in the Polri.

Second, there was a weak response to political dynamics due to lack of internal consolidation within the Polri. This situation gave the Polri a high level of political dependence on the regime and the control of the military. The position of chief of the Polri for some police was considered as 'political debt', which could be 'paid' by supporting the political policies of the ruling regime.[89]

Third, there was no boundary for the regeneration process of leaders at every level. The president could reflect this by rejections of candidates for chief of Polri. This in turn opened space for 'money politics mechanisms' that could defeat candidates proposed by the Wanjakti.

The New Order period presents a picture of a succession of efforts to further integrate the Polri into ABRI, at least as viewed from the regulations made by the government related to the position of the INP. From 1968 to 1998 the changes undertaken by the government can be divided into three phases.

First was the consolidation phase, between 1968 and 1986, when the Polri was under the Ministry of Security and Defence Affairs/Commander of the ABRI. The combined position of Minister of Security and Defence Affairs and ABRI commander was part of the New Order regime's integration of all policies related to the ABRI through a single umbrella organization.[90]

Second was the strengthening phase, between 1986 and 1996, when the New Order regime had been well organized and consolidated, so that the position of Polri was integrated completely into the ABRI.[91] This position made the Polri dependent in its leadership positioning on the ABRI headquarters through the Polri Supreme Board for Policy and Positioning (Wanjakti), which defined the various positions in the Polri institution and their duties.

Third, the supervision phase, between 1996 and the fall of Suharto from power. In the ABRI and the Ministry of Security and Defence Affairs, there was a discourse of gradually providing the Polri with more authority but still keeping it under the supervision of the Ministry of Security and Defence Affairs and ABRI headquarters. However, the Polri did not have a position outside the confines of the military structure.[92]

Notes

1 Based on Presidential Decree No. RI. 131/ABRI/1968. Hoegeng was a former Minister of State Finances and Polri Deputy Chief Operations. Tengku Abdulazis and Hoegeng were Polri officers of the same cohort. When Hoegeng was head of Reskrim of the North Sumatra Polda in 1956, Tengku Abdulaziz was head of the Medan Municipality Polres. *Pelopor Baru* (May 15, 1968), 'AKRI Ganti Panglima; Hoegeng Naik Pangkat'; Santoso *et al.* (2009).

2 *Pelopor Baru* (May 17, 1968), 'Tiga Pati AKRI Terlibat Gestapu'; *Warta Berita* (March 10, 1969), 'Pembersihan AKRI Terhadap Sisa-sisa G-30-S/PKI Jalan Terus'.
3 The indigenous police personnel in Papua considered they were being treated unfairly by the Polri, so they rebelled against their officers. Hoegeng investigated and took direct action against the corrupt officers. Hendrowinoto *et al.* (2007b), pp. 104–105.
4 These included three big cases which caused Hoegeng's problems with high officials of the New Order's political elite: car smuggling by Robby Tjahjadi, the Rene Louis Coenrad case, and a rape case involving an egg seller named Sumarijem, which later became known as the Sum Kuning Case. See *Angkatan Bersenjata* (July 1, 1969), 'Perlu Penegasan Lebih Lanjut tentang Tugas-tugas AKRI'; *Berita Yudha* (September 21, 1971), 'Kapolri Benarkan ada Pejabat-pejabat Terlibat Manipulasi 1.2 milyar'.
5 *Berita Yudha* (November 11, 1968), 'Putera Pak Harto Dihukum Denda Rp.300.-'; *Abadi* (December 18, 1970), 'Janji Kapolri Hoegeng: Taruna AKABRI yg Kroyok Rene Akan Diadili'; *Angkatan Bersenjata* (January 5, 1970), 'Peristiwa Sum Kuning: Polisi Juga dpt Dituntut Kapolri Hoegeng'.
6 Jenkins (1984); Dwipayana and Ramadhan (1989), especially Chapter 3; Elson (2001).
7 In 1969 the name of the Polri had been changed by Presidential Decree. No. 52/1969 from the National Police Force of the Republic of Indonesia (AKRI) to the Indonesian National Police (Polri), with their organic status and responsibilities in the Ministry of Security and Defence Affairs, and the title of its Head had been changed back from 'Commander' to 'Chief'.
8 *Berita Yudha* (October 4, 1971), 'Amanat Menhankam Pangab Jenderal TNI Soeharto pada Upacara Serah Terima Kapolri: Kepolisian Bertugas Mendorong Gerak Pembangunan'.
9 *Kompas* (June 19, 1972), 'Kapolri Komjen Mohammad. Hasan: Kewajiban Polri Mencari Diplomat Rusia yang Hilang'.
10 *Angkatan Bersenjata* (July 1, 1974), 'Polri Dalam Batas-batas Kemampuan Mencoba Memenuhi Keinginan Masyarakat'.
11 Internal Affairs included authority over local governments who were responsible to the Minister.
12 *Berita Buana* (December 2, 1972), 'Wapangab Jend. M. Panggabean Menyerahkan Bintang Jalasena Kl. I Kepada kapolri Komjen Polisi Mohamad Hasan'; *Angkatan Bersenjata* (May 21, 1974), 'Kapolri Resmikan Peleburan Komdak XII/Kalteng dan Komdak XIII/Kalsel'.
13 The Malari was an anti-Japanese protest demonstration about imported Japanese products, and also involved political turmoil due to miscommunication and internal conflict in the military between the Soemitro group and the Ali Moertopo group triggered by the role of President Suharto's personal assistant. See Cahyono (1998); Abdul Gani-Knapp (2007), pp. 126–132; *Tempo* (February 5, 2008) 'The Malari Mystery'.
14 Kopkamtib was established in October 1965, after G 30 S/PKI, to maintain national security and order and to ensure the New Order's Pembangunan Lima Tahun (Pelita) development programme ran well.
15 Security control was taken over by the ABRI, especially the army and Kopkamtib, led by General Soemitro, while other factions in the army led by Ali Moertopo and Soedjono Hoemardhani, personal assistant (aspri) of President Suharto, had advocated a hard line. For more about President Suharto's aspri, see Jenkins (1984), pp. 45–52; Elson (2001), pp. 168–170; Abdul Gani-Knapp (2007), pp. 125–130.
16 One of the military structure policies adopted was the merging of several provincial police forces; *Nusantara* (December 18, 1973), 'Kapolri Hasan: Eksistensi Kopkamtib Masih Perlu, Narkotika di Riau Didominir Cina'; *Merdeka* (June 13, 1974), 'Kapolri Jend. M. Hasan: Stabilitas Keamanan di Daerah Amat Penting'; *Angkatan Bersenjata* (May 24, 1974), 'Kapolri Resmikan komdak XV/Nusra di Denpasar'.
17 *Kompas* (July 2, 1973), 'Kapolri Moh. Hasan. Penjahat Sekalipun Harus Merasa Terlindungi Dalam Pemeriksaan Polisi'.

48   *Historical legacies and early* reformasi

18 The other was Sukahar, the head of the ABRI Academy and Widodo's predecessor as Jakarta Metro Kapolda.
19 Admiral Sudomo replaced TNI General Soemitro as commander of Kopkamtib after the Malari tragedy. Soemitro was dismissed and then retired from his military career. *Merdeka* (October 10, 1977), 'Gang Ala Mafia Dapat "backing" Oknum Polri'; *Tempo* (September 30, 1978), 'Sebuah Kasus Korupsi, Tapi Belum ...'.
20 *Angkatan Bersenjata* (September 29, 1978), 'Wibawa dan Kewenangan Polri Akan Ditegakkan Kembali'; Pour (1993); Sumarkidjo (2006).
21 In the East Timor Operation, the INP had a special detachment called the 'Alap-alap' focused on anti-riot measures and city fighting. See *Angkatan Bersenjata* (April 5, 1979), 'Jajaran Polri Hadapi Tantangan Berat'. Also see Hill (2002), pp. 34–39.
22 *Merdeka* (October 10, 1977), 'Gang ala Mafia Dapat "Backing" Oknum Polri'; for more information about corruption in the Polri in Widodo Budidarmo's period, see Jenkins (1984), pp. 241–247; Pour (1997); Djamin (1995).
23 'Prit jigo' was an idiomatic term to describe the negotiation of Polri traffic tickets in the street. *Berita Buana* (May 31, 1978), 'Seorang Polisi Sebelah Kakinya di Penjara, Sebelah Lainnya di Kuburan; *Kompas* (December 24, 1976), 'Para Anggota Polri yang Melanggar Hukum Hendaknya Ditindak Tegas'.
24 *Berita Buana* (May 31, 1978), 'Kapolri Memotret Oknum-oknum yang Sedang Lakukan Penyetopan Liar'; *Angkatan Bersenjata* (January 18, 1978), '60 Persen Uang yang Diselewengkan Berhasil Diselamatkan'.
25 Hasibuan *et al.* (2004); Sumarkidjo (2006). See also *Sinar Harapan* (August 1, 1976), 'Kapolri Yakin Pangdam dan dan Kadapol Menindak Bawahannya yang Terlibat'; *Sinar Harapan* (September 26, 1978), 'Belum Tercapai Cita-cita Membuat Polri Sebagai Polisi Ideal'.
26 *Angkatan Bersenjata* (August 22, 1979), 'Kapolri Mengenai Menurunnya Wibawa Polri'; *Angkatan Bersenjata* (September 25, 1979), 'Kapolri Adakan Dialog dengan Perwira Mabak'.
27 Pour (1997); interview on July 13, 2010 with Police General (retired) Prof. Dr Awaludin Djamin.
28 The expectations of Suharto and the Ministry of Security and Defence/Commander of the ABRI, M. Jusuf, were reflected in a speech delivered at various forums and meetings; see *Kompas* (September 11, 1978), 'Perlu Konsolidasi Menyeluruh di Tubuh Polri, Instruksi Menhankam/Pangab Jenderal TNI. M. Jusuf Kepada Kapolri Awaloedin Djamin'.
29 *Kompas* (February 21, 1979), 'Anggota Polri Akan Ditambah 12 Ribu'; Djamin (1995).
30 *Angkatan Bersenjata* (September 27, 1978), 'Pernyataan Kapolri Usai Pelantikan Sebagai Kapolri Oleh Presien Soeharto'; *Kompas* (September 27, 1978), 'Perlu Konsolidasi Menyeluruh di Tubuh Polri, Instruksi Menhankam/Pangab Jenderal TNI M. Jusuf kepada Kapolri Awaloedin Djamin'; Sumarkidjo (2006).
31 *Angkatan Bersenjata* (January 29, 1979), 'Dasar Fundamental Pembenahan Polri'.
32 *Angkatan Bersenjata* (September 29, 1978), 'Wibawa dan Kewenangan Polri akan Ditegakkan Kembali'.
33 *Angkatan Bersenjata* (September 16, 1981), 'Kepolisian RI Bukan Angkatan Perang'; *Angkatan Bersenjata* (October 24, 1981), 'Polri Tetap ABRI, Penugasannya Berbeda Dengan Angkatan'.
34 This included a plan for 142,333 personnel for the then roughly 160 million Indonesian population. *Kompas* (February 21, 1979), 'Anggota Polri Akan Ditambah 12 Ribu'.
35 *Berita Yudha* (September 8, 1979), 'Kerja Sama Pendidikan Kepolisian Dengan Inggris'; *Berita Yudha* (September 11, 1979), 'Tanggung Jawab Polri Makin Berat'.
36 *Kompas* (December 20, 1980), 'Sering dikaburkan Pengertian Antara Polsus dengan Satpam'; *Berita Buana* (May 28, 1982), 'Kapolri Tegaskan Status Tenaga Keamanan Swasta'.

37 *Warta Antara* (October 30, 1982), 'Kapolri: Kekuatan Polri Terletak Pada Dukungan Masyarakat'.
38 Tabah (1991), pp. 112–115; Handoyo (2003), pp. 95–104.
39 The government's response to Djamin's arguments: the Polri could not directly propose the budget to the government, but had to go through the ABRI Headquarters and then the Ministry of Security and Defence Affairs, after which the government needed time to discuss it. The increase in funding was for the development of units such as the Mobile Brigade, to increase the welfare of the Polri personnel, and for equipment needed for Polri field operations.
40 See Law No. 8/1981 about KUHAP. However, some of the contents were taken from the previous Dutch Colonial Criminal Procedures. *Sinar Harapan* (May 25, 1981), 'Kapolri: Polisi Siap Laksanakan HAP Baru: Perbaikan Secara Konsepsional Bukan Hanya Sekedar Tambal Sulam'.
41 Rekonfu had become a trademark for him, because this had been an operational concept he had applied since the early 1970s when he was kapolres of Malang District in East Java. See *Berita Buana* (January 18, 1983), 'Kapolri: Anggota Polri Harus Memiliki Tiga sikap Dasar'; Hendrowinoto *et al.* (2007c), pp. 70–75.
42 Members of the military broke into a mosque in North Jakarta where there had been objections to the imposition of the state ideology Pancasila, and desecrated it. In response, the people burnt motorbikes of the local military Babinsa, and crowds gathered to protest. There was a military attack in which protestors were beaten, shot, and killed and others were imprisoned.
43 For more discussion about the Tanjung Priok tragedy and the Petrus affair, see Barker (1998); Sulistiyanto (2007).
44 See Barker (1998); Van der Kroef (1957); *Warta Antara* (December 8, 1984), 'Kapolri: Kriminalitas Kita Kian Kompleks'; interview on July 13, 2010 with Police Inspector General (retired), Wik Djatmika, a lecturer at PTIK (Perguruan Tinggi Ilmu Kepolisian – Police University), Jakarta. According to Kontras (2007) there were almost a thousand victims of Petrus during 1983–1985, most of them with bound hands and shot.
45 The change from Kopkamtib to Bakorstranas was based on the New Order regime consolidation and low threat potential from communist organizations or radical Muslims aside from the dynamics of society. However, Bakorstranas had similar roles and functions to those of Kopkamtib. See Baker (1999), pp. 107–112; Rabasa and Haseman (2002).
46 In general, this programme's strategy was to optimize the effectiveness of the organization's efforts in a situation with minimum equipment. For more explanation of Opdin, see Hendrowinoto *et al.* (2007d), pp. 80–89.
47 *Antara* (September 11, 1986), 'Kapolri: Penanganan Kamtibmas Harus Dapat Perhatian Serius'; *Kompas* (January 18, 1987), 'Narkotik Senilai 8 Milyar Dibakar di Cilincing'; *Angkatan Bersenjata* (September 1, 1987), 'Ada Empat Kerawanan di Masyarakat'; *Angkatan Bersenjata* (August 9, 1990), 'Ada Kecenderungan Kriminialitas Berkembang Kepada Dimensi Baru'.
48 Beside Kunarto, there were four other candidates: Police Major General Kusparmono Irsan, Police Major General MH Ritonga, Police Major General Putera Astaman, and Police Major General Sedyo Utomo. See *Pelita* (February 20, 1991), 'Teka-teki Itu Telah Terjawab: Hari ini, Letjen Polisi Kunarto Dilantik Jadi Kapolri'; *Suara Pembaruan* (February 27, 1991), 'Sanoesi: Semoga Pengganti Saya Nanti Lebih Sukses'.
49 For more explanation of Kunarto's programme, see Hendrowinoto *et al.* (2007e), pp. 53–59.
50 See Hendrowinoto *et al.* (2007e), pp. 75–76.
51 In 1998, during his second period as head of the State Auditor Agency (Badan Pemeriksa Keuangan), Kunarto rejected attempts by Vice-President BJ Habibie who proposed his relative, Rivai Siatta, as Kunarto's deputy. This rejection shocked

50 *Historical legacies and early* reformasi

Suharto, and he asked Kunarto to find out about Rivai's capability first before rejecting him. However, Kunarto was firm and consistent, meeting the expectation of the public, who demanded eradication of corruption, collusion and nepotism (korupsi, kolusi dan nepotisme – KKN).

52 See Hendrowinoto *et al.* (2007e), pp. 81–83.
53 For the other candidates see *Angkatan Bersenjata* (April 6, 1993), 'Mengenal Mayjen Pol. Drs Banurusman Kapolri Baru'. For more explanation of banurusman programmes see Hendrowinoto *et al.* (2007f).
54 Law No. 14/1992 on road transport (Lalu Lintas dan Angkutan Jalan Raya, LLAJR). *Republika* (November 18, 1993), 'Kapolri: Indonesia Tidak Terlepas dari Kancah Kejahatan International'.
55 *Media Indonesia* (July 13, 1994), 'Banurusman: Polri Tak Persulit Izin Unjuk Rasa'; *Media Indonesia* (October 27, 1994), 'Denda Tilang Jutaan Rupiah Diberlakukan Sebelum Natal 1994'.
56 The case of Marsinah's murder put the INP in a dilemma. Several NCOs and officers of the Kodim of Sidoarjo were allegedly involved. Kodim personnel arrested ten people from CPS and forced them to confess to being murderers of Marsinah. The Sidoarjo Polres could do nothing and stated that it had been taken over by the Sidoarjo Kodim and the East Java 5, the Brawijaya military region command. See YLBHI (1994); *Tempo* (June 17, 2004), '"Kasus Marsinah": Kasus Pembunuhan Marsinah Pembela Mendesak Kapolri Agar Lasmini dan Susianawati Disidik'. See also VHR Media (2009), '16 Tahun, Marsinah Terus Menggugat', available at: www.vhrmedia.com/16-Tahun-Marsinah-Terus-Menggugat-opini1307.html (February 2, 2010).
57 Abdussalam and Zen Zanibar (1998), pp. 26–36; *The Jakarta Post* (March 24, 2000), 'Investigators Unsure of Marsinah Case'.
58 *Media Indonesia* (December 2, 1995), 'Kejahatan Transnational Diperkirakan Meningkat'; *Media Indonesia* (December 29, 1995), 'Suhu Politik 1996 Akan Memicu Angka Kriminalitas'.
59 Dibyo adopted the General Staff system used by ABRI. However, the name of 'General Staff' was changed to 'Directorate' in order to give impression of Polri as a civil institution.
60 The government issued Law No. 28/1997 to replace Law No. 13/1961 on the Polri. The government had issued Law No. 20/1982 on security and defence and Law No. 1/1988 revising it. The new law only reinforced the position of police under the Ministry of Security and Defence Affairs, the administration of the institution being under ABRI headquarters.
61 The Polri was in a dilemma because the government used military personnel to back Soerjadi factions against Megawati supporters. For more information, see Santoso *et al.* (1997); Bhakti (2000); *Koran Tempo* (July 27, 2005), 'Sembilan Tahun Peristiwa 27 Juli Diperingati'.
62 Azhari (ed.) (2003), pp. 23–27.
63 There are ethnicity-based conflicts in Kalimantan, religion-based conflicts in Maluku, Kupang and Poso, and separatist conflicts in Aceh and Papua. It was reported at the time, after investigations, that there was involvement of local and Jakarta political elites, including ABRI. Patebang (2000); Trijono (2001); *Suara Karya* (January 25, 2007), 'Tjahjo Kumolo: Bongkar Kelompok Elit yang Ambil Keuntungandari Konflik Poso'.
64 The Semanggi I incident happened in front of Atmajaya Catholic University, Jakarta, when thousands of students and others were demonstrating against the Special Parliamentary Assembly and Habibie as president. The military dispersed the crowd violently, killing 17 and injuring dozens more (Kontras 2007). The Semanggi II incident was the suppression of another demonstration, against the Anti-State Terror Bill (RUU Penanggulangan Keadaan Bahaya), near the same university, with one student shot and many injured. For more discussion of the Semanggi I and Semanggi II cases, see Luhulima (2001). See also Habibie (2006).

65 For example by Dr Zakarias Poerba, Head of the Special Program for Security Construction, Graduate Studies, PTIK (interviewed November 3, 2009); Koesparmono Irsan, a former deputy police chief of operations, and Rector of Bhayangkara University; and Dr Bambang Widodo Umar, ex-police officer and PTIK lecturer (interviewed November 3, 2009); see *Kompas* (November 16, 2009) 'Bambang Widodo Umar: Reformasi Polisi Indonesia'.
66 Kontras (1999). *Siaran Pers: Keharusan Pasca Pelepasan Polisi Dari ABRI*, available at: www.kontras.org/index.php?hal=siaran_pers&id=122 (February 26, 2010); *Republika* (July 1, 2005), 'Bambang Abimanyu: Polri dan Kultur Militeristik'; *MPR RI* (August 11, 2009), 'Siaran Pers MPR RI: Pemisahan TNI dan Polri Adalah Tuntutan Reformasi', available at: www.mpr.go.id/index.php?m=berita&s=detail&id_berita=875 (February 26, 2010).
67 Chrisnandi and Arifin (2005), pp. 35–46; *Tempo* (December 22, 1998), 'Letjen Susilo Bambang Yudhoyono: "Penghujatan Terhadap ABRI Tidak Lepas dari Politik Orba"'.
68 Syam (2008), pp. 56–70.
69 *Republika* (May 20, 1998), 'Kalangan Kampus Tetap Meminta Pak Harto Mengundurkan Diri'; *Gatra* (July 21, 2001), 'Tokoh Deklarasi Ciganjur Coba Kembali Dipertemukan'.
70 Badrun (2006); Suryadi (2002).
71 Djamin (2001a), pp. 7–12; see also *Kompas* (June 30, 1995), 'Awaloedin Djamin. Peringatan Hari Bhyangkara Ke-49: 50 Tahun Kepolisian RI, Citra, dan Wibawanya'; *Kompas* (April 3, 1999), 'Tak Perlu Ragu Tertibkan "Kakak"'.
72 When Benny Moerdani served as ABRI Commander, he stated that state apparatus, Polri included, should release their rigid approach to security and stay neutral in politics. The attitude was based on the absence of any real ideological threat. In 1988 the Kopkamtib was replaced by the Bakorstanas, reflecting low ideological threats against the New Order. See Pour (1993) and Pour (2007).
73 The Lemhanas was established in May 20, 1965 as the National Defence Institute (Lembaga Pertahanan Nasional) and was then directly under presidential supervision. In 1993 its name was changed to the National Resilience Institute and it was moved into the Ministry of Security and Defence Affairs. In 2001, the Lemhanas was changed to a non-ministerial organization on research and education in national strategic defence.
74 *Pelita* (July 1, 1995), 'Pakar Hukum: Polri Perlu Diberi Otonomi Penuh, Kalangan DPR: Ada Kesan Polisi Masih Diperalat Kelompok Tertentu'.
75 Consisting of Alwi Luthan, INP Expert Staff Coordinator (Korsahli), Adang Daradjatun, Assistant Planning and Finance (Asrena), S. Rijanto, Farouk Muhammad, and several other middle-ranking officers.
76 With the title 'Re-actualising the Position, Role, and Function of the Police' (Reaktualisasi Kedudukan, Peran dan Fungsi Polri).
77 An oppositional group of senior politicians and retired military general called themselves the National Front (Barnas) led by Kemal Idris, former Commander of Kostrad (the Army Strategic Reserves – Komando Cadangan Strategis Angkatan Darat), during the Special Parliamentary Session in 1998.
78 For example, Bhakti (2004).
79 For example, *Papua Pos* (2010), 'Hubungan TNI-Polri Masih Harmonis', available at: www.papuapos.com/index.php?option=com_content&task=view&id=1762&Itemid=0 (March 23, 2010).
80 For example, *Detik.com* (2010), 'Kasus RMS & Papua Upaya Giring Opini Pemerintahan SBY Lemah', available at: http://us.detiknews.com/read/2007/07/05/132136/801561/10/kasus-rms-papua-upaya-giring-opini-pemerintahan-sby-lemah (March 24, 2010).
81 For example, *Suara Merdeka* (October 7, 2005), 'Pengaktifan Koter TNI Bukan Jalan Keluar Cegah Teror'.

52 Historical legacies and early reformasi

82 A decree on Polri reform was issued by the Ministry of Security and Defence Affairs on December 14, 1998, to be implemented by April 1, 1999. *Tempo* (October 6, 1998), 'ABRI Ulang Tahun Di Tengah Hujatan.' It was implemented under Presidential Instruction No. 2/1999, which confirmed that the previous law would be updated and revised. This was followed by a decree of the Minister of Security and Defence Affairs and ABRI Commander, No. Kep/05/P/III/1999, on April 1, 1999, regarding the delegation of authority of police training from the ABRI Commander to the Ministry of Security and Defence Affairs.

83 Wiranto urged Roesmanhadi to assign Adang Daradjatun to work with the Polri reform team of Brigadier Generals Syafriadi and Drs Eddy Susilo, Chief Commissioner Drs Zaini, and other police officers. They published a 'Blue Book', entitled *Reform towards a Professional Police*. The process encountered many challenges, and therefore the police small team joined forces with experts such as Prof. Satjipto Rahardjo, Prof. Sahetapy, and Prof. Awaloedin Djamin. Just before July 1, 1999, the book was successfully completed at SESPIM and launched in Bandung. For more on this see Chapter 3.

84 Based on Presidential Decree No. 89/2000, the Ministry of Security and Defence Affairs became the Ministry of Defence Affairs, as the Polri was no longer under its supervision and the role of the three military components was only in national defence.

85 Departemen Pertahanan dan Keamanan (1966); Seskoad (1967).

86 During Sukarno's and Suharto's eras, counter-terrorism was always part of the military's role, but in the *reformasi* era, the Polri took over the role of counter-terrorism from the military. See Muradi (2009b), especially Chapter 5.

87 Sutanto and Sugiarso (2005).

88 For more discussion about the Polri position in the Guided Democracy era, see Chapter 1.

89 For more about Soetjipto Danoekoesoemo and Kunarto, see Chapter 1 and previous sections of this chapter. Rusdihardjo's term will be further discussed in Chapter 3.

90 Even though the Polri was integrated into ABRI from 1961, it was in practice not consolidated completely with ABRI, but was still controlled by the BPI (Central Intelligence Agency) and Sukarno's political circle. For more discussion about the process of integration of the Polri to the ABRI during the Guided Democracy era, see Chapter 1.

91 As stated in Article 3 of Law No. 13/1961, which was updated by Law No. 20/1982 on security and state defence, particularly in Article 29 Paragraph 4, and Law No. 1/1988 about the amendment of Law No. 20/1982 on Security and State Defence.

92 Law No. 28/1997 stipulated that in terms of its institutional administration, the Polri Headquarters was led by the commander of the ABRI, while the operations of the police were to be reported by the chief of INP to the Minister of Security and Defence Affairs.

Part II
Reformasi and its effect on the police

3 Politicization of the police
The struggle over control during the Wahid presidency

> The Police is accomplice of the Armed Forces ...
> The Police is accomplice of the Armed Forces ...
> The Police is accomplice of the Armed Forces ...
> The Police is abused and tortured by the Public ...
> (Student demonstration song before the fall of Suharto in 1998)

Reformasi was the gradual process of dismantling the New Order. In its early stages, this *reformasi* process produced an unstable situation in national parliamentary politics. Then, after the first election post-Suharto, the Indonesian Democratic Party of Struggle (Indonesian Partai Demokrasi Indonesia Perjuangan – PDIP), led by Megawati Soekarnoputri, emerged as the strongest party. However, Abdurrachman Wahid (Gus Dur or Wahid), leader of the smaller National Awakening Party (Partai Kebangkitan Bangsa – PKB),[1] was chosen to be president instead of her in a dramatic MPR session, which then elected Megawati as vice-president. The new team of Wahid as president and Megawati as vice-president may be seen as a symbol of political transition from an authoritarian to a democratic regime, but also as a symbol of the unstable and antagonistic nature of the early stages of that transition.

The Polri as one of the security institutions was affected both by the political changes and by their nature. President Habibie had agreed with ABRI's proposal for disassociating the Polri and putting it directly under supervision of the president's office after a two-year transition under the Ministry of Security and Defence Affairs, until it was ready and able to be an independent institution. The Polri itself had made almost no significant political contribution to this disassociation process, but had published its 'Blue Book' as guidance for its own reform in 1999, when ABRI headquarters had started to signal that the issue of disassociation could now be discussed.

This chapter will discuss the implementation of the 'Blue Book' as part of the Polri reform towards becoming a more independent and professional institution. It should first be noted that the reforms got under way during nearly two years of tumult in national politics, with tensions and conflict within the presidential 'team' and between parties leading to a final conflict between the president and the parliament, which only ended with Wahid's sacking. Therefore this chapter will first examine the politicization and the internal response of the Polri during the Wahid presidency.

The police and a new political configuration post-Suharto

The Polri anticipated that the election of Abdurrahman Wahid to the presidency would bring changes, with the Polri soon to be positioned directly under supervision of the presidential office. As an important element in his reformist programme, President Wahid had a clear commitment to free the Polri from a militaristic mindset and attitudes.

However, that expectation seemed to materialize only briefly; the comfortable assumptions about Wahid's adherence to the practices of democracy did not last long. He had a unique, personal and erratic leadership style with consequences for the Polri which can be seen from two perspectives: first as a threat against the foreseen independence and professionalism of the Polri, and second in the internal competition between senior Polri officers in their attempts to gain opportunities to get closer to the new political power.

Wahid asserted to Roesmanhadi that he did not want to replace him but that he was being urged to do so by a number of political parties in parliament, and asked him to suggest replacements. Roesmanhadi suggested two: S. Bimantoro, deputy chief of operations, and Bibit S. Rijanto, coordinator of expert staff. Following previous practices, both names were the result of the Polri Wanjakti meetings.[2]

However, a third name appeared: that of Noegroho Djajoesman, Kapolda (provincial head of police) of the Jakarta Metro. A source within Wahid's inner circle was quoted as saying that Bimantoro would be Polri chief while Bibit S. Rijanto would be deputy chief. All these rumours and information from the Palace eventually were overturned by the announcement on January 3, 2000 that Roesmanhadi was to be replaced by an unexpected candidate, Rusdihardjo, the head of the National Police School (SESPIM), with Bimantoro as his deputy. It was suggested that he had been proposed to Wahid by influential Nahdlatul Ulama Muslim clerics, and also that some money politics had been involved.[3]

Rusdihardjo's determination quickly collided with the wishes of the president. Although he performed his role in the Polri operation well, there was a proliferation of ethnic conflicts in Kalimantan;[4] there were also various political scandals involving the inner circle of President Wahid himself, in which there were pressures on the Polri to protect those involved.

President Wahid eventually wanted to replace Rusdihardjo after the latter refused to arrest one of Suharto's sons, Tommy Suharto, who was allegedly involved in a bomb explosion at the Jakarta Stock Exchange building. According to the president:

> The security situation is still not improving and this requires adjustment by the leader of police immediately. It should be presented to the nation that we all know the person [Tommy Suharto] whom we [the president] wanted

to investigate. But [my order] to examine was not carried out [by Polri], how about another problem? It was easy when it comes to that, please investigate, I have ever been arrested. But the leader of the police did not obey all that. Because of this, Chief of the Polri should be replaced [with] no doubt.

(*Forum Keadilan*, September 18, 2000)

In addition, there was a growing disharmony, including investigation into the State Logistics Agency (Badan Urusan Logistik – Bulog) and into corrupted aid payments from the Sultan Brunei Darussalam. These investigations, which became known as 'Bulog-gate' and 'Brunei-gate', involved members of Wahid's inner circle. A further contention was that Wahid was annoyed that Rusdihardjo always reported to the vice-president, Megawati, after reporting to him. Meanwhile, the disassociated Polri under Rusdihardjo was not succeeding in providing sufficient internal security, as there were still many cases of bombings and local conflicts.[5]

Rusdihardjo held the post of Polri chief for only seven months before Wahid replaced him with his deputy Bimantoro, a move that was also criticized as the president had again ignored both the Wanjakti and the parliament in making the appointment. The problem dissolved after Wahid approached Megawati Sukarnoputri, who had also had a close relationship with Bimantoro particularly during her difficult days in the New Order era.[6]

Loyalty to the president versus loyalty to the parliament

The struggle for power between President Wahid and the parliament intensified as ministers from other parties who had supported him were replaced[7] and a parliamentary special committee was set up to enquire into the Bulog-gate and Brunei-gate cases and Wahid's alleged involvement in them. The parliament subsequently approved the report of the special committee, which declared Wahid's involvement and that he had misled the community and misused his title as president.[8] The Polri had been involved only in using its legal enforcement procedures to ensure that the process had been run correctly, but Wahid considered that the Polri had not acted objectively when protecting public rallies that criticized him and by being ineffective in pursuing some notorious political cases in Jakarta,[9] and that there were moves within the Polri against him.[10]

Memorandum II gave the government one month to respond before parliament would impeach the president. Several attempts to bring the army in to support Wahid were unsuccessful, even after he offered to promote senior active or retired generals if they would support his issuing of presidential decrees of a state of emergency to protect his position and empower theirs. Wahid then turned to the police for support, initially through its chief, Bimantoro.

However, Bimantoro had long held the attitude that the issuing of a presidential decree would only make the situation less helpful and more miserable for the people. This made President Wahid irate and he demanded Bimantoro's resignation. Bimantoro rejected this firmly because it was not in accordance with the mechanism approved by parliament.[11] The issuing of a statement rejecting Polri politicization, signed by him and other senior Polri generals, then followed Bimantoro's first step.[12]

After trying and failing with Polri chief Bimantoro and those demonstrating solidarity with him, Wahid tried again, looking for support from other senior officers and promising them benefits. This attempt was more successful in the police than it had been in the army. One candidate was Chaeruddin Ismail, Head of the National Police School (SESPIM). Yasril Ananta Baharuddin, a politician of the Golkar Party, suggested his name to Wahid. Chaeruddin agreed to take up Wahid's offer of becoming initially both deputy chief and acting chief of the Polri, then becoming chief after the abolishing of the deputy position and a presidential removal of Bimantoro as chief. In a 2010 interview Chaeruddin told me how he had considered President Wahid's offer as an honour and an accomplishment, as he would be promoted to the highest rank and position.[13]

Bimantoro knew that the Polri had been dragged into the conflict between the president and the parliament and his only option was to take the side of one of these two forces. His choice was to get closer to the parliament, based on the flurry of overlapping presidential decrees on the validity of the organization and structure of the Polri, the appointment and dismissal of its chief, and the appointment of Chaeruddin Ismail as deputy chief of the Polri.[14] Bimantoro met Akbar Tandjung (Golkar), and Soetardjo Soerjogoeritno (PDIP), the chairman and vice-chairman of the parliament.

The president finally issued a presidential edict calling on the new minister to take all steps to 'coordinate the entire security apparatus ... to uphold public order, security and law as soon as possible', which had been proposed by cabinet members as a way to diffuse and divert President Wahid's original plan to issue a more extreme presidential decree.[15] Bimantoro decided that this presidential edict should be interpreted as only an ordinary command, not as something urgent and requiring an emergency response, so he merely ordered all Kapolda to raise their alert level to Number One Standby (Siaga I).

Chaeruddin was inaugurated as deputy chief of the Polri at a poorly attended ceremony.[16] Bimantoro had tried to contact and meet Chaeruddin before his inauguration, but failed. They finally had a meeting in Bimantoro's office, at his request, to settle the problem as soon as possible. This informal meeting came to a deadlock, because Chaeruddin felt he now had the legitimacy of being the deputy chief of the Polri. However, the meeting did reveal why Chaeruddin had accepted his appointment as deputy chief of the Polri: because it provided access to the prestigious position, rank, and opportunities which he would not have gained otherwise.[17]

Conflicts between the police and the president

Bimantoro acted cautiously on the process of complying with the new Polri structure and the presence of a rival 'acting chief' as his deputy. The organizational situation was paralysed, as on one hand, Bimantoro felt that he had not been formally replaced through a proper mechanism approved by the parliament so there was no obligation for him to hand over command to Chaeruddin. Chaeruddin Ismail thought that he had a strong legitimacy in his appointment by President Wahid as deputy chief and acting chief of the Polri. However, he could not exercise the authority like other chiefs of the Polri.[18]

The Polri tried to resolve the situation by arranging a meeting between Bimantoro and Chaeruddin, hopeful that they could work together. However, this did not succeed and they started a war of media statements about the handover of command and authority in the Polri. Bimantoro was very confident, as he was supported by most of the Polri officers, and would not give in to president's demand although the new coordinating minister, Agum Gumelar, had delivered it.

In general, the people in conflict inside the Polri can be divided into three groups.[19] The first comprised the high- and medium-ranking officers who supported Bimantoro as legitimate chief of the Polri.[20] The second group was the high- and medium-ranking officers who supported Chaeruddin as deputy chief and acting chief of the Polri and tended to support President Wahid's policies.[21] The third group was of the high- and medium-ranking officers[22] who tended to be a floating mass. They did not take sides in the internal politics, but had high bargaining power in their relations with the two conflicting groups.

Meanwhile, efforts made by some of Polri generals to accommodate Chaeruddin inside the the Polri structure by providing him space and asking him to deliver some of the tasks of the Polri leaders, such as representing the Polri chief in ceremonies, started to draw protests. Some of Chaeruddin's opponents filed a judicial review of the overlapping presidential decrees, a step supported by a number of retired police including Koesparmono Irsan.[23] Bimantoro had doubts about the professional ethics of this, as the presidential decree was in the political domain, but was willing to do it and action was taken by the Union of Retired Police (PP Polri) and the Police Graduates' Association (Ikatan Sarjana Ilmu Kepolisian).

The next move in the struggle between president and parliament over the Polri chief position came from two members of the military/police faction in parliament. The lobbying from Generals Taufiequrrahman Ruki and Posma Tobing eventually produced a July 7, 2001 agreement between all the seven parliamentary factions apart from Wahid's PKB that the president had violated procedures and mechanisms on the appointment and dismissal of chief of the Polri and had made a constitutional mistake in assigning Bimantoro as ambassador without asking advice from parliament.[24]

Another support for the parliament's position came from a meeting of senior INP officers, without Bimantoro or Chaeruddin, where they issued a public statement that accepted the president's legal authority to replace the police chief but declared that any such decision had to be agreed by Parliament. Bimantoro himself made a similar announcement to the media immediately afterwards.[25] Acting on these principles he remained in day-to-day control until parliament approved Wahid's decision. Chaeruddin's supporters were handicapped by not having access to all the top decision-making meetings within the Polri.

Agum Gumelar, as coordinating minister of political and security affairs, was caught between the interests of President Wahid and the political mainstream. He called Bimantoro and Chaeruddin to his office, along with two other Polri leaders. They discussed the settlement of the internal polemics that had developed in the Polri. Bimantoro and Chaeruddin finally accepted Agum Gumelar's proposal of a clear division of tasks between them. This partly repeated an agreement made several weeks previously but importantly also included agreeing that a third person accepted by both groups as neutral would be appointed as acting chief to mediate. Ahwil Luthan, from the 1968 Akpol class, was recommended.[26] The Wanjakti then proposed him, together with Yun Mulyana, and Chaeruddin, as suitable replacements for Bimantoro, who would retire with proper procedures having been carried out. For a short time it appeared that a solution had been found to the conflict that was acceptable to all within the Polri.

However, another problem emerged. At a rally in front of hundreds of Polri officers and news media, a group of middle-ranking Polri officers, the 'Group of Eight', staged a protest and expressed their disappointment.[27] Their statement was covered extensively by the media and dealt a blow to the nearly completed efforts for reconciliation and settlement of internal conflicts in the Polri initiated a few days previously by the coordinating minister.[28]

In practice, Chaeruddin was just an acting chief of the Polri without authority to consolidate. He recognized this and felt that the limitations were designed to prevent him having any authority.[29] Given the increasing political tensions related to the conflict between president and parliament, Chaeruddin held meetings with various Kapolda to coordinate activities to protect public security. He tended to protect President Wahid's policies, for example by trying to ensure security at national political events, such as the special plenary session of parliament or the carrying out of presidential decrees. He stated that the Polri did not take a position on the political agenda, but only on how to control mass rallies.

Chaeruddin tried to politically lobby a number of members of parliament, such as A.M. Fatwa of PAN (Partai Amanat National – the National Mandate Party), but these efforts proved useless since parliament still recognized Bimantoro as the Polri chief. Another member, Achmad Sumargono of PBB (Partai Bulan Bintang – Star Moon Crescent Party), even warned him that if President Wahid really inaugurated Chaeruddin and issued a decree to that effect, parliament would implement a special plenary session to impeach the president within hours.

The Group of Eight at first felt confident of the strength of their bargaining position regarding the demands of the middle-ranking officers. However, their confidence quickly faded as they realized that Chaeruddin did not have the support of the mainstream of parliament, and people wanted President Wahid to step down from his presidency.[30]

Chaeruddin's reliance on Wahid suddenly appeared successful when there was a claim in the media that the president had issued an order for him and the coordinating minister, Agum Gumelar, to arrest Bimantoro and the Kapolda of Jakarta Metro, Sofjan Jacoeb, for the legal offence of insubordination.[31] The coordinating minister Agum Gumelar said that he did not have the authority to do this and rejected the command, and President Wahid made a remark that became a political blunder.[32] Chaeruddin faced a dilemma: his efforts to act as chief of the Polri were not going to be a solution to the Polri's internal conflict.[33] Therefore, he decided it was not necessary to establish a board of honorary officers (DKP) to consider President Wahid's accusation of Bimantoro's insubordination.[34]

In the midst of this debate on the agenda of the session, President Wahid tried yet another political manoeuvre regarding the Polri chief's position by sending the parliament a letter requesting approval for the inauguration.[35] The parliament, increasingly infuriated with President Wahid's manoeuvres, responded with an ultimatum that if he inaugurated Chaeruddin as chief of Polri, the parliament would hold its special session at the same time.[36]

With or without the support of the parliament, President Wahid would keep Chaeruddin as chief of the Polri and, as he had been promoted after his inauguration to a four-star police general, he was already at the same rank as Bimantoro so there would be no formal obstacles to his undertaking further manoeuvres against Bimantoro and his supporters. Chaeruddin left his office quietly, in order to avoid the attention of the media and of Intelkam (Security Intelligence Unit) officers, to attend his inauguration as chief of the Polri at the Presidential Palace on July 22, 2001, after an approval from the chairman of the DPR, Akbar Tandjung.[37]

Chaeruddin was inaugurated without the presence of ministers, military commander, chiefs of other forces, or chief of the Polri. Even so, Chaeruddin remained confident and tried to perform a variety of preparations for security and in implementation of the presidential decree. One of these was to try to issue an instruction that the command of security and the execution of the decree were in his hands. This was directly countered by the Polri's deputy chief of operations, Sjahroedin Pagar Alam, who stated that command and operation still lay with the officially inactive chief of the Polri, Bimantoro, until further notification, and he continued to report on the security situation to Bimantoro.[38]

Claims and counter-claims spread among the elite leaders of the Polri as the conflict within this law enforcement institution increasingly mounted. Dozens of Polri officers held rallies, issued statements and lobbied in various efforts to have accepted and keep Chaeruddin in power as rightful chief of the Polri, while other leaders continued to join forces in efforts to keep Bimantoro as chief, urging the parliament to hold its special plenary session as soon as possible. Sofjan Jacoeb, Bimantoro's field operator, who was in command of the most powerful and local Polri force, the Jakarta Metro Polda, took various approaches to convince elites in the executive and legislative to reject any attempts by President Wahid to use his powers arbitrarily. Sofjan openly offered Brimob personnel as security guards to protect members of parliament.[39]

The final days of decision

President Wahid issued a presidential decree in the early hours of July 23, declaring a state of emergency, dissolving parliament and calling on the military and police to protect the state.[40] Chaeruddin immediately claimed that the Polri would secure the decree. However, at the same time, Widodo, as commander of the TNI, would not support the presidential decree. So, in practice, support for the decree came only from part of the Polri, from Chaeruddin and his supporters, among whom were those without commands or troops.[41]

In this highly tense atmosphere Bimantoro affirmed his continuing leadership. Bimantoro requested protection of the state broadcasting station (Radio Republik Indonesia – RRI), because word had spread that the RRI would be controlled to broadcast information related to orders from Chaeruddin. Bimantoro also sent an invitation to Chaeruddin through Chaeruddin's Akpol classmates, Kadaryanto and Wahyu Saronto, asking whether he would commit to joining with the Polri, or walk alone. Soon, Chaeruddin's colleagues reported back to Bimantoro to say that he would join the Polri and would not provide any resistance.[42] This somewhat relieved Bimantoro, because at least the Polri was solid in the midst of political uncertainty. However, personally, he still doubted the good intentions of Chaeruddin based on his experience that he often broke promises.[43]

After having a meeting with Vice-President Megawati on the Polri's readiness to secure the special plenary session, Bimantoro returned to Polri headquarters to meet Chaeruddin and reconfirm that he had joined the Polri side in this operation. The meeting was actually not very important for Bimantoro, but it would help to build the image that the Polri was solid under Bimantoro's leadership. Chaeruddin was invited to the Jakarta Metro Polda, where the Polri was continuously monitoring the situation of the special plenary session. Bimantoro's strategy was appropriate, since there were many news reporters at the Jakarta Metro Polda Office and he successfully presented an image of the Polri's solidarity, as well as striking back to President Wahid that the Polri remained solid under Bimantoro's leadership, despite the problems of Chaeruddin's inauguration.[44]

This chapter has argued that the reforms came into being during and after nearly two years of tumultuous period in national politics, with tensions leading to a final conflict between the president and the parliament that ended with Wahid's sacking. The chapter has argued that the leadership of the Polri was deliberately dragged into these politics and was divided and politicized by these rivalries in the newly democratizing Indonesia.

This chapter has shown that the rivalries within the Polri arose in connection with the internal Polri response to what President Wahid tried to do with the Polri. The Polri's response followed personal desire and opportunistic manoeuvring, due to lack of internal procedure in term of leader regenerations.

This chapter has argued that the conflict inside the Polri was easily heightened due to vertical mobility and the sentiments of the Akpol classmates and the different units. President Wahid realized this and attempted to use one of the factions of the Polri to support his regime, but this was wrong choice and made him fall from his presidency. However, the struggle of the Polri to keep clear and free of political intervention during Bimantoro's term was in part a way of ending the politicization of the Polri as attempted by President Wahid and as had affected previous chiefs of the Polri.

Notes

1 The PKB was based in the Nahdlatul Ulama (NU), a traditionalist Islamic organization operating mainly in Java, especially East Java, with a claimed membership of up to 30 million. Wahid Hasyim, a grand father of Abdurrahman Wahid, had founded it in 1926.
2 Kunarto (ed.) (2002), p. 45; Haramain (2004), p. 89; Sage (2003), p. 13.
3 Previous Polri chief; Kunarto (ed.) (2002), p. 48. Noegroho Djajusman (as cited in Sibarani et al. (2001), p. 74) asserted that the person who proposed Rusdihardjo to President Wahid was a banker, Yan Mandari. However, a PKB politician told me that the political rumours about the new Polri chief were not only about the NU clerics proposing Rusdihardjo to President Wahid, but also about money from Rusdihardjo and his supporters to put Rusdihardjo as a chief of the Polri. Interview on June 16, 2010 with a senior politician of PKB, Jakarta, and personal communication on September 4, 2010 with another senior politician of PKB.
4 *Tempo* (March 22, 2001), 'Temu Dayak-Madura Bukan Buat Cari Solusi Konflik'. *Tempo* (June 24, 2001), 'Pemerintah Belum Serius Tangani Konflik Dayak-Madura'.
5 For example, *Kompas* (September 19, 2000), 'Teka-teki Dibalik Pergantian Kapolri'.
6 Interview on November 6, 2009 with a senior politician of the PDIP (Partai Demokrasi Indonesia Perjuangan – Indonesian Democratic Party of Struggle), Jakarta. See also Hasrullah (2001), pp. 65–68.
7 For example Jusuf Kalla from the Golkar Party, Hamzah Haz from the United Development Party (Partai Persatuan Pembangunan, PPP), and Laksamana Sukardi from the PDIP, and also Wiranto. See Kunarto (ed.) (2002), p. 56; Haramain (2004), p. 91.
8 The Special Plenary Session overwhelmingly voted to accept the Special Committee's Report. The parliamentary faction of reserved seats of the military and Polri supported the declaration of Memorandum I. See Honna (2004), pp. 164–169; Haramain (2004), pp. 88–92; Rinakit (2005), pp. 100–104.
9 These included the bombing of the JSE building and the murder of a judge, with President Wahid accusing Tommy Suharto, son of Suharto, of being behind them. Wardaya et al. (2007), pp. 157–168.
10 There were rumours that President Wahid planned to replace the Jakarta Metro Kapolda, Mulyono Sulaiman, for not being firm and objective in dealing with mass rallies. This was not confirmed, but in a matter of months, Mulyono Sulaiman was pensioned and replaced by Sofjan Jacoeb, former Kapolda of South Sulawesi, and one of Bimantoro's Akpol classmates. *Koran Tempo* (March 16, 2001), 'Jawaban Memorandum: Presiden Tidak Bersalah'.
11 See the contents of Tap MPR No. VI/2000 and Tap MPR No. VII/2000. But see also the cynical interpretation from Luzuardi Adi Sage that Bimantoro was ambitious to hold the position for as long as he could, and was using the political situation to fight for this: Sage (2003), pp. 47–51.
12 Kunarto (ed.) (2002), Sage (2003), Sibarani et al. (2001), Budiyarso (2009).
13 Interview on June 13, 2010 in Bandung, with Police General Dr Chaeruddin Ismail, a former deputy and acting chief of the Polri.
14 Presidential Decree No. 40 and 41/Polri/2001 dismissing Bimantoro from his position, and temporarily replacing him with the deputy chief of the Polri, Chaeruddin

Ismail; Presidential Decree No. 77/2001 appointing Chaeruddin Ismail as deputy chief and then acting chief.
15 *Gatra* (May 28, 2001), 'Yudhoyono: Maklumat Bukan Dekrit Keadaan Darurat'.
16 Only the deputy himself and some ministers and their families attended the inauguration. The joint chief of staff and other chiefs of staff were not present and Bimantoro himself chose not to attend.
17 Chaeruddin Ismail argued in my interview with him that it would be impossible for him or his classmates to be chief of the Polri, because at that time the Wanjakti members were all Bimantoro's classmates.
18 For example, *Media Indonesia* (June 6, 2001), 'Chaeruddin Ismail Disambut Hangat'.
19 This can be compared to what happened in the early independent and Soekarno periods in Chapter 1, the stagnant grouping in Suharto's New Order period in Chapter 2, and also the grouping in early *reformasi*: see the next section of this chapter.
20 The Bimantoro group also has political support from the parliament and ant- Wahid groups such the Muslim Student Action Group (KAMMI), and groups from various universities, which have connections to KAMMI, PKS, and other anti-Wahid political parties. For more discussion about the anti-Wahid group, see Rinakit (2005), pp. 25–29.
21 The Chaeruddin group has support from NGOs and pro-democracy activists who closed with Wahid and so on. Sage (2003); Budiyarso (2009), pp. 72–89.
22 One of these was Alwi Luthan, from the Akpol class of 1968. Luthan was a popular general and respected by other groups. He was senior in the Polri, having graduated in 1968, but his age was similar to that of Bimantoro and his 1970 Akpol class.
23 *Media Indonesia* (June 27, 2001), 'Polri Ajukan Judicial Review Uji Keabsahan Keppres 77/2001'; *Media Indonesia* (June 29, 2001), 'Kapolri Disarankan Tetap Pilih Langkah Judicial Review'.
24 *Media Indonesia* (July 4, 2001), 'DPR Tetap Mengakui Bimantoro, Menhan Kecewa dengan Pernyataan Presiden'.
25 Bimantoro's statement was:

> Concerning my dismissal as Chief of the Polri, with respect, I personally accepted it as a fact and it was within the authority of the President to perform changes of positions of the Chief of the Polri, although Article 7 MPR Decree No. VII/MPR/2000 stipulated that the change should be based on the approval of Parliament. Therefore, as stipulated in Presidential Decree No. 49/Polri/2001 about my position, I asked police institutions, especially the relevant staff to do a review and followed up based on existing procedures. If the Decree No. 49/Polri/2001 conveyed by the Polri, then at the same time Mr President should announce immediately the definitive Chief of the Polri for the implementation based on the applicable procedures.

26 Kustiati and Effendi (2004), p. 228.
27 This Group of Eight had supported Chaeruddin Ismail in the hope of upgrading their careers. Interviews on November 3, 2009, with Police Chief Commissioner (retired) Dr Bambang Widodo Umar, a lecturer at the PTIK, and on June 12, 2010 with Police Chief Commissioner (retired) Alfons Loemau, both members of the middle-ranking Polri Group of Eight. The rally was driven by a number of the Polri officers who supported Chaeruddin, such as Alfons Lemau, Bambang Widodo Umar, Bandjarnahor, Parlindungan Sinaga, Badaruzzaman Haidir, Herman Koto, Nurdin Umar, and Salihin.
28 Their assertions were: (1) Dismissal of Bimantoro as chief of the Polri by Presidential Decree, legal administrative procedures no longer being an issue because the Polri was under presidential supervision at the time. (2) The statements of several generals some time ago on behalf of the chairman of the Union of Retired Police rejecting the removal of the Polri chief Bimantoro conveyed an improper, unfair and authoritatarian attitude,

because they was not in accordance with the aspirations of more than 200,000 officers of the Polri. (3) The officers of the Polri rejected efforts on bringing the Polri into the political arena in the parliament, the Polri being under supervision of the president desk, not the House of Representatives. (4) They respectfully requested that parliamentary interference blocking the removal of the chief of the Polri should stop because it was not proportionate. The Polri required that parliament strive for an opportunity to develop the INP into a professional civilian police force accountable to the public. The listing of the Kompolnas in the MPR Decree No. VII/MPR/2000 was never questioned when the Kompolnas was an independent commission that oversaw the Polri on law enforcement. (5) They agreed and demanded that the former chief of the Polri, General Bimantoro, and several other high-ranking Polri officers who supported him, should abandon their disgusting attitudes of defiance and let the Polri be led by a younger generation. They should not contaminate the Police Oath (Tri Brata), Police Code of Conduct (Catur Prasetya), and 'Remember!', the Police Attitude (Satya Prabu), (6) They respectfully asked President Wahid to revoke the recent decree on the INP's organizational structure and return the Polri to its previous form of organization.

29 Interview on June 13, 2010 with Police General (retired) Dr Chaeruddin Ismail, former deputy chief of the Polri.
30 Interview on June 13, 2010 with Jenderal Polisi (retired) Dr Chaeruddin Ismail, former deputy chief of the Polri. See also Sage (2003), pp. 90–93; Budiyarso (2009), pp. 175–178.
31 *Suara Pembaruan* (July 14, 2001), 'Agum Tidak Setuju Bimantoro Ditangkap'. However, Chaeruddin said he had never received an order to arrest Bimantoro and Sofjan Jacoeb; it was only media propaganda against him and the INP group who supported President Wahid. See interview on June 13, 2010 with Police General (retired) Dr Chaeruddin Ismail.
32 Kustiati and Effendi (2004), p. 213; *Suara Pembaruan* (July 14, 2001), 'Agum Tidak Setuju Bimantoro Ditangkap'.
33 Interview on June 13, 2010 with Police General (retired) Dr Chaeruddin Ismail, former deputy chief of the Polri. *Media Indonesia* (July 14, 2001), 'Wakapolri Bingung Dengan Perintah Presiden'.
34 Interview on June 13, 2010 with Police General (retired) Dr Chaeruddin Ismail, former deputy chief of the Polri; *Media Indonesia* (July 17, 2001), 'Mabes Belum Polri Perlu Bentuk DKP'.
35 See letter from President Wahid No. 188/Setmil/A/VII/2001 dated July 19, 2001 to the chairman of DPR, Akbar Tandjung. A day later, Akbar Tandjung responded that DPR would never give support to the appointment of Chaeruddin as chief of the Polri by Wahid because that letter was wrong. President Wahid should ask the DPR to agree to the candidacy of chief of the Polri first, and Wahid would then consider his candidacy, as shown by Tap MPR No. VI/MPR/2000 and Tap MPR No. VII/MPR/2000.
36 *Rakyat Merdeka* (July 19, 2001), 'Jika Chaeruddin Diangkat Jadi Kapolri, SI MPR akan Digelar'.
37 *Rakyat Merdeka* (July 21, 2001), 'Eh, Sumpahlah Demi Presiden'; also *Tempo* (July 29, 2001), 'Chaeruddin di Senjakala Presiden, Pelantikan itu Memicu SI MPR'.
38 *Tempo* (July 29, 2001), 'Chaeruddin di Senjakala Presiden, Pelantikan itu Memicu SI MPR'.
39 *Business News* (July 21, 2001), 'Gus Dur Bersilat Lidah Terus Untuk Bertahan'.
40 *Kompas* (July 23, 2001), 'Presiden Berlakukan Dektrit'. See Hardilani *et al.* (2003), p. 29.
41 *Koran Tempo* (July 24, 2001), 'Banser Magelang Apel Mendukung Dekrit Presiden'. *Kompas* (July 23, 2001), 'Forum Silaturahmi Ulama Dukung Dekrit'. *Kompas* (July 23, 2001), 'MPR dan DPR Tolak Dekrit'.

42 Interview on June 13, 2010 with Police General (retired) Dr Chaeruddin Ismail.
43 At almost at the same time, the Secretary General of the Polri, Yun Mulyana, sent a telegram to all Kapolda, the leaders of the Polri in each province, asserting three things: first, the Polri Command remained under Bimantoro; second, to secure the entire course of the Special Plenary Session, the Polri had initiated 'Steady Operation Brata VIII' (Operasi Mantap Brata VIII); third, unity and cohesion among officers of the Polri should be maintained.
44 *Tempo* (July 29, 2001), 'Saya Akan Menyerahkan Tongkat Komando ke DPR'.

4 Developing a more independent and professional police force

While this drama was being played out, modernizing and professionalizing as proposed in 1999 by the Polri 'Blue Book' were starting to be put in practice. When the Polri had first presented these proposals it was still effectively under the control of ABRI and the proposals could not be effectively acted on. It was only post-disassociation that the Polri had enough authority over itself. Beginning in the era of President Wahid, the Polri had relatively more chances to practise and implement their proposed developments aimed at becoming more independent and professional. These developments will be discussed separately and in more detail later in the book.

Revision of the police code of ethics

A fundamental change was to make changes to the contents of its *Catur Prasetya*, the Polri Professional Code of Ethics.[1] This had included a promise to be faithful to the country and leaders of the country, homeland, and nation, and not to be bound to anything except the people, the nation and the state. This formulation was considered less relevant, especially promises that required national police loyalty to leaders of the state, in that the police should not become a political tool of power because they were non-combatant.[2]

New police act

The steps to revise Law No. 28/1997 on the Polri were finally halted when disassociation of the Polri from the ABRI was reinforced by MPR Decrees Nos VI/2000 and VII/2000.[3] These made Law No. 28/1997 irrelevant, because the Polri had now been completely disassociated from the ABRI and the Ministry of Security and Defence Affairs, which later became the Ministry of Defence.[4] Although somewhat hampered and interrupted by political turmoil and intervention in the Polri, Law No. 2/2002 on the Polri was finally issued in conjunction with the publication of Law No. 3/2002 on state defence.

The new law also affirmed the various oversight mechanisms and the roles and functions of the Polri within the scope of democratic policing; however, the sources of funding for the Polri were not explained in detail.[5] Although clearly the Polri budget came out of the state budget, the new law did not close the opportunity for the Polri to legally get extra-budgetary financing from local governments, from the community, or from businesses owned and run by the Polri. From this situation a terminology developed in the community associated with extra-budgetary funding received by an individual member or by the institution of the Polri: Public Participation (Parmas), Friendship Participation (Parman), and Criminal Participation (Parmin).[6]

Rise of internal conflicts

One consequence of Polri's disassociation from the military was the greater flexibility for those becoming leaders inside the Polri. This caused conflict between classes at Akpol, conflict between Akpol graduates and non-academy recruits, and conflict between units of the Polri as people attempted to gain better positions. The conflict among Akpol classes occurred among high-level officers, particularly at Polri headquarters, while conflicts between graduates of Akpol and non-Akpol recruits occurred from the level of Polda down to Polsek (precinct).[7]

Another serious impact of the disassociation was the formation of cliques and regroupings inside the Polri, especially at the national level, but without clear bases for the groups.[8] When the Polri was part of ABRI, cliques or groups were based mainly on Akpol classes and Polri units. However, post-disassociation, groupings in the Polri were based on the orientation and characteristics of each officer as they considered the future of the Polri. This corresponded to a desire to build the Polri as professional and independent, not merely through slogans, with conscious and confirming choices made by each officer associated with his orientation towards building and developing the Polri.[9]

Changes in the responsibility of the post-disassociation Polri also changed access to political and economic power. When it was part of the ABRI, Polri headquarters was highly dependent on the ABRI; post-disassociation, Polri was directly related to the power of the president and the parliament. The groupings after disassociation had no direct institutional foundation but fell into three categories: the Status Quo,[10] the Moderate[11] and the Radical.[12]

One interesting feature of this grouping is that it is based mainly on the personal character of the individuals and does not necessarily indicate where individuals would or would not be in an internal conflict. As an illustration, Chaeruddin Ismail and Bimantoro were actually included in the Status Quo group. Conversely, the eight Polri officers who took part in conflict were positioned among the radical officers who wanted the Polri to be a professional and independent institution.

Increased number of personnel

In 1998, the Polri had 250,000 police officers, while ten years later there were 380,000. This gave a ratio between police officers and population of 1:574, although in some provinces the ratio was only half as big (see Table 4.1).[13] It

Table 4.1 Ratio between Polri officers and population at the national and selected provincial levels

Province	Ratio
National	1:574[1]
East Kalimantan	1:300
Bali	1:300
Maluccas	1:300
Central Sulawesi	1:500
Central Kalimantan	1:750
West Java	1:1,100
Central Java	1:1,100
North Sumatra	1:1,200
South Sumatra	1:1,200

Source: IPW (2008); Mabes Polri (2009).

Note
1 Mabes Polri (2009), p. 13.

was expected that if the ratio between police officers and population could be brought close to the ideal of around 1:400 in all provinces, the role and functions of Polri would be optimized and maximized.

Development of community policing model

The implementation of the community policing model was part of a paradigm change related to the roles of the Polri in the community. Before the start of *reformasi* the model had been in the form of the Polri's Security, Development and Public Order NCOs (Babinkamtibmas), which paralleled the army's system of Village Developer NCOs (Babinsa) as implemented by the army's Territorial Command.[14] In addition, efforts to develop safety in the community and in industrial areas were implemented in such programmes as the Neighbourhood Security System (Siskamling) and Licensed Security Guards (Satuan Pengamanan – Satpam).[15] However, there was a growing awareness that the Polri must have a winning programme that would reflect the new paradigm within the Polri itself. The community policing programme was an integral part of the democratic policing that was implemented by the Polri after its disassociation from the armed forces.

Increased budget

Over the first ten years after the fall of the Suharto presidency, there was an increase in the Polri budget of more than 3,000 per cent. In 1998, when it was still part of the ABRI, the Polri budget was only Rp.9 billion;[16] in 2008, the Polri budget was Rp.27 trillion. The rise in budget provided for a gradual development of the Polri organization and increases in the number of officers. However, the budget was still considered not enough based on the organizational development over the ten-year period.[17]

Table 4.2 The Polri budget, 1998–2008

Year	Amount (million Rp.)	Increase (%)
1998	Rp.9,000	–
1999	Rp.3,200,000	355.6
2000	Rp.3,200,000	–
2001	Rp.4,630,000	30.88
2002	Rp.7,170,000	35.40
2003	Rp.9,000,000	20.30
2004	Rp.10,645,000	55.50
2005	Rp.11,165,000	4.89
2006	Rp.16,778,000	10.23
2007	Rp.18,230,000	8.65
2008	Rp.27,000,000	48.10

Source: BPK (2008); Mabes Polri (2009); DPR (2009).

Changed basis of financial management

Post-disassociation there was a change of financial management in the Polri from being centralized to being based more on work units. This step was a part of reducing the level of distortion and leakage of the Polri budget when funds were received by the Polri headquarters from the Finance Ministry and distributed to their units.[18]

One risk of the national model for the Polri was in its centralized institutional controls. These had included a centralized financial management, which opened spaces and opportunities for diversion and leakage as it was passed down through several levels until personnel received it, whether in the form of salaries, allowances, or other state-funded local budget lines. Most often the reason for the leakages was direct cuts from the state that had to be accepted by the authorized receivers. The new financial management model allowed all working units and units in the field to take a direct monthly budget from the Finance Ministry.[19]

Changes in recruitment and training

After disassociation, the Polri revised its curriculum, its teaching manuals, and the quality of its recruitment system. These were all evaluated and better adjusted to the needs and conditions of more civilian police values. Although in some cases there were disagreements among leaders related to education policy, gradually there were adjustments and improvements.[20]

Some changes were associated with efforts to respond to public demands that the Polri should realize their determination to be an independent and professional force. One policy was related to education for bachelors and masters graduates at the Akpol. This policy overlapped with the roles of other schools such as the PTIK, which would provide bachelor graduates in police science, and the SESPIM, which awarded a managerial-level qualification equivalent to a masters degree, despite changes in policy that involved focusing on acceptance of Akpol cadets from high school who later would hold a Diploma qualification, with an enhanced function of the PTIK to strengthen its policing science programme.[21]

Increasing anti-terror capabilities

The INP's anti-terror unit was given increasing capabilities. In addition to the existing Brimob, which had an anti-terror unit, the Polri also established the 88 Anti-Terror Special Detachment (Densus 88 AT) as part of a response to rampant acts of terror.[22] The capability of Densus 88 AT later became recognized as one of the Polri's achievements and was even used as an exemplar in counterterrorism efforts in Asia and the Pacific.[23] The Anti-Terror Training Centre at Semarang, the capital of Central Java Province, and the Jakarta Centre for Law Enforcement Cooperation were established as part of the agreement made between the Minister of Foreign Affairs and 25 countries in the Asian Pacific.[24]

Changes in the promotion and disciplinary system

There were improvements in the mechanism of rewards and punishments in the Polri. When the Polri was still part of the ABRI its system was based on the existing pattern in the ABRI, which positioned the Polri as an integrated part of the ABRI and had a negative impact on the psychology of police officers. The most striking change was in starting to use civil courts to try various allegations of irregularities in the public behaviour of Polri personnel, while hearings about alleged breaches of the Polri code of ethics were conducted by the Profession and Ethics Division (Propam: Profesi dan Pengamanan) of the Polri headquarters, with Propam also investigating alleged irregularities in the performance Polri officers.[25]

Various awards could now be made to police officers, starting with awards, promotions and improved positions, with increases in remuneration depending on the level of achievement.[26] This extra remuneration was part of Polri efforts to improve the performance of its officers on duty by motivating them to be effective and work hard in the field.

Locally based appointments

The Polri revised its locally based personnel assignment under a policy of 'local boys for local jobs' and implementation of more effective structures for this.[27] While the Polri was a dependent part of ABRI its implementation of locally based personnel had been hampered by interventions from ABRI leaders at various levels, from headquarters to local.[28] After its disassociation, the Polri reinforced its local assignment mechanisms to apply to low-ranking police officers, with the assumption that they would be working at the operational level in the field, while the assignment of police officers from the first middle rank and up was under the authority and supervision of the Polri headquarters.[29]

Moreover, the assertion of a 'minimum structure, rich implementation' function was part of the Polri policy to focus on how police in the district or city and provinces could effectively apply the mechanisms of the function. One of these was to give wide authority to local police heads in formulating operational policies in the field but to keep supervision and direction in police headquarters in the form of public policy. The 'minimum structure, rich implementation' function was later reaffirmed by emphasizing the role of district police units (Polres) as the Basic Police Unit (Kesatuan Operasional Dasar), with all supervision by Polda (the level above) as the umbrella unit, and the Polsek (Precinct) as key in carrying out police roles and functions. The policy was later confirmed by the abolishing of the Sub-regional Police (Polwil) level of administration, which no longer had legitimacy under the revised civil administrative structure from 2010.[30]

Grand Strategy of police development

The legal implementation of the Grand Strategy of Polri development was based on the Polri's 'Blue Book'. The Grand Strategy sets out the stages of the Polri's efforts to become an independent and professional police force. When referring to the 'Blue Book',[31] police reform and development was divided into three areas: structural, instrumental and cultural.[32] Reforms were conducted in a series of stages to achieve goals in the development of Polri towards being independent and professional. The Grand Strategy contained several phases of development: Trust Building, Partnership and Networking, and Striving for Excellence.[33]

De-militarization of Brimob

As a paramilitary police unit, the Brimob had been directed as a combat unit. The strong militaristic culture of this elite unit of the Polri was often remarked on negatively, including it being mentioned in various reports on violence and human rights violations by Brimob personnel. Some NGOs, such as Kontras (Komisi untuk Orang Hilang dan Korban Tindak Kekerasan – Commission for 'the Disappeared' and Victims of Violence) and Imparsial, categorized Brimob's human rights abuses and violent activities as being similar to those perpetrated by the ABRI.[34]

Based on this perceived problem, the approach to changing the unit was to change its leadership, which had a military character and appearance, to one using various civil approaches to adjust to the changes and challenges of the main institution, the Polri. Two crucial turning points were the motto 'civilize Brimob' and the implementation of community policing.[35] So far, there have been some changes in behaviour patterns and approaches in the field by Brimob personnel, but in general the practice of violence by the personnel of Brimob and other units has remained relatively high, especially in conflict and mining areas.[36]

Increase in the number of women police

Post-disassociation, the number and role of police women (Polwan) in the INP has been increased. Before disassociation Polwan were no more than 1 per cent of all Polri officers, but by 2008 this had been increased to 3.5 per cent. It is planned that the number will increase to 10 per cent. The Polwan have crucial roles and functions in the Polri's development, with the opening of Special Assistance Units (RPK: Ruang Pelayanan Khusus) for children, women and senior citizens who are victims or have faced crime. The RPK units are fully led and controlled by Polwan officers.[37]

Activation of the National Police Commision

The activation of the National Police Commission (Kompolnas) was based on the belief that one of the conditions in a democratic state is that the police force needs to be publicly monitored.[38] However, the Kompolnas had a very limited role and no supervisory duties. The commission has the duty to assist the president in setting the policy for the Polri and to provide considerations in the appointment and dismissal of the chief of the Polri. The Kompolnas also has a duty and limited function to collect and analyse data as a material consideration for the president in developing the Polri, and to provide advice in creating an independent and professional police force. On the other hand, the Kompolnas also deals with complaints from the public on the performance of the Polri roles.[39]

Changes in oversight and supervision of police performance

The oversight of Polri performance has been increased post-disassociation. Although it was recognized that public monitoring of police performance had increased, there were many people who blamed the Polri for a variety of aberrations, in terms of the institution and its personnel. Institutionally, the Polri has two surveillance inspectorates: the General Supervision Inspectorate (Ikatan Sarjana Ilmu Kepolisian, known as Irwasum), a unit to supervise various activities related to the role and function of police officers; and the Profession and Ethics Division (Propam), which had repressive functions related to breaches of the professional codes of ethics of police officers.

The president, assisted by the Kompolnas, the ombudsman, the commission of the DPR, and the public, conducts the external oversight of the Polri as part of a layered supervision. Nevertheless, an essential point is the weakness of the external institutions that oversee Polri's performance. The implementation by the president, as he/she was the chief of the Polri, often positioned the Polri, directly or indirectly, in the way of politicization and intervention.[40] The Kompolnas, which was expected to be an effective watchdog, was only positioned as a prompter and adviser to the president.[41] The ombudsman finds it difficult to solve problems beyond legal issues due to the limits of its authority. Moreover, the ombudsman tends to send all reports from the public relating to the Polri to the President as the direct supervisor of the Polri.[42]

Meanwhile, monitoring by parliament often created stagnation with Polri's poor understanding of security issues, especially in relation to the Polri. This weakness was caused by lack of knowledge related to internal security, which tended to be more specific than the scope of national security as both internal security and defence or of external security.[43] In other words, although there was increased oversight in quantity, the quality was still far from expectations. The quality of oversight was generally more in the tradition that had been running, with a few changes that are not significant, and gave a far from ideal impression.[44]

Changes in relations with the military and local government

Post-disassociation patterns of relations between the Polri and other institutions were changed. Importantly, the Polri took over many roles of territorial or dual functions that had been previously dominated by ABRI. Continuing tensions in this area resulted in various clashes in the field between police and military personnel relating to their new roles.[45] Being still a national police, the Polri's relations with local governments also experienced a change, from a combination of the consequences of the disassociation and the implementation of more decentralization, both central elements of *reformasi*. The change was to a direct and potentially complicated relationship, which had to be negotiated in each case.[46]

Summary of developments

The progress made by 2009 towards the Polri becoming a more professional and modern police institution, and related changes, are shown in Table 4.3.

This chapter has shown that the development of a more independent and professional Polri was started in the *reformasi* era, especially during President

Table 4.3 Changes in the Polri post-disassociation, 1999–2009

Implemented steps	Progress
Revision of the Polri code of ethics	Completed
New police act	Completed
Rise of internal conflicts	Still happening
Increased number of personnel	Ongoing
Development of community policing model	Ongoing
Increased budget	Ongoing
Changed basis of financial management	Completed
Changes in recruitment and training	Under development
Increasing anti-terror capabilities	Under development
Changes in promotion and disciplinary systems	Under development
Locally-based appointments	Completed
Grand Strategy of Polri development	Completed
De-militarisation of Brimob	Completed
Increased number of women police	Ongoing
Activation of national police commission	Completed
Changes in oversight and supervision of Polri performance	Under development
Changes in relations with the military and local government	Ongoing
Strengthening of politicisation	Still happening

Sources: Mabes Polri (1999); Meliala (2008); Mabes Polri (2008); IPW (2009).

Wahid's term, with some changes inside the Polri. However, these were also followed by political intervention from President Wahid in relation to the position of Polri support for his administration. The situation got worse due to the Polri having not yet consolidated and being still in post-disassociation euphoria.

This chapter has argued that to keep the Polri free from politicization, it should have been more active as a political player and supported one of the groups in the national political turmoil. The Polri realized that the consequence of this was that it was trapped in dualism of its leadership, and conflict within the Polri arose.

Notes

1 For more discussion of 'Catur Prasetya' of the Code of Ethics of the Polri, see Kunarto (1997). See also *Koran Tempo* (November 4, 2010), 'Mempolisikan Polisi'.
2 In fact, the Polri could not hide from the political interests of the regime, even in the democratic transition regimes from Presidents Wahid, Megawati, and Yudhoyono. See also Mabes Polri (2008), pp. 16–19; *Pikiran Rakyat* (January 2, 2005), 'Polisi Harus Pahami Lagi Tri Brata'.
3 Rusdihardjo and S. Bimantoro, chiefs of the Polri at the time, had tried to revise Law No. 28/1997 to make sense of the Polri's role and its position directly under presidential supervision. The political turmoil made them lose focus on this; the New Police Act was finally issued in Da'i Bachtiar terms in President Megawati's era.
4 For more discussion of the process of disassociation of the Polri from the ABRI, see Chapter 2.
5 For more explanation see Law No. 2/2002 on the Polri, especially Chapter VI and Article 40.
6 External support for the Polri at local level will be further discussed in Parts IV and V. See also Haseman and Lachica (2009).
7 Interview on November 2, 2009, with Police Inspector General (retired) Drs Ronny Lihawa, M.Si. Secretary of the Kompolnas, Jakarta. Interview on November 5, 2009, with Police Commissaries General Drs E. Winarto, SH, M.Si, Head of Human Resources of the Polri Headquarter, Jakarta.
8 More discussion about the regrouping of the Polri in local areas will be provided in Chapters 10 and 11.
9 This grouping was further emphasized by the accelerated politicization of the Polri, which might have been good, but also could be negative because the impact of the grouping also led to more dynamics in the Polri. For more discussion of this, see Chapter 3.
10 The Status Quo group is defined as a group of officers in the Polri who have a tendency to support any policy associated with political power and to engage in political dynamics for personal or group interests.
11 The Moderate group is defined as a group of individuals who accommodated themselves to various trends of thought and career orientation and were neither opportunistic nor radical.
12 The Radical group is defined as those police officers who wanted to keep Polri on the right track as they saw it, in accordance with the mandate of police reform: to realize the Polri as an independent and professional organization.
13 The ratio between the police and the population in each province is different because each province has a different population. See Muradi (2009b), pp. 11–12; *Pikiran Rakyat* (September 7, 2003), 'Polri Baru Memiliki 80.000 Pucuk Senjata'.
14 Sutanto and Sugiarso (2005), pp. 172–178.

15 Djamin (1995), pp. 239–245. For more discussion of relations between the private security guards and the Polri see Jansen (2010, unpubd), especially Chapter 3.
16 The Polri budget increase of more than 3,000 per cent was not only because of government policy, but also because of the inflation of the Indonesian currency. *The Jakarta Post* (December 8, 1999), 'I Putu Gede Ary Suta: The Capital Market versus the Banking System'.
17 *Pikiran Rakyat* (July 2, 2003), 'Bersihkan Lembaga Polri'. *The Jakarta Post* (October 13, 2010), 'National Police want Rp.30 trillion Budget'.
18 Suprananto (2005).
19 See Joint Agreement between Chief of the Polri and Minister of Finance No. 14/KMK.06/2005 on the changed basis of financial management, and also Chief of the INP Decree No. Pol. Kep/5/I/2005 on the procedure of using state funding in the Polri.
20 *Suara Merdeka* (December 10, 2009), '2010, Akpol Hanya Terima Lulusan SMA'.
21 *Sinar Harapan* (December 10, 2009), 'Penerimaan Akpol 2010 Akan Diubah'.
22 This was later confirmed by the INP as the main institution to deal with terrorism, as stipulated in Law No. 15/2003 on combating acts of terrorism. See *Pikiran Rakyat* (September 12, 2003), 'Pemerintah Siap Bekukan Aset Teroris di Indonesia'. *Pikiran Rakyat* (September 17, 2003), 'Polri Dinilai Kebablasan Dalam Penanganan Kasus Terorisme'; Muradi (2009b), Chapter 5.
23 *Suara Merdeka* (July 3, 2004), 'Menengok Sekolah Anti Teror, Diikuti 21 Peserta Mancanegara'.
24 *Detik Online* (2010), 'Ada "Teroris" di Akpol Semarang', available at: http://us.detiknews.com/index.php/detik.read/tahun/2006/bulan/07/tgl/27/time/190222/idnews/644618/idkanal/10 (April 19, 2010).
25 For example, *Antara News* (2010), 'Propam Kepri Amankan Oknum Polair Diduga Perompak', available at: www.antara.co.id/berita/1265915950/propam-polda-kepri-amankan-oknum-polair-diduga-perompak (April 19, 2010). See also *Inilah.com* (2010), 'Kapolsek Johar Diadukan ke Propam Polda', available at: www.inilah.com/news/politik/2009/04/07/96927/kapolsek-johar-diadukan-ke-propam-polda/ (April 19, 2010). *Pikiran Rakyat* (May 26, 2003), '3 Anggota Polres Kuningan Hadapi Proses Pemecatan'.
26 *Tempo Interaktif* (2010), 'Hari Bhayangkara, Kapolri Beri Penghargaan pada Bintara Polisi Cacat', available at: www.tempointeraktif.com/hg/nusa/2009/07/01/brk,20090701-184668,id.html (April 19, 2010). See also *Solo Pos* (2010), 'Polri Siap Berikan Remunerasi Pada Jajarannya', available at: www.solopos.com/2009/channel/nasional/polri-siap-berikan-remunerasi-pada-jajarannya-1085 (April 19, 2010).
27 For more discussion of the implementation of this 'local boys for local jobs' policy, see Part IV.
28 For example *Kompas* (June 17, 1974), 'Mutasi Besar-besaran di Lingkungan Polri'; also *Pikiran Rakyat* (February 27, 2003), 'Komandan Korp Brimob Pecat Bharatu Mintori'.
29 Interview on November 4, 2009 with Police Inspector General Drs Andi Chaerudin, Coordinator of Expert Staff for Chief of the Polri.
30 *Kompas* (February 2, 2010), 'Polri Likuidasi Polwil'.
31 For more discussion of the publication process of the 'Blue Book' of the Polri, see Part II.
32 For more discussion of three problems of the Polri as explained in the 'Blue Book', see Part II.
33 For more explanation of the Polri's Grand Strategy, see Mabes Polri (2004).
34 Kontras (2007); compare those with *Pikiran Rakyat* (August 21, 2003), 'Brimob Polda Antisipasi Bencana Alam'.
35 For more explanation of the Polri's Brimob, see Jones et al. (2004); Wenas (2006); Muradi (2009b).

36 *Pikiran Rakyat* (January 28, 2008), 'Warga Minta Penarikan Anggota Brimob'. *Republika* (October 26, 2006), 'Warga-Brimob Bentrok di Poso, Empat Warga Tertembak'.
37 Harsono (2004), pp. 29–36. *Pikiran Rakyat* (February 20, 2003), 'Supratiningsih, Kapolres Wanita Pertama di Indonesia'. *Pikiran Rakyat* (September 2, 2003), 'Peran Polwan Belum Maksimal, Kapolda: Polwan Akan Ditempatkan pada Tugas Operasional'.
38 As a consequence of Law No. 2/2002 on the Polri, it was necessary to establish a commission to supervise police performance. The creation of Kompolnas was the mandate of Articles 37 and 38 of Law No. 2/2002 on the Polri.
39 See Presidential Decree No. 55/2006 on the establishment of the National Police Commission (Kompolnas).
40 Interview on November 5, 2009, with Police Inspector General Drs Jacky Murdono, former advisor to the Minister of Security and Defence, Jakarta.
41 Interview on November 4, 2009, with Mufti Makarim, Executive Director of the Institute of Defence, Security, and Peace Studies (IDSPS), Jakarta.
42 Interview on November 3, 2009, with Junaidi Simon, Coordinator of Research on the Security of Imparsial, Jakarta.
43 For more discussion of the definition of security as internal and external roles, see Buzan (1997).
44 Interview on November 4, 2009, with Mufti Makarim, Executive Director of the Institute of Defence, Security, and Peace Studies (IDSPS), Jakarta. Interview on November 3, 2009, with Junaidi Simon, Coordinator of Research on the Security of Imparsial, Jakarta. *Tempo* (May 27, 2002), 'Da'i Bachtiar: "Sofjan Jacoeb Hanya Menjelaskan"'. *Kompas* (February 7, 2011), 'Polri Harus Buka Data "Rekening Gendut"'.
45 Interview on November 3, 2009, with Chief Commisioner (retired) Dr Bambang Widodo Umar, lecturer at the PTIK, Jakarta. Local relationships between the Polri and the ABRI post-disassociation will be discussed in Part IV.
46 These new relationships are described and discussed in more detail in Parts IV and V.

Part III
Consolidation, development and corruption

Part III

5 Resolving the divisive issues of the rival chiefs and the Group of Eight

> The relationship between leader and subordinates in the Police [in the *reformasi* era] is still bad, because they still apply 'the science of the frog' in their career path, namely: bowing and scraping to the leader, eliminate all competitors, and then bring them down.
>
> (Sartono Mukadis, 2006)

The inauguration of Megawati (PDIP) as president and Hamzah Haz (PPP) as vice-president marked the end of Wahid's presidency, which had lasted less than two years. Several hours before the inauguration, Sofjan Jacoeb, the Jakarta Metro Kapolda, asked for confirmation of the re-establishment of Bimantoro as the Polri chief. According to Sofjan Jacoeb, this would be part of the reorganization of the Polri and would reduce conflicts caused by President Wahid's political interference.

Soon after that, the command of the Polri was retransferred to Bimantoro. Although Megawati stressed that the fate of Chaeruddin would be decided later, her true meaning, as interpreted by Bimantoro, was that he should resolve the problem by himself.[1] Bimantoro then translated this into taking an informal approach to Chaeruddin's situation, with the hope that Chaeruddin would resign his post and end his political adventures of the last six months.[2]

After consultation and approval from Megawati, Chaeruddin was finally relieved of his position based on Presidential Decree No. 60/2001 and Bimantoro was officially reactivated as chief of the Polri.[3] As he would be retiring in three or four months, a replacement had to be selected using acceptable procedures. The Polri's Wanjakti proposed five possible names: Chaeruddin Ismail, Ahwil Luthan, Sjahroedin Pagar Alam, Sofjan Jacoeb and Yun Mulyana.[4]

Resolving the problem: military or civilian approaches?

Compared with the more informal moves taken against Chaeruddin, a different treatment was received by the Group of Eight who had supported Chaeruddin against Bimantoro. They were arrested and charged with violation of the Polri code of conduct and with insubordination, the charges being processed internally. The arrest of these eight officers was a turning point in strengthening the power of Bimantoro in the Polri.[5]

The arrest invited criticism from several parties because it was considered unfair and discriminatory. Forty lawyers, members of Legal Assistants for the Truth, supported these middle-ranking police officers, including Taufik Basari and Irianto Subyakto from the YLBHI (Yayasan Lembaga Bantuan Hukum Indonesia – The Indonesian Legal Aid Institute Foundation), conducting pre-trial litigation against the chief of the Polri over a number of issues about the treatment, accusations and arrests of the eight officers.[6] Several of the eight including Herman Koto, Alfons Loemau, and Badarudin Zaman held a hunger strike as a protest against their treatment.[7] Although the Polri headquarters rejected the complaints, debates and consequences strengthened.[8]

The Polri gave five reasons why these middle-ranking police officers must undergo an examination by the Officers Honour Board (DKP):[9] first, their rallies and statements discrediting the Polri chief, which were considered to be insubordination; second, their meetings with activists against the attitude of police criticizing the validity of the special plenary parliamentary session of MPR; third, spreading word or writings against the rule, trying to thwart Polri activities when securing the parliament in Operation Mantab Brata VIII; fourth, officially or unofficially refusing official orders, that is, the order to stop giving press releases or publicity beyond their authority;[10] fifth, allegations regarding the ethics code of the Polri and criminal offences against the law.[11]

Following personal approaches by the Polri leaders to the Group of Eight, they finally withdrew their legal action against the Polri and chose to follow an internal trial to discipline violations.[12] However, the Group of Eight filed a lawsuit against the chief of the Polri, because approaches made to them by Bimantoro and the Polri leaders were followed by their removal from their jobs. This lawsuit was based on three issues. First, following the disassociation of the Polri from ABRI, according to MPR Decree No. VII/2000, every police officer was subject to the civil court rather than a military court. Second, they had been accused of committing an abuse of power in the form of a press release as defined in Information Letter of the Polri Chief No. Pol.: SE/09/VI/2001 on 'Authority of Press Release' dated July 1, 2001, signed by Bimantoro, and they considered that at the time when the letter was issued, Bimantoro was a non-active Polri chief. Third, the officers complained about the method of their arrest and about illegal intimidation of themselves and their families.[13]

Although their lawsuit was rejected by the South Jakarta Court, the confusion and problems between the Group of Eight and Polri leaders continued.[14] Moreover, the DKP recommended three options: dishonourable discharge, dismissal with honour, or another sentence based on a decision from Bimantoro.[15] Bimantoro's decision was to suspend the detentions, and the Polri reassigned the officers with conditions. One was that there would be no career advancement.[16] The decision was accepted by the eight officers because most of them were nearing retiring age and their posts would no longer be upgraded in any case, although there was a possibility of extension stipulated in Law No. 28/1997 and discussion of this for the legislation which was to replace that Law.[17]

Rivalries between classes and regeneration issues

Some of the internal conflict was related to the nepotic rivalry of groups who had been together in the same Akpol class. It was common when a chief of the INP was inaugurated for him to assign his classmates to strategic and important positions. This would have followed his selection through the Wanjakti and his appointment would have involved support from these classmates. In addition to supporting his policy measures and programmes, such appointments were intended to strengthen the leadership of the chief of the Polri. This made for competition between classes, especially between what was seen as the 'younger generation' versus 'older generation' (even when the difference between such 'generations' would be only a year or so of cohort and age). As the normal age for compulsory retirement from the Polri was only 55, by the time someone reached the top there was usually only a short time left before he, and thus his classmates, would have to retire.

The internal importance of these Akpol classes could handicap regeneration processes inside the Polri. This happened several times due to the appointment of a chief from a senior 'generation' or from the same 'generation' as the previous chief. Consequently, there were some officers who could not wait any longer and tried various manoeuvres in order to gain position and title earlier, using political lobbying, money, or sentiment between and within Akpol classes.

Changing political context

The political situation led to a more publicly open and visible competition for the chief's position. After its disassociation from the ABRI, the Polri became more open to internal competition involving external influences. The replacement of Roesmanhadi by Rusdihardjo was not through the internal mechanism of recommendation by the Wanjakti and proposal by the retiring chief of the Polri, and was a precedent. Subsequent appointments came through a combination of demands from the president, the public, and political parties, as seen in President Wahid's decisions about Roesmanhadi, Rusdihardjo and Bimantoro. In the case of Bimantoro, there was fierce resistance that led to internal conflict in the Polri and contributed to Wahid's fall from the presidency.

It should be recognized that, after the era of Dibyo Widodo, the weakening of the Polri leadership led to poor leaders in the Polri. There were three reasons for this: political reciprocation, the appointments of Polri chiefs not following the recommendations of the Wanjakti, and the appointees' insufficient capabilities. This had become common during the eras of Suharto and the New Order, as Suharto's rule relied on it, but it changed in the *reformasi* era, where democracy was becoming the main pillar. It still happened, in two variants. The first was in a sense of inferiority felt by the chief towards those who had appointed him.

The second variant was an agreement between the president and the candidates for chief of the Polri.

Consolidation and reforms

After Bimantoro had settled the case of the Group of Eight, the issue was then who would replace him as chief of Polri. As described above, at first, the Wanjakti recommended Chaeruddin (Akpol 1971), Yun Mulyana (Akpol 1970), Ahwil Luthan (Akpol 1968), and Sjahruddin Pagar Alam (Akpol 1970). However, younger candidates such as Sutanto (Akpol 1973) and Da'i Bachtiar (Akpol 1972) were then brought up.[18] Sofjan Jacoeb (Akpol 1970) was also proposed.[19] There was also a growing demand among the public for extension of Bimantoro's term. However, the latter was just in public discourse and not reflected internally.[20] Moreover, the three-star general Kadaryanto (Akpol 1971) was the strongest candidate.[21]

The eventual decision by President Megawati to appoint Da'i Bachtiar surprised many people, inside and outside the Polri. It was interesting that the in nomination process of Da'i Bachtiar, President Megawati submitted only his name to the DPR, and none of the names proposed by the Polri's Wanjakti. This was a shock inside the Polri and provoked some serious internal debate. Bimantoro asserted that Da'i Bachtiar had been one of the names proposed and recommended by the Wanjakti to President Megawati, although this claim has been disputed.[22]

Although this was an unusual act due to her choice not to take the candidate proposed by the Polri Wanjakti, it was part of the prerogative of the president.[23] There were now opportunities for political institutions, including the presidency, to propose candidates who they might expect to support their preferred policy positions. This would make the Polri a politicized institution, with intervention like that practised by President Wahid.[24]

There were a numbers of reasons why Megawati did not take any of the candidates proposed from the Wanjakti. The first reason was that she wanted an end to all internal conflicts in the Polri left by President Wahid. Some members of the inner political circles saw the option of Da'i Bachtiar as a good choice because he was not directly involved in the conflict.

The second reason was that President Megawati did not want to interfere in the internal dynamics of the Polri in any way that could disrupt the programme of internal security. Da'i was a figure expected to be acceptable to all parties in the Polri, which would facilitate internal consolidation by solving a variety of problems and allow the Polri's focus to be on realizing its programme and performance.[25]

The third reason was that Megawati wanted the Polri chief to be in control in accordance with a good administrative mechanism, in which the prerogative of the president could run effectively, with no interruptions, and also be safe from the internal resistance of the Polri. The fourth reason was that President Megawati wanted the reform programme to work well. The option of Da'i Bachtiar became a political gamble, with President Megawati hoping that he would steer the Polri towards becoming a professional and independent institution.[26]

The fifth reason was for the regeneration in the Polri. President Megawati had practically no choices but to choose Da'i Bachtiar or Sutanto, who represented a younger generation and hope to the Polri. The choice of Da'i Bachtiar was part of that planned framework.[27]

Da'i Bachtiar was elected smoothly to be chief of the Polri based on a joint meeting of the parliament's First Commission on Defence and Security Issues and Second Commission on Law and Government Issues. The various negative opinions expressed in the meeting were overcome and the former Kapolda of East Java became the leader of the Polri.[28]

It is interesting that the process by which President Megawati appointed Da'i Bachtiar, who was considered as being close to the president, was repeated in the subsequent appointment of Sutanto in the era of Susilo Bambang Yudhoyono. Like President Megawati, President Yudhoyono did not choose a candidate proposed by the Wanjakti, but had his own: Sutanto. He was a 1973 classmate of Yudhoyono in the Akademi Angkatan Bersenjata Republik Indonesia (Indonesian Armed Forces Academy). The pattern of politicization in the Polri involved the past and personal proximity factors as well as just a meeting of interests.

Internal consolidation and new politicization

However, psychological comfort in carrying out similar work for running the government also had an effect. In this context, we can see how there was uncertainty inside the Polri as to how to act as a professional and independent institution with a continuing proximity to power. The desire to reposition the Polri as defender of the current regime re-emerged in the *reformasi* era, as in the era of President Wahid.[29]

During Da'i Bachtiar's era, there were political mobilizations within the Polri to choose Megawati as president in the 2004 election, but Susilo Bambang Yudhoyono eventually won this.[30] Sutanto, although he was less obvious, ensured the direction of policies, which kept the government of Yudhoyono assured of protection from security problems caused by political conflicts and other security threats. A strong indication that Sutanto was close to and supportive of Yudhoyono was that after he retired he was on the successful campaign team of President Yudhoyono in 2009, and was then appointed Head of the National Intelligence Bureau (BIN).[31]

In the era of President Wahid, the politicization of Polri post-disassociation was an open model. Wahid tried to position the Polri to gain support for the government, against those he saw as opposed to him and what he stood for, and eventually support for his survival, against those he saw as enemies who were trying to bring him down. President Wahid's replacing of Roesmanhadi with Rusdihardjo and Rusdihardjo with Bimantoro caused small ripples but no polemic or conflict. However, his third attempt – to replace Bimantoro with

Chaeruddin Ismail – met with resistance and rejection from the Polri and also from parliament.

President Megawati applied a more closed model in her politicization of the Polri. She looked for control over the Polri without setting off resistance and internal conflicts over it. It seemed that Megawati exercised sufficient prudence when selecting Da'i Bachtiar to replace Bimantoro. Da'i realized that, as far as possible, he should show his support for the president and tried to help her win in the presidential election of 2004.[32] Other than that, Da'i Bachtiar ensured that the Polri could perform well in fulfilling the government's aims, through his success in dismantling the terrorist network and forming an elite anti-terror unit (Densus 88 AT) which had a positive effect for Megawati's administration.[33]

In the era of President Yudhoyono, the politicization of the Polri was a mixture of an open and a closed model. Yudhoyono had asked Sutanto to become his Polri chief before he became president. A friend of Sutanto recognized that there was a desire to help Yudhoyono become president, as this was believed to have positive effects on other colleagues in the Polri. However, this friend, a retired two-star police general, stated that in the era of President Megawati the Polri gained more freedom and benefits, politically and economically, than during Yudhoyono's presidencies.[34]

During Megawati's presidency, the Polri under Da'i Bachtiar was not clearly directed to do political work. Yudhoyono assigned Sutanto to investigate APBD-gate issues.[35] The ruling regime built political bargains with a coalition of other political parties in order to not interfere with President Yudhoyono and Vice-President Jusuf Kalla.[36]

The APBD-gate issues were used by President Yudhoyono to arrest several members and former members of the Dewan Perwakilan Rakyat Daerah (DPRD – district or provincial assembly), bupatis or mayors, utilizing the Polri headquarters and the local police (Polda and Polres).[37] In the era of Da'i Bachtiar, such pursuit of cases of alleged corruption by local or national government had not been carried out under the Megawati government; alleged corruption cases such as those of Indosat and Temasek (involving the Minister for State Enterprises, Laksamana Sukardi, who was claimed to have corruptly taken billions of rupiah from the state budget) had not been processed.[38]

One of the economic benefits for the Polri was an increased budget; although at a smaller percentage compared to the era of President Megawati, it provided more possibilities to build international cooperation and associated international assistance, particularly to the development of Densus 88 AT.[39] However, the basic foundation, which had been built in the era of Da'i Bachtiar, was then developed by Sutanto, who focused his programme on combating drugs and gambling, and increased counter-terrorism capabilities.[40]

New policies and programmes

The first policy undertaken during Megawati's presidency was to resolve the internal conflicts based on taking smoother approaches. If in the era of

Bimantoro the settlement was completed but not correctly, then in the era of Da'i everything was clarified, with relations between the Polri and the governments, both national and local, and internal relations within the Polri becoming conducive and consolidated.

After thus resolving internal conflicts and consolidation, Da'i Bachtiar focused on developing programmes for the future. Terrorism was a new form of security threat for countries with major and complex problems such as Indonesia, and became a serious part of what had to be addressed by the Polri. The new challenges faced by the Polri during the terms of Da'i Bachtiar, Sutanto, and after him can be divided into seven categories.

The first challenge was the completion of the institutionalization of the Polri, which had not yet been established. In addition to referring to MPR Decrees Nos VI/MPR/2000 and VII/2000, the INP also referred to the old Police Act, Law No. 28/1997, which was no longer relevant.[41]

Second was the settlement of communal conflicts and conflicts caused by political euphoria in the democratic transition in Aceh, Papua, Kalimantan, Poso, Central Sulawesi and Maluku.

Third was strengthening prevention and counter-terrorism in Indonesia. The attack on the World Trade Center in New York on September 11, 2001 had set off a new war against terrorism. This opened opportunities for the police to build the momentum to develop their own anti-terror forces, Densus 88 AT.[42]

Fourth was the formulation of a Grand Strategy for the Polri. Having been distracted by political minefields laid by the attempted interventions of President Wahid, efforts to develop the Polri's organizational strategy were stressed again.

Fifth was the strengthening of commitment to the eradication of corruption and power abuses. This challenge became a serious matter to be addressed, because the Polri was an institution that must first be cleansed before having a convincing commitment to eradicate corruption and abuse of power.[43]

Sixth was the implementation of community policing programmes. As part of modern policing, the Polri could no longer hide from direct interaction with the public in its independent protection of the security environment. The community policing programme emphasized the importance of community participation in the creation of a secure environment.

Seventh was the development of programmes and units that could be successes for the Polri in the future. These were important for at least three of the Polri's roles and functions: security and the creation of a sense of security in 'conflict areas' post-conflict and separatism, conducted by the Brimob; combating terrorism and transnational crimes that included acts of terror in internal security, conducted by the Densus 88 AT; and the eradication of corruption (including corruption in the Polri) and of environmental crimes such as illegal logging, illegal mining, illegal fishing, and drugs crime, conducted by the Bareskrim.

Sutanto continued to demonstrate firm commitments as a Polri chief. In addition to being anti-corruption, several times the Densus 88 AT were involved in efforts to combat gambling and social crimes.[44] With its various successes, the

Densus 88 AT became better known by the international world. Sutanto also developed patterns of community relations with the Polri, in the form of community policing.[45] This was officially introduced to the public as a programme to build and improve the image of the Polri. In the context of the development of the Brimob, Sutanto strived for it to cover tasks and functions that were not being done directly by the Densus 88 AT.[46]

Constraints on reform

However, Da'i Bachtiar and Sutanto were faced with similar problems and obstacles constraining their attempts to provide leadership in developing a modern police force.

First, the proximity of the Polri to the president, particularly the chief of the Polri, made the Polri prone to politicization. This was proven in both the 2004 and 2009 elections, when both individuals and institutions in the Polri became politicized. In contrast to the politicization of the Polri in the Wahid era, under Megawati and Yudhoyono the closed models became a 'reciprocation politics' that tied institutions and individuals into it.

A second constraint was in the relation between the Polri and local government. Although Da'i Bachtiar confirmed the existence of mechanisms of *dekonsentrasi* (semi-autonomy) of the Polri at all levels, from the lowest Polsek (precinct) up to the Polda, in practice there were still tendencies to adhere to a centralized hierarchy working down from the Polri headquarters.[47] Moreover, the actual implementation of the *dekonsentrasi* policy was strongly influenced by the local Polri leadership.[48]

A third constraint was the corruption and deviation from correct procedures that could not be eradicated from within the Polri. This fact still gave the Polri a negative image among the public, who could see and feel the direct impact of a range of irregularities and corrupt practices.[49] It appeared to many that the culture of corruption and irregularities was institutionalized and would require a high commitment of all parties to overcome.[50]

This chapter has reported on the internal consolidation and development of the Polri, which has been successful in several ways but is still facing major constraints from both outside and inside. From the outside, the Polri is always shadowed by politicization due to being directly under the president's office. Internally, the biggest constraints have been the pervasive practices of corruption and extortion practices, which have increased due to a lack of adequate budget support and gaps in welfare for leaders, officers and personnel.

Notes

1 *Koran Tempo* (July 26, 2001), 'Soal Bimantoro Sebagai Kapolri, Mega Harus Tunggu Keputusan MA'; interview on November 6, 2009 with a senior politician of the PDIP (Partai Demokrasi Indonesia Perjuangan – Indonesian Democratic Party of Struggle), Jakarta.

2 *Kompas* (July 26, 2001), 'Bimantoro Tak Jawab Status Chaeruddin'; *Media Indonesia* (July 26, 2001), 'Chaeruddin Tak Akan Diperiksa'. However, Chaeruddin Ismail told me that he had never been approached or summoned by Bimantoro. He claimed that everything that he did was purely on his own initiative. Interview on June 13, 2010 with Chaeruddin Ismail.
3 Bimantoro removed Chaeruddin's nameplate as deputy chief in a closed room. One interesting aspect was that Bimantoro did not seek legal approaches against Chaeruddin.
4 *Republika* (August 6, 2001), 'Empat Jenderal Masuk Bursa Kapolri'. Ahwil Luthan graduated in 1968 and Chaeruddin in 1971; Sjaroedin Pagar Alam and Yun Mulyana were in the class of 1970 with Bimantoro.
5 *Tempo* (August 5, 2001), 'Serangan Balik Jenderal Bimantoro'. Interview on November 4, 2009 with Chief Commissioner (retired) Dr Bambang Widodo Umar, Jakarta. Interview on June 12, 2010 with Chief Commissioner (retired) Alfons Loemau, Jakarta.
6 Polri had mechanisms to process personnel and officers who had been accused of acting against internal rules and policies, and also had its own lawyers for personnel and officers. The Group of Eight hired lawyers from YLBHI, making leaders of the Polri unhappy: if external lawyers were used, this would open up the case for public consumption. *Suara Pembaruan* (August 1, 2001), 'Polri Siap Menghadapi Gugatan Pra Peradilan'. Budiyarso (2009), pp. 14–135.
7 *Koran Tempo* (August 1, 2001), 'Mogok Makan Sebagai Protes'; *Suara Karya* (August 7, 2001), 'Perlakuan Polri Tidak Adil'. Alfons thought that protesting at least made the media focus on their case. Interview on June 12, 2010 with Chief Commissioner (retired) Alfons Loemau, Jakarta.
8 *Koran Tempo* (August 2, 2001) 'Mabes Polri Bantah Ada Aksi Mogok Makan'. See also *Suara Pembaruan* (August 2, 2001), 'DKP Siap Ke Sidang'.
9 The members of DKP were Police Inspector General Jusuf Manggabarani, Police Brigadier Generals Yusuf Muharam, John Lalo, Soekamto, Dachroen Riva'I Siregar, Mudji Hardjadi, E. Winarto J, Djuain Arief, and five chief commisioners from the Law Directorate, Human Resources, and Inspectorate General of the Polri. Interview on November 5, 2009 with Police Commissioner General E. Winarto, Head of Human Resources of the Polri.
10 *Media Indonesia* (August 3, 2001), 'Terancam Pidana Militer, Mereka Melanggar Empat Aturan'.
11 *Rakyat Merdeka* (August 1, 2001), 'Bimantoro Balas Dendam, Korek Dua Kasus Terkait Gus Dur'; *Rakyat Merdeka* (August 19, 2001), 'Akhirnya Pendukung Chaeruddin Benar-benar Digantung Bimantoro'.
12 Normally, as active Polri officers, they were not allowed to use external lawyers or to direct lawsuits against their own institutions. But Alfons and Bambang Widodo Umar said that they realized that Polri Headquarters was not really going to solve the problem as smoothly as it could. Polri Headquarters wanted to put all eight of them in jail, so it would be useless for them to follow the normal rules and pattern related to their cases. Interview on November 3, 2009 with Chief Commisioner (retired) Dr Bambang Widodo Umar, a lecturer at the PTIK, Jakarta; interview on June 12, 2010 with Chief Commissioner (retired) Alfons Leomau, Jakarta.
13 Interview on November 3, 2009 with Kombes Pol. Dr Bambang Widodo Umar, a lecturer at the PTIK, Jakarta. Interview on June 12, 2010 with Alfons Leomau, Jakarta. Sage (2003), pp. 185–189.
14 *Sinar Harapan* (September 4, 2001), 'Kuasa Hukum Polri: Gugatan Harus Ditolak'.
15 The three recommendations from the DKP were as follows. First was dishonourable dismissal as a maximum sentence recommended for serious violations made by the eight. The punishment was prescribed by law related to their political manoeuvres and mandated the removal of all rights held by the eight as members of the police,

including the right to receive retirement benefits. The second recommendation, honourable dismissal based on the violations made by the eight police officers, was still tolerable. For the DKP, a continuation of these officers' careers could produce many difficulties because they would cause disruptions inside the Polri; a sentence of dismissal with honour was recommended, where the officers still kept their rights from having served as officers and their pension rights. The third recommendation was to give the decision on punishment to Bimantoro as chief of the Polri. *Tempo* (August 29, 2001), 'Hari Ini Delapan Pamen Polri di-DKP-kan'.

16 This was not totally true, because one of them, Police Chief Commissioner Salikin Moenits, had a promotion to Police Brigadier General a year later. However, others remained stuck in their careers until they retired. *Pelita* (November 7, 2002), '9 Jenderal Polri Naik Pangkat'.

17 Alfons Lemau, Herman Koto and Badaruzzaman Haidir were from the 1974 Akpol, while their five other friends varied between the classes of 1968 and 1971; Salikin Moenits, who served in the BIN before retiring with the rank of Brigadier-General, was from the Akpol 1972 class.

18 *Rakyat Merdeka* (September 2, 2001), 'Kapolri Baru, Sutanto atau Da'i Bachtiar'.

19 *Rakyat Merdeka* (October 4, 2001), 'Tinggal Pilih Bimantoro Atau Sofjan'.

20 *Forum Keadilan* (October 21, 2001), 'Kapolri Bimantoro Masih Berpeluang'.

21 *Rakyat Merdeka* (October 10, 2001), 'Mega Mendadak Panggil Calon Kapolri'.

22 *Media Indonesia* (November 13, 2001), 'Pergantian Kapolri Dibicarakan Tertutup'; *Sinar Harapan* (September 20, 2001), 'Bimantoro: Satu Nama, Calon Kapolri Yang ke DPR'; *Sinar Harapan* (October 29, 2001), 'Da'i Bachtiar Siap Jadi Kapolri'. Adrianus and Jacky Murdono told me that Bimantoro's claim that Da'i Bachtiar had been recommended by the Wanjakti was not true; it was made to gain the good opinion of the public.

23 President Megawati's political move of naming only one candidate was a sign that he had gone through existing mechanisms correctly as described in the MPR Decrees No. VI/MPR/2000 and No. VII/MPR/2000.

24 *Sinar Harapan* (November 11, 2001) 'Dicurigai Ada Konspirasi Politik Pencalonan Kapolri'. See also interview on November 6, 2009 with a senior politician of the PDIP, Jakarta.

25 *Rakyat Merdeka* (November 27, 2001), 'Calon Kapolri Diplonco Orang-orang Malas'. See also interview on November 2, 2009 with Police Inspector General (retired) Ronny Lihawa, a Secretary of the Kompolnas Jakarta.

26 *Media Indonesia* (November 27, 2001), 'Komisi Gabungan Setuju Da'i Menjadi Kapolri'; *Kompas* (November 28, 2001), 'Da'i Bachtiar Disetujui Secara Aklamasi'.

27 *Sinar Harapan* (November 27, 2001), 'Da'i Bachtiar Hampir Pasti Jadi Kapolri'. Interview on November 6, 2009 with a senior politician of the PDIP, Jakarta.

28 *Kompas* (November 28, 2001), 'Da'i Bachtiar Disetujui Secara Aklamasi'.

29 For more on the position of the Polri in terms of the regime during Sukarno and Suharto's New Order eras, see Chapters 1 and 2.

30 *Koran Tempo* (July 29, 2004), 'Kasus VCD Banjarnegara'. See also *Suara Merdeka* (July 30, 2004), 'Kapolwil Banyumas Dicopot Terkait VCD Pro Mega'.

31 In Yudhoyono's first presidency, Sutanto got a first reward from Yudhoyono as chief of the Polri because he had successfully backed Yudhoyono as president. As a second reward, when Sutanto retired, President Yudhoyono made him a commissioner in PT. Pertamina, a state oil and mining company. A third reward, after Yudhoyono won his second presidency, was being appointed as head of the State Intelligence Bureau (BIN). He was the first ex-police officer to lead the state civil intelligence body since Sutarto, a police officer who was close with the PKI (Partai Komunis Indonesia – Indonesian Communist Party) in Sukarno's era. See Chapters 1 and 2; see also *Republika* (June 15, 2009), 'Akhirnya Sutanto Pilih Pertamina'; *Detikcom* (2010), 'Jadi Timses SBY-Boediono, Sutanto Didesak Mundur dari Komisaris Pertamina',

32 *Gatra* (July 30, 2004), 'Politik Tersembunyi VCD Polisi'. *Koran Tempo* (July 30, 2004), 'Panwaslu Selidiki 13 Orang Terkait VCD Banjarnegara'.
33 For more discussion of Da'i Bachtiar's policies related to counter-terrorism, see Muhammad and Sulistiyo (eds) (2006).
34 For more discussion of the Polri budget, see Chapter 4. Interview on July 7 and 8, 2010 with a retired two-star police general, Jakarta. He gave the example that under the Megawati presidency, the Polri had succeeded from the issuing of the Polri Act up to the establishment of Densus 88 AT.
35 'APBD-gate' was the misuse of APBDs (local annual budgets) of provincial, district or municipality governments that involved former or incumbent bupati or members of DPRD, mostly from the PDIP and the Golkar Party who won the 1999 and 2004 elections.
36 For the first time, Kalla as a chairman of the Golkar Party supported policies aimed at ridding government of corruption and misuse of policy, but when the policies were applied and many local leaders from the Golkar were arrested by the Polri or the KPK (Komisi Pemberantasan Korupsi – Corruption Eradication Commission). Kalla realized that the policies served only for Yudhoyono's political benefit. See Lebang (2006), pp. 8–13.
37 For more discussion of APBD-gate and what the Polres and Polda did relating to that issue, see Part IV.
38 *Koran Tempo* (August 7, 2002), 'Laksamana: Penjualan Indosat Tetap Tahun ini'. *Koran Tempo* (August 8, 2002), 'Kementerian BUMN Keluarkan Buku Putih Privatisasi Indosat'.
39 Muhammad and Sulistiyo (eds) (2006). See also *Detikcom* (2011), 'Berantas Judi, Alasan Sutanto jadi Kapolri', available at: http://us.detiknews.com/index.php/detik.read/tahun/2005/bulan/07/tgl/05/time/080930/idnews/396602/idkanal/10 (May 5, 2011).
40 *Jawa Pos* (April 8, 2008), 'Ketika Kapolri "mencuekin" Kapolda Gara-gara Illegal Logging'.
41 Institutionalization was the ideal positioning post-disassociation from the ABRI. This was based on cases of politicization in the era of President Wahid, who took advantage of MPR Decree No. VI/2000 and MPR Decree No. VII/2000. For more information, see Law No. 28/1997 on the Polri and MPR Decree No. VI/2000 and No. VII/2000.
42 Karnavian *et al.* (2008), especially Chapter 1; Muradi (2009b), Chapter 5.
43 During the New Order, there were corruption cases inside the Polri from Hoegeng's term until Dibyo Widodo's. The biggest case arose when the deputy chief of the Polri, Siswadji, and several higher- and middle-ranking officers were arrested due to their being involved in corruption. This happened during Da'i Bachtiar's term, when his head of Bareskrim (the national Criminal Investigation Board), Suyitno Landung, had been arrested when he was in charge of the case of money-laundering in Bank Negara Indonesia 1946 (BNI 1946).
44 Some cases of anti-corruption stance were labelled as being politicization of the Polri by Yudhoyono in his pursuit of his political opponents in APBD-gate cases, rather than developing the Polri as a modern police force. *Sinar Harapan* (June 4, 2010), 'Densus 88 Segera Dilikuidasi'. *Antara News* (2011), 'Da'i Bachtiar: Hindari Konflik Untuk Cegah Terorisme', available at: www.antaranews.com/berita/1256987736/dai-bachtiar-hindari-konlfik-untuk-cegah-terorisme (May 5, 2011). Suaedy *et al.* (2010).
45 See Sutanto and Sugiarso (2005), pp. 172–178. See also Chief of the Polri Decree (Skep Kapolri) No. 737/2005 on the implementation of community policing.
46 See Chief of the Polri Decrees (Skep Kapolri) No. Pol.: Kep 53/X/2002 on the new structures of Brimob and No. Pol.: Skep/27/IX/2002 on Brimob reform. For more

discussion of Brimob reform, see Jones *et al.* (2004); Muradi (2008, unpubd), *The Reform*; Muradi (2009c).
47 The *Dekonsentrasi* mechanism became the programme of Da'i Bachtiar continued by Sutanto. *Dekonsentrasi* was defined as a sharing of authority between the Polri and provincial, district, and precinct police so the local police were able to independently conduct negotiations and cooperation related to the role and functions of police in the areas.
48 Interview on November 11, 2009, with Prof. Adrianus Meliala, PhD, Head of Criminology Department of University of Indonesia, Depok, a former chief of the Polri advisors. Interview on June 15, 2010 with Neta S. Pane, a coordinator of the Indonesian Police Watch (IPW).
49 Pane (2009), pp. 115–118.
50 Students of the PTIK class of 39A investigated such practices in 2004, with this being their conclusion. *Pontianak Post* (February 27, 2004), 'Heboh Skripsi Mahasiswa PTIK soal KKN di Tubuh Polri'; see also Pane (2009), pp. 115–118.

6 Corruption in the police

Do not ask, but do accept when given.[1]
(Chaeruddin Ismail, former acting chief of the Polri, 2010)

The practice of corruption and irregularities in the Polri post-disassociation from the ABRI tended to increase compared to what had happened in the Suharto era.[2] This should be viewed in the context that the Polri as an institution did not change significantly in a better direction.[3] The phenomenon of practices of power abuse and corruption in the Polri after disassociation from the ABRI indicates two things. First, after disassociation the Polri tended to be a free agent due to minimum supervision and control. Second, the post-disassociation Polri went through a period of euphoria.

In the New Order era, there was not much practice of corruption. Even if there were cases, the amounts were not big. An example is the case of Police Commissioner General Siswadji, who was deputy chief in the era of Widodo Buddhidarmo and Awaluddin Djamin.[4] There was a previous case in the Hoegeng term involving illegal importing of luxury cars by Robby Tjahyadi, who had been backed by crooked military officers. Moreover, there were some influential military officers involved in the case.[5] The corrupt practices by police officers also happened at the lower levels, for various motives, including enriching themselves and 'saving' for education, promotion and assignment.[6]

Characteristics, patterns and models of corruption in the police post-disassociation

Corruption in the Polri post-disassociation were often open and closed with the involvement of third parties, either directly or indirectly. These third parties, partners of the Polri and people who have access, could give a guarantee to such practices. These third parties were known as case brokers (*makelar kasus*), and were present in the post-disassociation Polri at all levels from the Polri headquarters to local.[7]

There is a wide variety of irregularities committed by police in their position as law enforcement and internal security agents. Indonesian Police Watch (IPW) has divided these into eight categories: illegal payments, extortion, brokering, manipulation, collusion, corruption, fraud and evidence embezzlement. The National Ombudsman Commission's categories are delaying investigation of a case, arbitrary acts, deviation from procedures, unjust acts, abuse of authority, collusion and nepotism, and illegal payments.[8]

Corrupt practices in the services, roles, functions, inter-institutional relations and operational assistance can be categorized as external Polri corruption, with corrupt practices related to recruitment, education, promotion and misuse of police budgets being internal corruption.[9]

Corrupt practices in the Polri were entrenched and tended to lead to the formation of cartels. This occurred in the recruitment of new members of the police, from the lower level of police brigadier down to the level of the ordinary police officer. Money also needed to change hands for specialty schools such as for investigator and detective skills, paramilitary police skills, intelligence skills, or schools such as the Brigadier Police School (SEBA), Police Inspector Candidate School (SECAPA), Police Inspector School (Sekolah Inspektur Polisi: SIP), Police Academy (Akpol), Police University (PTIK), Police Advanced Officers School (SELAPA), Police Staff Leadership College (SESPIM) and Police School for Staff and Chairmen (SESPATI).[10]

A guarantee for promotion and assignment to be confirmed by the Polri headquarters applies only to the 20 best students in all recruitment stages, whether in the SEBA, SECAPA, SIP, Akpol, PTIK, SELAPA, SESPIM or SESPATI. The rest have to fight for higher positions and ranks. In observations and discussions with personnel of the Polri, from brigadiers to officers at lower, middle, and higher levels at Polri headquarters, Polda, and Polres offices, I found that the roles of the personnel bureau were dominant compared with those of the Propam. In fact, almost every unit and most individual personnel in the bureaus play roles as intermediaries, brokers and fixers, who become liaisons and problem-solving agents for promotion, assignment and education inside the Polri at all levels.

Moreover, the utilization of Polri budget allocations from the state budget, in the form of operational funds and operational support funds (Dukop) coming from the Polri headquarters to the local police from Polda down to Polsek levels, is also prone to irregularities. This is especially true for the Dukop, which is paid into private accounts of the chief of the Polri, Kapolda, kapolres and Kapolsek and is very vulnerable to misapplication. Problems then arise when the limited budget of the Dukop runs out through the financial year.[11] Extra funding is then obtained, with a term used at each level in the Polri: 'We do not ask, but if given we accept!' – which is a justification for crooked police at all levels to corrupt and abuse their authority.[12]

External corruption practices were associated with normal services including the creation or extension of police clearances (Surat Keterangan Catatan Kepolisian); creation and renewal of driving licenses, vehicle registration, motor vehicle owner documents (Bukti Pemilikan Kendaraan Bermotor) and other letters; complaints and reports of loss; and 'case trading'. In this context, the practice of corruption involved not only crooked police, but also third parties that are known as brokers (*calo* or *makelar*) or problem-solvers (*fixer*). The roles of these third parties are varied, from acting as a broker to searching for a 'victim' or solving payment problems.[13]

The Polri's relationships with government agencies involve additional, external supporting grants for operation of the Polri, Polda, Polres and Polsek from, among other sources, local government;[14] community aid;[15] kickbacks from night amusement centres such as discos and nightclubs; and kickbacks from illegal activities such as prostitution and gambling.[16] The main problem of this operational aid and the relationship between local governments and the appropriate levels of the Polri is that it is built within the leadership circle only. In practice, these relationships very much depend on how active the police leaders are in conducting and maintaining good relations with local business managers, who also want to maintain good relations with the police.

The practices of corruption in the post-disassociation Polri are likely to exhibit characteristics, patterns and models comparable to those of other security institutions.[17] This weakness applies especially to Kompolnas. Although there have been efforts to strengthen its authority, it is still an 'ivory tower' because neither the government nor the Polri are happy with the formation of a Kompolnas that would perform the function of supervision and control effectively.[18] The public relies entirely on there being supervision by higher institutions in the hierarchy, with the Polsek office being supervised by Polres which, in turn, is supervised by the Polda, as well as on mechanisms that entitle local police leaders to punish offenders, but which rely on subjectivity and remain far from public expectations.

The possibility of the police selecting cases to report or investigate was to maintain a good image and influence for decision-making based on two mechanisms: first, giving the government more power to supervise and control local police, and, second, giving the Polri more money for its local personnel. The first proposal, to engage government supervision more, was rejected by the Polri, although they did send proposals supporting the second, increasing the operational budget for the welfare of personnel at local level.

There are six characteristics of the irregularities and corrupt practices that occur in the Polri (see Table 6.1).

Table 6.1 Characteristics, patterns and models of corruption and extortion practices and abuse of authority in the Polri post-disassociation

Characteristics	Patterns	Models
Decentralised	Internal initiatives	Open
Mutual benefit	Third party initiatives	Closed
Economic	External initiatives	Mixed
Massive		
Strong rivalry		
Using third parties		

Source: compiled from Widoyoko (2003); IPW (2007); the RIDEP Institute (2007); PSKN UNPAD (2008).

First, the corruption is decentralized. Each level of Polri uses the possibilities of the new autonomy and discretion in the *dekonsentrasi* policies and applies them in independent practices of corruption and abuse of authority at each level. Three of these practices involve coordination at the local level, assistance to the local operational budgets, and local denials.

- Police officers, whether for personal or institutional benefit, negotiate payments to arrange that some activity will be either carried out or not carried out for the benefit of someone.
- Corrupt activities which can contribute to meet the operational budgets of each unit will reduce the spending that unit requires from the local police chief's general Operational Support Fund, Dukop, which is a discretionary fund to fill the gaps in local units' funding from their inadequate annual operational budgets.
- With the impact of decentralization, investigation of practices of corruption in region become the responsibility of the local chief, who is likely to have been the recipient of some payments from these practices but can deny that they are occurring or claim that he knew nothing about them, and the responsibility will be placed on the lower-level personnel who actually carried them out.

Second, there are mutual benefits between the personnel and members of the public that 'use' or are 'being used' over these corrupt practices. Based on economic principles, corrupt practices create a 'market' where 'seller', 'buyer' and 'intermediaries' gain benefits by taking advantage of the processes. This makes the practices more difficult to clean up.

Third, the corrupt practices in the Polri are based on economic factors alone, with individual officers enriching themselves and preparing the 'provisions' needed to pave their ways to achieving higher rank, positions and education. The post-disassociation Polri is entrapped in corrupt practices that are caused by internal economic factors. There is also a trend of corruption that leads to political advantage, but as this occurs only after several years of retirement, it could be happening not only to the INP but also to military retirees.

Fourth, corruption occurs at all levels and is massive. It starts from 'negotiating a ticket' at the police station or on the street with a police patrol, and goes up to the very high-cost manipulation of cases and brokering practice at Polri headquarters involving high-ranking officers. Almost irrespective of the level, the motives are similar: to enrich themselves and save for further education, promotion and rank.

Fifth, there is a strengthening of internal rivalry and conflict as an impact of the rampant and pervasive corruption in the Polri. If previous internal conflicts were based on class in the Academy and unit in the Polri, the post-disassociation practice of corruption has brought new factions such as 'bad cop and good cop', intellectual police and field police officers, etc.

Sixth, the practice of corruption in the Polri almost always involves third parties. These can be internal to the police, as active or retired officers or civil servants, as well as many externally who have developed connections into the Polri. They are called by various names including intermediary, liaison officer, problem-solver, fixer or broker – even the Mafia.

As discussed above, it has become obvious that a pattern of corruption has become an integral part of the Polri in its post-disassociation era. There are three patterns of corruption in the Polri post-disassociation (see Table 6.1).

- Corruption on the initiative of police within the Polri to take advantage related to their handling of cases, services and police roles in ways that exploit suspects or members of the public who need services from the Polri.
- Corruption on an initiative from a third party. This is conducted by 'packaging' the case or services to be sold by a third party to make it look attractive and easy, and which will be negotiable to an interested member of the public.
- Corruption on an initiative from an external source, such as relatives of a suspect or person who wants to use the police service, accessing a 'special path' to avoid punishment or red-tape bureaucracy from the service.

These patterns are then reinforced by the practice of extortion and corruption, setting up a willing market among the public. In addition, there is also a growing assumption in the public that these situations were created inside the police and, more widely, in the state administration by the state, so the saying 'If it is complicated, why should it be made easier!' (*Jika bisa dipersulit, mengapa harus dipermudah!*) is also applied in the Polri.

There are three models of corruption and abuse of authority post-disassociation (see Table 6.1). First, there is an open model of corruption and extortion practices, which is clearly seen by the public. The existence of the internal Polri slogan of 'Do not ask, but do accept when given' has become a confirmation that the Polri understands and accepts the support of external income.

Second, there is a closed model. In the practices of corruption and extortion, the crooked police tried to manipulate the element of corruption within a bureaucratic approach that ultimately ends the practice of bureaucracy and leads to corrupt or extortion 'transactions' instead.[19]

Third, there is a mixed model, containing both closed and open elements. This model occurs when a corrupt practice is originally open, based on initiatives taken by crooked police, but then is closed due to a change in circumstances and situations and managed through intermediaries or third parties. A closed practice may also become open: after deciding that having an intermediary who would take part of the payments is not worth it, corrupt police personnel might take over the transaction themselves.

The 'Markus' in the police

The term 'Markus' is an abbreviation of *makelar kasus*, literally 'case trader' or 'case broker'. The term itself refers to case brokering that arranges links between various parties to reach common ground and agreement, and is usually applied to brokers involved in major cases at national level. In various cases handled by the Polri, from criminals to political or economic problems, a Markus is attached to the suspect or charged person and positions them to take advantage of the processing procedures and issues related to police roles.

The Markus at Polri headquarters usually have a background as retired police, former high officials, businessmen or politicians, especially the first two categories. In recent times, based on my observations at Polri headquarters, it is very difficult to distinguish between police officers and people who work as Markus. A senior officer told me that there were only a few Markus identified in the Polri headquarters. One of them had been arrested for his involvement in a case with the former Bareskrim head Susno Duadji.[20] Meanwhile, two other Markus are a businessman of Chinese descent and a former high-ranking officer in the Polri. Neither of them has yet been revealed because they have specialities in handling cases at Polri headquarters. The businessman focuses on economic cases, such as the smuggling of luxury cars and electronic goods. The retired officer mostly deals with criminal cases and narcotics, as well as procurement of communication equipment, network communications, and various other tenders in the Polri.[21]

The existence of Markus at Polri headquarters reflects a view that the Polri is as an institution that is not transparent, clean, or strongly committed to becoming a professional and independent institution. The Polri is easily infiltrated, and many personnel want to take advantage. The presence of Markus after the Polri disassociated from the ABRI become stronger than in the era of the New Order or the previous regime.

The process of case handling by Markus involves establishing a personalized access and relationship with the suspect. There are three stages of case handling that attract the attention of Markus. First, the case is still at filing stage and is being explored by the Polri, while the suspect has not yet been detained by police. In this context, the fee demanded is not too large, depending on the case.

If a Markus becomes involved in the second stage of a similar case, when the case filing is already complete and the Polri is deciding whether the suspect should be detained or not, the Markus' fee will be higher, not less than Rp.1 billion.

Third, if the 'P21' stage has been already reached, when the prosecution file has been completed and is ready for the trial process, which means that it will be delegated to the Attorney General, the suspect will have to pay more than Rp.5 billion because prosecutors and courts will now have to be paid off as well as the Polri headquarters.

These stages open opportunities for Markus and crooked police to take advantage. The three-stage Markus role is significant in that it ensures crooked police can take advantage of the case to enrich themselves. Some of the money obtained is used to fix and renovate facilities. In November 2009 and mid-2010, I went into the Bareskrim building and talked with some middle-ranking officers there. The problems of Markus, funds from illegal practices, and the 'coordinating budget' of Markus became issues raised during the discussion that followed in the cafeteria near the mosque in the Polri headquarters. Some of these middle-ranking police officers reported they were in a dilemma, where on one side, the Polri personnel and officers need 'side income' due to their inadequate salaries.[22]

Police businesses and the problem of welfare

Since the establishment of the Guided Democracy regime under Sukarno in 1959 the Polri has managed a variety of businesses in the form of foundations (*yayasan*), cooperatives (*koperasi*), and private limited companies (*Perseroan terbatas* – PT). There were a number of businesses managed directly by the ABRI and the Polri headquarters, extending down to local business activities. At national level, for example, there were the Polri Brata Bhakti Foundation, Kemala Bhayangkari Foundation (a foundation managed by wives of Polri officers) and the Graha Purna Wira Foundation. These three foundations were spread from national to the local level and managed a variety of businesses, including education from kindergarten to college level, construction development, and distribution of many goods and services.[23]

The Polri financial resources, apart from the state budget, are extortion practices and donations from the community as well as management of businesses it owns. Those owned by the Polri in the New Order were discussed above, where they were like those managed by the military.[24] The difference between businesses owned by the Polri and other three forces in the military was in the management.

The business structure as owned by the Polri is still similar to that of the military. The business activities managed by the Polri take three forms: formal businesses, informal businesses, and criminal activities (see Table 6.2). Formal business is the category that involves the police institutionally in its business management, whether in the form of foundations (*yayasan*) or co-operatives (*koperasi*). After the Polri was disassociated, this controlling relationship between the Polri and the company was changed, and then was confirmed in the Foundations Law that prohibits interference from a parent institution to foundations and companies under it. So, the relationships between the leaders of the Polri and the foundations and companies have become weaker and more informal.[25]

Pre-disassociation some companies under Polri foundations were led by generals and middle-ranking police officers who were in their pre-retirement period, but there were interventions in these appointments by the Polri chief.[26] However, after the disassociation, Polri foundations and companies could continue to provide regular allowances to Kapolda and the Polri chief.[27] The amounts of these benefits varied, but were between Rp.50 and 250 million per month. However, the value of company profits that are managed and distributed under the foundation each year is estimated to be more than Rp.20 billion.[28]

Other types of Polri business are the co-operatives, which are structured and formally associated with police leaders at all levels; at headquarters, for the Main

Table 6.2 Polri business activities post-disassociation

Form of business	Type of business	Business cores
Formal	Brata Bhakti Foundation	General trading; forestry; hoteliers; insurance; banking; plantations[1]
	Main Police Cooperative (HQ level) Police Cooperative Centre (provincial police) Primary Police Cooperative (district level)	Public transport; petrol stations; restaurants; stationery shops; delivery services; credit financing; agencies to make and extend driving licenses, car registrations and documents[2]
Informal	PT. Salwa Arowana Lestari (SAL)	General trading (Makbul Padmanegara)[3]
	PT. Para Group	Holding company (S. Bimantoro)[4]
	PT. Pertamina	State-owned oil company (Sutanto)[5]
	PT Metro Security Nusantara (PT MSN)	Security service company (Hindarto)[6]
	PT Dhatama Adiyaksa	Forestry (Awaloedin Djamin)[7]
Criminal	Extortion in conflict zones	Extortion on security posts in Aceh and Poso together with the TNI[8]
	Illegal logging	Especially in conflict areas, and along the border of Kalimantan[9]
	Luxury-car smuggling	Especially in Aceh, conflict areas, and Batam[10]
	Illicit drugs	Especially in Aceh and ex-conflict areas[11]

Notes

1 The companies under the Yayasan Brata Bhakti are: PT. Tansa Trisna; PT. Bhara Induk; PT. Bhara Union; PT. Braja Tara; PT. Braja Tama; PT. Bhaki Bhayangkara; PT. Sapta Pursa Mandiri; PT. Bank Yudha Bhakti; PT. Surya Satria Timur Corporation; Bimantara building Management; PT. Brata Jaya Induk. Widoyoko *et al*. (2002), pp. 51–54. See also written interview on May 10, 2011 with a former Head of Inkopol at Polri headquarters.
2 *Serambi Indonesia* (June 15, 2010), 'Koperasi Polri Masih Dibutuhkan'; *Fokus Indosiar* (2011), 'Koperasi TNI/Polri Terlibat Pengoplosan Minyak', available at: www.indosiar.com/fokus/23420/koperasi-tnipolri-terlibat-pengoplosan-minyak (May 25, 2011).
3 Makbul Padmanegara was a former deputy chief of the Polri when Bambang Hendarso Danuri led it. He has 50 per cent ownership of PT. SAL.
4 *Viva News* (2011), 'Kenapa Chaerul Pasang Jenderal di Carrefour', available at: http://us.bisnis.vivanews.com/news/read/145298-kenapa_chairul_pasang_jenderal_di_carrefour (May 9, 2011). S. Bimantoro is a former chief of the Polri. He is one of the PT. Para Group commissaries in the Carrefour Supermarket, which has more than 40 per cent of its ownership in PT. Para Group Holding Company led by Chaerul Tandjung.
5 Sutanto was a chief of the Polri. When he retired, President Yudhoyono made him one of the commissaries in PT. Pertamina for a year before he left to be Head of BIN in President Yudhoyono's second term. *Kontan* (September 25, 2008), 'Setelah Endriartomo Pergi'.
6 Hindarto was a Kapolda Jakarta Metro after graduating from the PTIK in 1962. He was a founder and also commissary of PT. MSN, which runs the security guard company 'Metro 911' in Jakarta. PT. MSN has a good relationship with the Polda Jakarta Metro, and PT. MSN is also a place to be for officers who have retired and get new jobs as private security officers. For more discussion of PT. MSN, see their website: www.metro-911.com/index.php.
7 Awaloedin Djamin was a chief of the Polri. He is president-director of PT. Dhatama Adiyaksa, a timber company which operates in Central Sulawesi. See Aditjondro (2005).
8 Widoyoko *et al*. (2002), p. 38. see also Aditjondro (2005); Aditjondro (2006), pp. 25–42.
9 Tacconi (ed.). (2007), pp. 69–109. See also *Okezone* (2011), 'Oknum Polisi Diduga Terlibat Illegal Logging', available at: http://international.okezone.com/read/2010/08/02/340/358963/oknum-polisi-diduga-terlibat-illegal-logging (May 10, 2011). *Waspada* (March 19, 2011), 'Oknum Aparat Bekingi Illegal Logging di Aceh'.
10 Widoyoko *et al*. (2002), p. 40. *Tempo* (July 13, 2004), 'Bea Cukai Akui Banyak Penyelundupan Mobil Mewah di Batam'.
11 Widoyoko *et al*. (2002), p. 40. McCulloch (2002), pp. 11–13.

Police Cooperative (Inkopol); at Polda level, for the Police Cooperative Centres (Puskopol); at Polres level, for the Primary Police Cooperatives (Primer Koperasi Polri, known as Primkopol). Assets and activities of the business units under the cooperatives are estimated to be more than Rp.1,000 billion.[29]

However, co-operatives in government agencies and other security institutions provide benefits first for leaders, then personnel, and then staff. No wonder, then, that there is a saying related to police cooperatives as an abbreviation for Village Unit Cooperatices (KUD) as also 'KUD' standing for *ketua untung duluan* ('chairman gets first benefit'). This was recognized by a former chairman of Inkopol who told me that until recently, cooperative management would be appointed and dismissed by leaders of Polri at each level, and the title used by some managers in the cooperatives to lobby their superiors for a promotion. So the idea and purpose of cooperatives for improving the welfare of personnel at various levels was being distorted and corrupted. The dissatisfaction among personnel mounted, with protests demanding increases in their welfare and rights as members of the cooperatives.[30]

The third form of business activity is economic crime, usually in the form of protection provided for a fee by members of the police to organized practices that are against the law. Such economic crimes usually thrive in conflict areas, former conflict areas, and border regions. Perpetrators are not only members of Polri, but also of other security forces, including the military and local government officials.[31] The practice of illegal logging also exists in West Kalimantan, which resulted in the Kapolda being removed from his position and the arrest of seven middle-ranking police officers who were involved in backing and taking advantage of illegal logging practices.[32]

However, as discussed above, businesses managed by Polri have not been able to solve the problem of distributing welfare more evenly between leaders and personnel, even when referring to the salary and benefits between leaders and personnel based on government regulations. In practice, the businesses managed by the Polri tend to become a tool to enrich the leaders, whether in the form of allowances granted by the foundation and companies under it or through unfair advantage since police leaders at various levels became supervisors of the cooperatives. Hence the extortion practices carried out by crooked police outside the criminal economy have tended to increas since the Polri was disassociated from the ABRI, with various motives and goals not just at Polri headquarters level but also in small local police posts.

This chapter has examined claims that practices of extortion and corruption in the Polri tend to be greater since the disassociation of the Polri from the ABRI. Those problems are due to the state budget for the INP being inadequate; businesses managed by Polri are not able to solve the problem of uneven welfare between leaders and personnel and inadequate operational budgets at all levels. The internal mechanisms and systems for gaining education, promotions and ranks are still open to kickbacks which the officers and personnel need much money to pay for; and there is also a minimum of effective oversight by the public.

Notes

1. The Polri's Officers and Personnel Principles relate to extortion and corruption practices.
2. *Pontianak Post* (February 27, 2004), 'Herman Koto, Alfons Loemau, and Badarudin Zaman, Skripsi Mahasiswa PTIK soal KKN di Tubuh Polri'.
3. The results of research by PTIK students in 2004 reflected the anxiety of the younger generation of the police after disassociation from the ABRI. For more discussion of the definition of corruption, see Lobe and Manuel (1987), pp. 1–79. Seligson (2002).
4. For more discussion of corruption in the Polri in the era of New Order, see Chapter 2.
5. For more discussion about Hoegeng's term, see Chapter 2.
6. Interview on July 13, 2010 with a retired police two-star general, Jakarta.
7. Interview on November 5, 2009 with a senior high-ranking officer of the Polri, Jakarta. Interview on June 18, 2010 with a retired senior high-ranking officer of the Polri, Jakarta.
8. Pane (2009), pp. 138–142.
9. More discussion about corruption and extortion practices in local areas will be provided in Parts IV and V.
10. For more discussion of the Polri education system see Presidential Decree No. 70/2002 on the INP organization system, and Chief of the INP Decree No. 4/2010 on the Polri educational system. In Polri education, the newest structure, SELAPA, was brought together with SESPIM and turned into SESPIMMA; SESPIM itself change its name into SESPIMMEN and SESPATI became SESPIMTI (Sekolah Staf dan Pimpinan tingkat Tinggi – School for Higher Rank Police Staff and Chiefs).
11. The Dukop budget in the Polri headquarters was Rp.500 million up to Rp.2 billion per year. Interview on November 5, 2009 with a senior high-ranking officer, Jakarta.
12. Most of the money from corruption and abuses of police authority had been used for their personal activities, from personal affairs such as having mistresses to building houses and having fun.
13. More discussion of fixer and broker activities in the Polda and Polres will be provided in Part V.
14. More discussion of the support budget from local government to the Polres or Polda will be provided in Part IV.
15. More discussion of public support to the Polri in local areas will be provided in Part V.
16. More discussion of support from night and criminal activities to the Polri will be provided in Part V.
17. See *Antara* (June 12, 2008), 'Menguak Tabir Busuknya Korupsi Kejaksaan Agung'. *Koran Tempo* (July 2, 2008), 'Emerson Yuntho: Membersihkan Korupsi Kejaksaan'.
18. Interviews on November 2, 2009 and June 21, 2010 with Police Inspector General (retired) Ronny Lihawa, a Secretary of Kompolnas, Jakarta. Written communication on June 25, 2010 with Dr La Ode Husein, a member of Kompolnas, Jakarta. *Suara Pembaruan* (February 4, 2011), 'Kompolnas Dapat Terlibat Penyelidikan'.
19. Interviews on November 2, 2009 and June 21, 2010 with Police Inspector General (retired) Ronny Lihawa, a Secretary of Kompolnas, Jakarta. Written communication on June 25, 2010 with Dr La Ode Husein, a member of Kompolnas, Jakarta. Interview on November 11, 2009 with Prof. Dr Adrianus Meliala, Jakarta. Interview on June 15, 2010 with Neta S. Pane, a coordinator of the IPW, Jakarta.
20. Interview on July 21, 2010 with a high-ranking officer of the Polri. See also *Solo Pos* (April 8, 2010), 'Komisi III Sebut Markus Mabes Polri Berinisial SJ'. *Kompas* (April 8, 2010), 'Mabes Polri Periksa Markus Palsu di "TV One"'.
21. *Kompas* (April 4, 2010), 'Edmond Dikenal Semua Tersangka, tapi Raja Tidak'. *Gatra* (2011), 'Peran Raja Dalam Rekening Gayus', available at: www.gatra.com/artikel.php?id=137305 (May 7, 2011).

22 For more information about Polri personnel's salaries, see Presidential Decree No. 24/2007 on Polri personnel salary and allowances. Polri salaries and allowances from lower to higher ranks are Rp.3 million up to Rp.15 million.
23 Widoyoko *et al.* (2002).
24 For more discussion of the history of TNI's business following Suharto's New Order, see McCullough (2000); Misol (2006).
25 Transcript of interview on May 10, 2011 with a former head of Inkopol, at Polri Headquarters. See Law No. 16/2001 on Yayasan, and Presidential Decree No. 63/2008 on the implementation of the Yayasan Law.
26 For example, at the University of Langlang Buana and Bhayangkara University some strategic positions such as Rector and vice-Rector are filled by former Kapoldas of West Java and middle-ranking Polri officers who are close to retirement. See http://unla.ac.id/pages/tentang-unla/pimpinan.php.
27 *Gatra* (January 11, 2002), 'BPK Tetap Pantau Yayasan TNI/Polri'. Denny Indrayana, a special advisor to President Yudhoyono, wrote in his blog that Sutanto had spectacularly increased his property and wealth by more than 150 per cent. Da'i Bachtiar also gained big money while and after he served as chief of the Polri, having more than Rp.1,000 billion in properties and money, similar to the alleged wealth of former Polri deputy chief Adang Dorodjatun. As Polri chiefs they could not have earned such spectacular wealth, because they made no more than Rp.50 million per month, and before that, as Kapolda, no more than Rp.30 million per month. Indrayana and Denny (2011), 'Sutanto, Terus Berjuang Jenderal', available at: http://dennyindrayana.blogspot.com/2007/03/sutanto-terus-berjuang-jenderal.html (May 11, 2011). See also Governmental Decree No. 29/2001 on salaries in the Polri; Governmental Decree No. 12/2007 on revisions to the decree on the IN Salaries; Presidential Decree No. 28/2007 on the financial support of the Polri.
28 For example, see *Oke Zone.com* (2011), 'Polri Ternyata Punya Bisnis Asuransi', available at: http://news.okezone.com/read/2010/07/01/337/348469/polri-ternyata-punya-bisnis-asuransi (May 11, 2011). *Mata News* (2011) 'Bongkar Bisnis Petinggi Polri', available at: http://matanews.com/2010/07/09/bongkar-bisnis-petinggi-polri/ (May 11, 2011).
29 When I asked a former head of Inkopol about the total assets of the Polri cooperatives, he did not answer, but when I asked 'around' or 'more than' Rp.1,000 billion, he choose 'more than'. Transcript of interview on May 10, 2011 with a former head of Inkopol, The Polri Headquarters.
30 Transcript of interview on May 10, 2011 with a former head of Inkopol, Polri Headquarters. See also *Viva News* (2011), '70 Polisi DiperiksaTerkait Demo Brimob', available at: http://us.nasional.vivanews.com/news/read/3764–70_polisi_diperiksa_terkait_demo_brimob (May 11, 2011). *Detikcom* (2011), 'Mabes Polri Sesalkan Demo Anggota Brimob Sulsel', available at: http://us.detiksport.com/read/2008/10/17/150511/1021769/10/mabes-polri-sesalkan-demo-anggota-brimob-sulsel (May 11, 2011).
31 See Aditjondro (2005), p. 13.
32 *Oke Zone* (2011), 'Tersandung Illegal Logging, Kapolda Kalbar Dicopot', available at: http://news.okezone.com/read/2008/04/16/1/101025/tersandung-illegal-logging-kapolda-kalbar-dicopot (May 11, 2011). *Detiknews* (2011), '7 Polisi Diendus Terlibat Illegal Logging Kalbar', available at: http://us.detiknews.com/index.php/detik.read/tahun/2008/bulan/04/tgl/04/time/150233/idnews/918465/idkanal/10 (May 11, 2011).

Part IV
Local government perspectives

7 Cosmetic changes

Roles of the police in local areas

> Institutional changes in the Polri, after the disassociation from the Armed Forces, happened only in Jakarta. The Polri in Local areas actually acted as if they have the right to do anything, starting from violence to arbitrary arrest.
> (Ahmad Syabbuddin Alwy, Chairman of the Cirebon Arts Council, 2010)

As it was a national police force, reform in the Polri should have started from the headquarters level and then progressed down the hierarchy to the lower levels. However, the process did not run properly. No wonder that, after disassociation from the ABRI, its reform changes occurred only at the headquarters level. In local areas, changes occurred only in the form of physical organization, not in the form of improvements in the role and functions of the police. The local government needed to ensure that their power was not disturbed in various ways, especially through law enforcement and corruption.

The pattern of relationships, motives and different interests between the Polri, national and local government was based on the policy that the Polri in local areas could improvise in the form of discretionary and semi-autonomous operation, but still remain within the corridor and essence of the Polri as national police. Although Indonesia adopted the concept of a national police, the Polri in local areas tends to be influenced by dynamics that occured at local level. The Polri maintained their *esprit de corps* but also controlled economic access, whereas in the past they had had to share this with the military.[1]

Along with other factors, the Polri is also influenced by the characteristics of each leader in the local institutions.[2] This chapter will also outline the estuary of interests between the Polri and politics at the local level, together with various problems faced by the two institutions.

Local government perspectives on the police post-disassociation

As a national institution, the Polri's organizational changes at the national level also have effects on changes in the smaller parts of the Polri organization. West Java Province, located close to the national capital, was directly affected by the changes. The Polri in West Java is represented by the West Java Province Police Office (Polda Jabar) and five sub-regional police offices (Polwil) in Bogor, Purwakarta, Bandung Municipality, Priangan and Cirebon, including numbers of district or municipality police (Polres) based on the number of districts and municipalities in West Java Province.[3] With the characteristics of a national police, the Polri institutionally did not experience much difficulty in implementing various organizational changes, because these did not clash with the culture of bureaucracy in the regions.[4] Commonalities can be found in a decentralized police model, as in federal states or a combined state police system.[5]

Bandung is the capital of West Java Province. In 2010 it had a population of nearly 2.4 million within its city area of 168 square kilometres, and was the third largest city in Indonesia after Jakarta and Surabaya. Relating specifically to the police, Bandung is also the site of the SESPIM and the SESPATI.[6] Since the 2004 elections, the city parliament (the DPRD) has been dominated by members of Islamic parties: the Justice and Prosperity Party (PKS) and others including the National Mandate Party (PAN – Partai Amanat National) and the Crescent-Moon Party (PBB – Partai Bulan Bintang). However, in the 1999 elections, the first held after the fall of Suharto, the secular PDIP won in the DPRD and then, in 2003, in the election of the mayor, Dada Rosada, by the members of the DPRD. In 2008 Dada Rosada was re-elected in the first direct election with a coalition between PDIP and the Golkar Party.[7]

Garut District mainly voted for the Golkar Party from the start of the *reformasi* era until 2008, when the Garut bupati from the Golkar Party, Agus Supriadi, was jailed for corruption and abuse of power. He was replaced by a bupati and vice-bupati who were not affiliated with a political party and were elected in the local election, although the Golkar Party, the United Development Party (PPP), and the PDIP are still dominant in the district's DPRD.[8]

Tasikmalaya District is the largest and most important district in East Priangan. Its had a population of 1.9 million in 2009; from 1998 to 2008 its annual economic growth was around 3–5 per cent. Most of it is a lush green, especially from agriculture and forestry, and farmers are the majority of its population. It is a main base of the moderate Islamic party PPP in West Java, joined by the PDIP in a steady political coalition, which controls both Tasikmalaya District's local DPRD and its executive government.[9]

In 2008 Ciamis District had a population of 1.5 million. From 1998 to 2008 its annual economic growth was 3–5 per cent. Ciamis Distict is in the southeast area of West Java. Large parts of the district are highlands, but there are coastal areas in the south and southeast, including those of the Gulfs of Pangandaran, Parigi and Pananjung. Pangandaran Beach is the main tourist destination in Ciamis District and a major one in West Java. Since the 1999 elections of the *reformasi* era, both the district's DPRD and its local government have been dominated by the PDIP.[10]

Cirebon District had a population of two million in 2010 and economic growth of around 4–9 per cent a year from 1998 to 2008. It lies in the eastern part of West Java. Cirebon District lies on the very busy main road along the north coast, which carries much of the traffic between Central and West Java and passes through the district's Losari sub-district.[11] Since the 1999 election, the PDIP has been the main party in Cirebon District, in both its local government and its DPRD.

Cirebon Municipality, population about 300,000 with annual economic growth during 1998–2008 of around 4–14 per cent, is the second largest city in West Java Province after Bandung.[12] Cirebon Municipality provides much potential for investment in sectors such as hotels, restaurants, shopping centres and education. From 1998 to 2009 the DPRD of Cirebon was chaired by coalitions of the PDIP and the Golkar Party, but from 2009, the Democrat Party (the party of President Susilo Bambang Yudhoyono) led the Cirebon parliament although the PDIP continued to control the local executive government.[13]

The Polri's changes in role and function were implemented with extreme caution, given previous experience when the Polri was under the shadow of the ABRI.[14] Indarto, the deputy kapolres of Cirebon Municipality, and Ari Wibowo, the deputy kapolres of Ciamis District, said that the Polri had to report to the Kodim (Komando Distrik Militer – Military District Command) or the Korem (Komando Resort Militer – Military Sub-regional Command) when handling certain cases during Suharto's era. As a law enforcement unit, such an act would affect the objectivity of police in handling criminal cases when actually it no longer needed to report and coordinate with local military units.[15]

However, it was reported to me that in many cases, there were still psychological pressures both verbal and non-verbal exerted by the military commander or the personnel of Korem or the Kodim in local areas post-disassociation, as experienced by the Polres in Garut, Tasikmalaya, Ciamis, Cirebon District and Municipality, and Bandung Municipality.[16] However, leading newspaper critic Budhiana Kartawijaya asserted to me that in major cities such as Bandung the Polri does not experience any psychological pressure because media access and coverage are open in the area. The situation was quite different in other districts and municipalities, so processes were also different.

On a practical level, the formal relationship between the Polri and other institutions in the area was supposed to be dealt with in the Forum of Local Leaders (Musyawarah Pimpinan Daerah, known as Muspida), whose members were from elements of the local government, the military, the police, prosecutors and the immigration department.[17] After the disassociation from the ABRI, the coordination between local leaders and the Polri became easier and as stakeholders in the region, local government directly got positive and negative effects. Aside from easier coordination, the boundary between the Polri authority and the military's role also become very clear.[18]

However, the disassociation of the Polri from the ABRI also brought problems for local government. Sunaryo, deputy mayor of Cirebon Municipality, complained that at several meetings of senior officials in Cirebon, the kapolres of Cirebon Municipality was often absent and just sent the head of the Community Security Development and Partnership Unit (Kasat Bina Mitra). Sunaryo said that the kapolres of Cirebon Municipality was an 'arrogant person', because a retired army colonel had claimed that the Muspida forum was an important meeting for local leaders, but the kapolres never came. This situation made Sunaryo think that the disassociation of the Polri from the ABRI had not made the Polri in his region any better informed or closer with communities and other local leaders.[19]

The police, local government and internal security

In contrast, the bupati of Cirebon, Dedi Supardi, actually saw the Polri presence on the Muspida forum becoming more effective after disassociation from the ABRI. Dedi asserted that, as bupati, he had the right and obligation to maintain security and order in his territory. Dedi realized that every officer who was appointed to be the kapolres in Cirebon had different leadership characteristics. So, as the central stakeholder in the region, he must take the initiative for coordination and communication with the kapolres.[20]

Based on the Polres perspective in general, the Muspida forum is no longer the boring forum it used to be in the New Order era. The forum is now used by the Polres leaders to establish intensive coordination and communication, especially at certain potentially unsettled moments such as the local elections, Idul Fitri, Christmas, and New Year's Eve. Explicitly, the scope, role, and function of the Polri are focused on internal security.[21] Many things associated with the role and functions of the Polres in the area are submitted in the forum, either regarding security coordination, communication, or budget support for Polres operations.[22]

It was also recognized that there was a gap between the Polres leaders and regional leaders, and other government agencies, except the military as some of the kapolres and the commanders of Kodim or Korem had been classmates at the Military Academy.[23] Maturity and age differences also become obstacles in building communication and coordination between kapolres and local leaders. In some cases, kapolres even considered local leaders to be like parents influenced by a patrimonial system in which older persons had to be respected by young persons. However, in a relationship between institutions that may be inappropriate and is sometimes not good.[24]

In addition, a consequence of the affirmed roles and functions of the Polri in internal security was tensions over the presence of municipal police units controlled by local government (Satpol PP) that had very similar roles and functions.[25] It is no wonder that in a variety of assignments, the Satpol PP were always backed by the INP because of limitations in the scope of the former's duties and functions as set out in their government regulations.[26]

However, the implementation in each province, district or municipality required more operational talks between the local government and the Polri in the Muspida forum. The consequences of these talks is that the Polri has gained support from local government, especially supporting the local governments' own Satpol PP as part of the Polri's role, with varied allocations ranging from personnel meals and money for transport allowances of various amounts depending on the form of security back-up provided by the Polri.[27]

In addition to coordination with and support for the Satpol PP, the Polres locally also build relationships with other institutions with the aim of early detection and prevention as part of the local intelligence community (Kominda), coordinated by the provincial deputy governor or vice-bupati and municipality deputy mayor, with the head of the local Bakesbangpol Linmas as Kominda secretary.[28] The Kominda consists of intelligence elements in the military, police, the State Attorney's Office, the judiciary, the BIN and local government.[29] The role of Kominda was to be an inter-institutional coordination forum facilitated by local government to undertake various efforts to establish a conducive and calm atmosphere in the area.

In Kominda, the Intelkam (Security Intelligence) Unit was no longer dictated by military intelligence or the BIN, because each unit has different tasks and functions. However, they are still in the framework of efforts to maintain security through coordination and early detection. However, after the law on counter-terrorism had been enacted, in practice the Polri was one step ahead of the military and BIN in counter-terrorism and as the law stated, the Polri is the agency that is involved in the counter-terrorism programme and the other agencies must just support the Polri.

Meanwhile, interaction between the Polri and the community was then translated into the community policing programme in the form of a security partnership.[30] Long before that, the Polri had programmes based on security partnerships with the community, starting with Village Police (Poldes) and the Environmental Police and Citizen Security Partnership (Mitra Pollingga), the name of which was spoofed into 'crooked police rob (their) citizen partners' (*kemitraan polisi maling warga – mitra pollingga*) because the existence of Mitra Polingga was supposed to be like a partnership but many INP officers carried out various negative activities such as blackmail, extortion and violence in the name of the law.[31]

The development of community policing, although it was not optimal, gave power to kapolres at district level to maximize their local programme as a tool for making a good image for the Polri.[32] In Cirebon, almost all community groups (RW – Rukun Warga) have police officers allocated to them under the programme called the RW police. Residents in a RW implement informal approaches to access the police.[33] In Bandung, an obvious presence of the Polri and their office exists due to open and 'permissive' attitudes of the public associated with the presence of the Polri in their area.[34] The negative stigma associated with the previously general opinion of the Polri was no longer dominant, although there are still some people who think that the police are always taking benefits from the community. This was partly because there were still crooked Polri officers practicing exortion by taking advantage of the community's ignorance related to law.[35]

In the other areas studied, in the Garut, Ciamis, Tasikmalaya and Cirebon districts, the programme tends to be stagnant and to rely more on relationships between community leaders such as Islamic preachers to build links between communities and the Polres. In the East Priangan areas of Garut, Tasikmalaya and Ciamis, the role of Islamic preachers (Kiayi) makes a significant contribution in building constructive relationships between the Polres and the community.[36] Meanwhile, in Cirebon District, beside preachers, there are also Village Heads (Kepala Desa or Kuwu) who traditionally reduce the inter-village brawls in the district that always occurred during the harvest season when many people held harvest celebrations.[37]

In this context the mechanism of decision-making in the local police becomes important. The semi-autonomy (*dekonsentrasi*) policy initiated by General Da'i Bachtiar, when he was chief of the Polri (2001–2005), asserted that the authority of Polres as the new Basic Police Unit (Kesatuan Operasional Dasar) would be more capable in service to the community and carrying out the basic tasks and duties of the police in district areas.[38]

Thus, this *dekonsentrasi* policy had become the answer to the criticisms made by NGOs and political observers. Although this might not be an answer desired by the public, the Polri only coordinates local activities based on the scope and limits of both the Polri and the local government authority, which is governed by laws and political decisions.[39] Consequently, local governments should allocate budgets for police operations in their districts.[40]

The proposal for local leaders and DPRD being able to appoint and dismiss kapolres was then rejected by the Polri headquarters and the Ministry of Internal Affairs. This was then supported by the national parliament passing the Polri Act in 2002, confirming that the position of the Polri relative to the local government was only in the area of coordinating.[41] The same assertion had been made in the Local Government Act of 1999, which was modified in other aspects in 2004 but still stated that security is the domain of central government.[42] The implementation of the national policy of a *dekonsentrasi* of the Polri was translated by leaders of the Polri at provincial (Polda), district or municipality (Polres) level to their being authorized to conduct negotiations related to the position and situation of the Polri at their level within the wider policy and implementation of decentralization and its empowerment of local governments.

The second policy was aimed at forming a more effective structure with more functions, called 'Small Structure, Rich Functions'. This was to emphasize that the Polri was aware that its lower institutional levels required more roles, not only in security, but also in all public problems. However, in practice, this policy was implemented to provide stimulation to NCOs and officers of the Polri to get used to performing more than one role and function.[43] According to the deputy Kapolsek of the Cirebon Municipality, with the policies of 'local boys for local jobs' and 'Small Structure, Rich Functions', the Polri in Cirebon Municipality divides up all personnel according to the number of residential RW, to optimize the role and functions of each member of the Polri in the RW police programme.[44] Therefore, the police officers could take care of not only the security problems, but also other domestic issues such as childbirth, taking sick people to hospital, domestic violence, or community disputes.[45]

These policies also show that the Polri's principal roles and functions have not changed much over the decade 1998–2008, except in certain cases such as relationships between institutions in local areas, where the Polri tend to have more power to accelerate the development of their roles and functions.[46] This fact may ultimately be viewed inside the Polri, especially in West Java, as showing that its presence is as an integral part of the dynamics of society and that the Polri is now in a position to adopt several of the changes explained above appropriately and in line with the expectations and desires of the public.

Notes

1 For the national and local role of the military during Suharto's New Order era, see Chapter 2.
2 These include internal dynamics, relationships in the hierarchical agency and local government.
3 In 2010, the Polri liquidated the Polwil and the Polwiltabes. See Mabes Polri (2010), pp. 10–15. See also Presidential Decree No. 22/1963 on liquidating the sub-regional level of the government system, and Law No. 32/2004 on local government.
4 As has already been noted in Chapter 5 regarding the organizational changes as part of the disassociation of the Polri from the ABRI.
5 Interview on July 3, 2009 with Chief Commisioner (retired) Dr Zakarias Poerba, a lecturer at the PTIK. Interview on November 11, 2009 with Prof. Adrianuas Meliala, PhD. See Bayley (1992).
6 See Lubis *et al.* (2000). For more information on the SESPIM and the SESPATI, see Djatmika (2007).
7 In 2012, Dada Rosada left the Golkar Party and joined Yudhoyono's Democrat Party for his part in political interests in the West Java governor's election one year after, but his political strategy of being nominated by the Democrat party was not realized because the Democrats already had their own candidate. He is now facing a bribery case from his periods as Bandung mayor and has been summoned by the KPK (Komisi Pemberantasan Korupsi – Corruption Eradication Commission) as a key witness. For more information see *Jakarta Post* (2013), 'Dada Questioned Again by KPK', available at: www.thejakartapost.com/news/2013/06/05/dada-questioned-again-kpk.html (accessed June 3, 2013).
8 Agus Supriadi's corruption and abuses of authority as bupati will be discussed in a later section of this chapter. Aceng H.M. Fikri, his successor as bupati, was elected as a non-party candidate but later joined the Golkar Party. See *Tribun Jabar* (January 15, 2011), 'Bupati Garut Jadi Pengurus Golkar'.
9 For example, *Pikiran Rakyat* (October 11, 2010), 'Koalisi Besar Bubar, PPP Jalin Koalisi dengan PDIP'.
10 *Radar Tasik* (February 22, 2009), 'DPRD Ciamis Harus Koordinasi'. *Pikiran Rakyat* (July 18, 2010), 'Elit Politik Ciamis Terus Berjuang'.
11 *Pos Kota* (October 10, 2010), 'Duduki Posisi Baru, Bupati Cirebon Lantik 113 Pejabat'.
12 For more discussion on the Jabodetabek areas, see *Koran Tempo* (January 16, 2011), 'Kajian Greater Jakarta Disangsikan'. *Koran Bogor* (February 11, 2011), 'Bupati dan Walikota Bogor Siap Terima Konsep the Greater Jakarta'.
13 For example, see *Radar Cirebon* (October 21, 2010), 'Bantah Adanya Koalisi'.
14 For discussion of the change in name of the ABRI to TNI, see Honna (2004); Haramain (2004); Rinakit (2005); Sebastian (2006); Mietzner (2009).
15 Interview on November 9, 2009, with Police Commisiaries. Indarto., SIK., M.Si, deputy of kapolres of Cirebon Municipality. Interview on June 24, 2010 with Police Commissioner Ari Wibowo, S.IK, deputy of kapolres of Ciamis.

16 Interview on June 22, 2010 with Police Commmisioner Eka Mulyana, SIK, deputy kapolres of Garut. Interview on June 24, 2010 with Police Commisioner Hadi Syafriadin, SIK, deputy kapolres of Tasikmalaya. Interview on June 22, 2010 with Police Commisioner Ari Wibowo, SIK, deputy kapolres of Ciamis, West Java. Interview on July 2, 2010 with Police Commisioner Subiantoro, SH., SIK, deputy kapolres Cirebon District. Interview on June 25, 2010 with Bahrul (pseudonym), an army officer in Tasikmalaya.

17 *Pikiran Rakyat* (January 5, 1999), 'Tahun ini, Gangguan Kamtibmas di Jawa Barat Meningkat'; *Pikiran Rakyat* (January 12, 1999), 'Gangguan Kamtibmas di Bandung Tertinggi'.

18 *Radar Tasik* (June 14, 2004), 'Polda Tetapkan Tiga Tersangka'. *Kabar Priangan* (June 19, 2004), 'Ramai-ramai Kembalikan Kelebihan Anggaran'. Interview on June 24, 2010 with H. Iing Syam Arifin, vice-bupati of Ciamis, West Java. Interview on June 24, 2010 with Gandjar M. Yusuf, vice-chairman of the Ciamis DPRD and a MP from the Golkar Party in the Ciamis DPRD (FRG of Ciamis DPRD).

19 Interview on June 30, 2010 with H. Sunaryo, S.IP, deputy mayor of Cirebon Municipality, West Java. Interview on November 9, 2009, with Police Commisioner Indarto, SIK., M.Si, deputy of kapolres of Cirebon Municipality. See *Radar Cirebon* (July 14, 2010), 'Muspida-Ormas Gagal Bertemu'.

20 *Radar Cirebon* (May 2, 2006), 'Sikap Kapolres Dilaporkan ke Mabes'. Interview on July 1, 2010 with Drs Dedi Supardi, bupati of Cirebon.

21 The assertion of the INP's working area being internal security was set out by Law No. 2/2002 replacing Law No. 28/1997 that overlapped the functions of defence and security.

22 Interview on June 22, 2010 with Police Commisioner Eka Mulyana, SIK, deputy kapolres of Garut. Interview on June 24, 2010 with Police Commisioner Hadi Syafriadin, SIK, deputy kapolres of Tasikmalaya. Interview on June 22, 2010 with Police Commisioner Ari Wibowo, SIK, deputy kapolres of Ciamis.

23 In the New Order era, recruitment for Polri officers was through the same process as in the military. See Djatmika (2007).

24 Interview on June 24, 2010 with Police Commisioner Hadi Syafriadin, SIK, deputy kapolres of Tasikmalaya. Interview on July 2, 2010 with Police Commisioner Subiantoro, SH., SIK, deputy kapolres of Cirebon.

25 Satpol PP; see Barker (1998). See also Government Decree No. 26/2005 on standard operational procedure for the Satpol PP and Law No. 32/2004 on local government.

26 Interview on June 23, 2010 with Imam Gadjali, Head of Kesbangpol Linmas of Tasikmalaya District, and Ali Rochman, Head of the Satpol PP of Tasikmalaya District. See also *Kabar Priangan* (July 1, 2004), 'Rekruitmen Satpol PP tak Jelas'. *Radar Tasik* (June 2, 2008), 'Pol PP Tunggu Instruksi Walkot'.

27 Interview on July 20, 2010 with a senior mid-ranking officer in West Java Polda. The local government would provide support material and accommodation for Polres if they called Polres to be a supporting agency in the Satpol PP Program.

28 Under the New Order, the Bakesbangpol Linmas was called the Office for Social and Political Activities (Kantor Sospol) and was controlled by the military. The change of the Sospol office into the Bakesbangpol Linmas was part of the military reform taking place in Indonesia. Interview on June 22, 2010 with Suherman, Head of the Kesbangpol Linmas of Garut District. Interview on June 23, 2010 with Imam Gadjali, Head of Kesbangpol Linmas of Tasikmalaya District. Interview on June 30, 2010 with Adam, Head of the Kesbangpol Linmas of Cirebon Municipality.

29 In the New Order, the function of the Local Intelligence Community (Kominda) was controlled by the Coordinating Board of State Intelligence Services (BAKIN). After Suharto stepped down, BAKIN had its name changed to BIN, and focused only on state issues. For more explanation of Indonesia's intelligence agencies see Conboy (2004); Widjajanto (ed.) (2005).

30 See Chief of the Polri Decree No. Pol.: Skep/737/X2005 on the community policing programme in the Polri. In practice, this programme is not spread around Indonesia yet. It collided with the previous culture of the Polri, so that it still has problems. More explanation on it is in Chapter 5; see also Sutanto and Sugiarso (2005), pp. 25–27.
31 *Buletin Blakasuta* (Editioni 24, Oktober 2009) 'Rekam Jejak Polmas: dari Gagasan Menuju Perubahan', published by Fahmina, Cirebon, West Java. Interview on November 2, 2009, with Police Inspector General (retired) Drs Ronny Lihawa, M.Si, Secretary of the Kompolnas, Jakarta. Interview on July 1, 2010 with Erlinus Thahar, Community Policing Program Officer of Fahmina, Cirebon.
32 Prihatono and Evangeline (2008), pp. 274–276.
33 *Pikiran Rakyat* (January 13, 2003), 'Polsek Gandeng Tukang Ojek Untuk Menjaga Kamtibmas'. *Pikiran Rakyat* (January 13, 2003), 'Polisi Tindak Pengganggu Ketertiban'. Interview on November 9, 2009, with Police Commisioner Indarto., SIK., M.Si, deputy kapolres of Cirebon Municipality. Interview on June 30, 2010 with H. Sunaryo., S.IP, deputy mayor of Cirebon Municipality, West Java. Interview on July 1, 2010 with Erlinus Thahar, Community Policing Program Officer of Fahmina, Cirebon, West Java.
34 Karisma (2010, unpubd), especially Chapter 1.
35 *Radar Bandung* (July 9, 2009), 'Polmas Baraya Urang Dukung Kepolisian'. Interview on August 1, 2010 with Ade, chairman of Association of Motorcycle Taxis Union of Bandung Municipality (Persatuan Ojek Bandung Raya).
36 Interview on June 22, 2010 with Eka Mulyana, deputy kapolres of Garut; interview on June 23, 2010 with Hadi Syafriadin, deputy kapolres of Tasikmalaya; interview on June 24, 2010 with Ari Wibowo, deputy kapolres of Ciamis; interview on June 23, 2010 with KH. Hilman Farid, Islamic Preacher of Tasikmalaya; interview on June 22, 2010 with Suherman Head of Kesbangpol Linmas of Garut.
37 Interview on November 9, 2009, with Police Commissioner Subiantoro, deputy kapolres of Cirebon. In that situation, I saw that the Kuwu have an important position in front of the people in Cirebon. They had enough charisma to calm down the angry people, hand-in-hand with the Polsek and Polres. There are other Kuwu who take a lead in inter-village brawls because they reason they should protect and build solidarity among their people; however, there are not many of these.
38 Djamin (2007), p. 68.
39 Djamin (2007), p. 69.
40 Until post-disassociation all the budget of the Polri from headquarters was covered by the national government. There is more explanation in the following section. Also see Ismail (2001), pp. 12–13.
41 See Law No. 2/2002 on the INP, especially Articles 2 and 3.
42 See Law No. 32/2004 on local government, especially Article 10, and Law No. 22/1999 on local government.
43 *Pikiran Rakyat* (June 15, 2008), '247 Anggota Polisi RW Dikukuhkan'; interview on November 9, 2009, with Police Commissioner Indarto, deputy kapolres of Cirebon Municipality; interview on July 1, 2010 with Erlinus Thahar, Community Policing Program Officer of Fahmina, Cirebon.
44 Interview on November 9, 2009, with Police Commissioner Indarto, deputy kapolres of Cirebon Municipality; interview on July 1, 2010 with Erlinus Thahar, Community Policing Program Officer of Fahmina, Cirebon.
45 Interview on November 9, 2009, with Police Commissioner Indarto, deputy kapolres of Cirebon Municipality; interview on June 24, 2010 with Police Commissioner Hadi Syafriadin deputy kapolres of Tasikmalaya; interview on June 22, 2010 with Police Commissioner Ari Wibowo, deputy kapolres of Ciamis.
46 More discussion on the extortion practices of crooked police will be provided in Chapter 8.

8 The budget, local politics and jealousy

Different from the model of the relationships at national level between the military, Polri headquarters and national government, at the local level the relationship between the military's Kodim or Korem, Polres and local government tends to be dynamic in terms of their respective positions, which do not depend on each other. However, these three institutions make every attempt to gain influence on each other. The relationship between local government and Polres has developed different characteristics and tends to be on a more equal level, having been turned into being a political transactional relationship, especially in the handling of sensitive cases such as corruption and abuse of power.[1]

The model of the local relationship between police and military, Polres and Kodim or Korem, is also different from that between the Polri and the military at the national level. Efforts by the military to influence the Polri have occurred at the national level but not at the local level. There is even a high confidence when Polres personnel are face to face with Kodim or Korem personnel in the field, which in some cases has led to a conflict. Nevertheless, the relationship model built between Polres post-disassociation and Kodim or Korem is to accept equivalence and try not to intersect each other's roles.

The police, local supports and the military

The most crucial issue in the role and functions of the Polres is to build effective relationships with the Kodim or the Korem and the local government. There have been problems in how to build working relationships with them, based on a political configuration that has changed since the democratization process; this configuration has been relatively dynamic and has directly or indirectly made relationship patterns change.[2]

Institutionally, the Polri in West Java followed the hierarchical structure of the existing government system; the Polri in the regions related to the direction and goals of the local government. In this context, the relationship between the provincial and local governments with their respective Polda or Polres should work well, because in the domain of internal security they have very similar interests. Moreover, the governmental functions in maintaining security and public order (*kamtibmas*), peace and good order (*ketentraman dan ketertiban*, known as Trantib), as well as protection, safety, and community service are integral parts of both institutions. The only difference is in the focus of the role and functions of each institution.

Relationships developed between the Polres and local government in the post-Suharto era have made significant progress in terms of the patterns of the professional relationships of both institutions. Especially when the Polri was disassociated from the ABRI, the desire to build a new relationship between the Polres and local government was strengthened. Although it was later hit by the position of each institution at the national level, historically the Polri and the Ministry of Internal Affairs were separated for a long time and had different functions.[3]

However, it must be admitted that the appointment of a kapolres usually is for not more than two years, due to the policy of tours of duty and refreshing the system, and in several ways this complicates the cooperation between a kapolres and a local government. This is where the real political maturity of a local leader is tested, in how to help a newly assigned kapolres to quickly understand the situation and start the job.[4] Iing Syam Arifin, vice-bupati of Ciamis, told me that the tour of duty policy was not really a problem as long as there was good communication between bupati and kapolres.[5] Dedi Supardi, bupati of Cirebon, stated that the local government should have the initiative to start the communication with kapolres formally or informally, although kapolres are replaced every two years under the tour of duty policy of the Polri headquarters.[6]

Another problem related to rotation and tour of duty is the internal pressure felt by a number of leaders at the Polres from the overload of work on deputy kapolres. Several informants implicitly and explicitly acknowledged that the task of a deputy kapolres is to support the task of their kapolres. Nevertheless, it was also admitted that the delegation of duties from the kapolres to deputy kapolres indirectly provides a useful exercise for them in case they will be appointed as kapolres in the future.[7]

The evidence indicates that the relationship developed between the Polres and local government in the six areas studied runs well. The indicator was that local government openly helps the operation of the Polres. One area of material supports was in the form of grants of land and buildings for the construction of a Police Post, Polsek Office, and Polres Office, and even for a Polda Office. There was even extra self-interested assistance provided from another source: the support for the development of several Police Posts from real estate developers who built these Police Posts near new real estate complexes, in the hope that it would help them be safe against threat of crime.[8]

The difficulty for local governments and DPRD to reject proposals from government agencies was based on the benefits in supporting the performance of these two institutions in carrying out their role and functions, including that they could attempt various efforts to derail the local government and DPRD with threats and terror supported by elements in the two institutions.[9] Although at the national level the two institutions have committed to run the reform agenda, in reality, in local areas their attitude has not changed yet.[10] This was especially the case for the Polres: they were able to apply psychological pressure to the local DPRD members and heads of government in their area to not reject the proposals. There were several DPRD members in the 'APBD-gate' case, with local heads including Agus Supriadi, bupati of Garut, who was inflexible in budgeting, becoming suspects and being arrested in a number of cases of corruption.[11]

From the cases mentioned above it can be seen that in practical terms, the Polres are still following the same patterns and approaches as they were when part of the ABRI. The only difference is in the motive; in the New Order era the emphasized motive was to pressure local legislators for a commitment in maintaining political and security stability, while in the current era, the motive is in the interests of money for Polres members. However, in discussions with me, all three kapolres deputies in the East Priangan Districts studied, Eka Mulyana (Garut), Hadi Syafriadin (Tasikmalaya) and Ari Wobowo (Ciamis), denied that there were any examples of suspected graft by members of their staff.[12]

Other local government supports related to the operation of Polres were in the operational budget support for them associated with religious holidays and political activities. As the buffer area for the national capital Jakarta, West Java becomes one of the most strategic crossing areas for people who want to celebrate great days of religion such as Eid Mubarak, Christmas and New Year's Eve.[13] The Polri performs a variety of security measures on the highway lanes that are used to go to the east of Java, such as the Java North Coast Line (Pantai Utara Jawa, Pantura) through Cirebon, and alternative pathways on the Java South Coast Line through Garut, Tasikmalaya and Ciamis. There are two patterns of support from these areas' local governments to Polres for a variety of security activities, as follows.

First, local governments call on kapolres to conduct coordination and cooperation in security using funds from the governments' Harkamtibmas (*pemeliharan keamanan dan ketertiban masyarakat* – maintenance of public order and safety), a fund of Rp.75 million to Rp.3 billion depending on the financial capacity of the local government, disbursed every three months after a proposal is submitted.[14] In the Ciamis District the smallest amount was Rp.75 million in 1999; this had risen to Rp.200 million by 2008. Payments from the Cirebon Municipality government to its local kapolres had also risen from Rp.75 million in 1999 to Rp.300 million by 2008. Garut government's support went up relatively even more, from Rp.80 million in 1998 to Rp.400 million by 2008. Tasikmalaya's Rp.75 million in 1999 went up to Rp.375 million in 2008, while Cirebon District's Rp.250 million increased to Rp.1,000 million over the same period. Understandably, Bandung Munipality government's Rp.350 million was the highest amount in 1999 and its allocation from its annual budget for Rp.3,000 million was the highest in 2008.[15]

Second, the Polres takes the initiative to submit a proposal to the bupati or mayor and asks legislators to invite the kapolres to present the programmes in a DPRD session. In this second pattern, usually the kapolres has a relatively good personal relationship with both local government leaders and DPRD leaders, both formally and informally.[16]

The second issue was to cover budget shortfalls from the Polri headquarters. Although the Polri budget became much better after the disassociation from the ABRI, it still does not fully cover the operational needs in the field and Polri headquarters urges creativity and initiative on the part of police leaders at lower levels in order to cover the operational needs and welfare of their staff. One of the major recognized channels is through this cooperation and assistance from local government.[17]

From the local governments' perspective, apart from the reason to keep security in the region sufficient against possible security threats, there is also a political motive. As known in the post–New Order era, the meaning of 'local autonomy' has been widely interpreted to be an attempt to build small empires in power, and it tends to corrupt.[18] Unscrupulous NCOs or officers of Polres exploited this to enrich themselves by designing and carrying out extortion activities.[19] However, it was claimed that although it was investigators from the Reskrim unit of Polres who did such activities, this was with the acknowledgement of the kapolres and his deputy.[20]

However, operational and territorial command positions and the number of military battalions needed to maintain security and order in these areas are now being questioned. This relates to the principle of justice, because the Polres receive grants and funding assistance for their operational budgets in amounts that are sometimes more than twice the budget given to the military.[21]

In district capital towns such as Garut and Tasikmalaya, the relationship between the Kodim or the Korem and the Polres is like fire under the husk; although they look fine and peaceful, actually there is jealousy among the military related to the different standard of facilities given to the Polres and the Kodim or the Korem.[22] Especially in those towns, there is almost no night-life such as discotheques, nightclubs or bars as potential sources of informal income for Polres and Kodim. There are also some middle-class entrepreneurs who provide additional funds for the Polres and Kodim operations. In Garut there is a geothermal power plant run by the multinational company Chevron International, but this does not provide any financial feedback to the local Polres and the Kodim, because they were blocked by their respective headquarters in Jakarta.[23]

In Bandung, the protection business was based on the city being divided into monopolized zones with zealously guarded boundaries. Feri, a source interviewed, who gave me information about the Polres and the Kodim controlling the security of some night-life adult amusement areas in Bandung, said that there were relatively few fights between the Kodim and the Polres because they paid respect to restrictions that had been informally discussed and mutually agreed, except on the outskirts of Bandung which was not considered as a source of revenue, but only for shows of force.[24]

Cirebon is not as big as Bandung; a harmonious relationship between the Polres and the Kodim also exists there, but for a different reason. There are not many entertainment centres in Cirebon, and usually there is mutual cooperation between the Kodim and the Polres personally or institutionally in securing the evening' entertainment centres in a different way from Bandung. Cirebon is also known as 'The Muslim City' (*Kota Santri*), so they must look after its name and public image and not be seen to be supporting rampant night-life activities. The local governments realized that in order to keep the nightclubs safe, they must involve personnel of both institutions, as if they used only one then the other would cause dangerous trouble.

Therefore, it can be said that the Polres interaction with the Kodim was not in line with the policy that operates at the national level. Local relations between the Polri and the TNI are based on the following characteristics. First, the characteristics of the district and municipality will make for a good or bad relationship. These characteristics are related to whether a district or municipality is a busy business centre like Bandung or Cirebon Municipalities, with shopping centres and night-life activities, and whether there is a more strongly religious background of much of the population such as in Garut, Tasikmalaya, Ciamis and, nearly to the same extent, Cirebon District.

Second, are there any territorial commands or combat battalions in those areas? If there are, they may trigger a negative relationship between military and police in the area because sometimes although both leaders have a good and harmonious relationship this is not so between the personnel of the military battalion and the Polres in the area. In the context of the whole of West Java, from 1998 until 2008, there have been more than 25 times when clashes between the military personnel and the police were recorded officially.[25] One relatively large clash that became national news was between personnel of the Infantry Airborne Battalion 330 Kujang I Kostrad based in Cicalengka, Bandung, against Brimob personnel.[26]

Third, what are the characters of the leaders of each institution, whether of local government, Kodim or Polres? Various steps have been taken by local governments to accommodate complaints from the Korem or the Kodim by providing assistance funds based on the financial ability of the local government and DPRD for their operation. Greater assistance is provided to the Polres because they are fully responsible for peacefulness and security in the areas.[27] The relationship between some leaders of Kodim and Polres established when they were still in the Military Academy together allows them to use approaches which can mute turmoil among their men.

This chapter has discussed the different dynamics that have occurred among all levels in the Polri. The influence of political reforms which provide for a strengthening of local autonomy have affected the patterns of relationship between the Polri and local government and the military; these relationships are becoming totally different from those of the New Order era. The economic euphoria in the Polri post-disassociation from the ABRI, and the political euphoria which swept leaders both in local governments and DPRD without being sustained by political and legal controls to build mutual benefits, were not found in any other countries' models of relationships between their police, local government and military.

On the other hand, the strengthening of the Polri at the maximum, especially in a material sense, including its physical facilities and equipment and the welfare of its personnel, has made it much better off compared to when it was part of the ABRI. This has produced an anomaly, with the Polri being built up to be a more independent and professional institution, while its image is far from better.

Notes

1 This will be discussed in subsequent paragraphs.
2 For more discussion of regime change and the position of the Polri, see Chapter 2.
3 For more discussion on relationships between the Polri and the Ministry of Internal Affairs in the early Republic, see Chapter 1.
4 Interview on July 1, 2010 with Drs Dedi Supardi, bupati of Cirebon; interview on June 24, 2010 with H. Iing Syam Arifin, vice-bupati of Ciamis; *Priangan* (April 8, 2008), 'Kombes Anton Kapolwil Priangan'.
5 Interview on June 24, 2010 with H. Iing Syam Arifin, vice-bupati of Ciamis.
6 That policy was still influenced by the military's culture, in which the tour of duty system is part of the effort to refresh personnel with changes of atmosphere and scene. Interview on July 1, 2010 with Drs Dedi Supardi, bupati of Cirebon.
7 Interview on November 9, 2009, with Police Commissioner Indarto, deputy kapolres of Cirebon Municipal; interview on June 24, 2010 with Police Commissioner Hadi Syafriadin, deputy kapolres of Tasikmalaya; interview on June 22, 2010 with Police Commissioner Ari Wibowo, deputy kapolres of Ciamis.
8 Interview on June 24, 2010 with Ayi Vivananda, deputy mayor of Bandung Municipality; interview on July 21, 2010 with Tedy Rusmawan, an MP from the PKS Faction of the Bandung Municipality DPRD. In my observations in some housing complexes and estates around Bandung municipality, the developer would always spend money and provide material for building police offices or supporting the police post or Polsek near their developments.
9 Interview on June 22, 2010 with a senior politician from East Priangan District; interview on June 23, 2010 with Irfan, MP from Nation Awakening Party in the Ciamis DPRD (FPKB DPRD Ciamis); interview on June 23, 2010 with Demi Hamzah Rahardian, MP from the National Mandate Party in the Tasikmalaya DPRD; interview on June 30, 2010 with Muhamad Arif Rahman, MP from the Prosperity and Justice Party in the Cirebon DPRD of (FPKS DPRD Cirebon).
10 Interview on July 1, 2010 with Ahmad Syabuddin Alwi, chairman of the Cirebon Art Council; interview on July 2, 2010 with two NGO activists in Cirebon; interview on July 7, 2010 with a senior official of Bandung Municipality Goverment.
11 See *Joglo Semar* (March 25, 2010), 'Reformasi Polri Jalan di Tempat'; *Radar Bogor* (August 23, 2010), 'Galang Dukungan Desak Reformasi Polri'; *Koran Tempo* (June 18, 2010), 'Kejaksaan Siap Telusuri Aliran Dana Bantuan Sosial Tasikmalaya'.
12 See *Republika* (July 7, 2007), 'Penyidikan Korupsi di Garut Terhambat Ijin Presiden'. *Kompas* (July 9, 2007), 'Audit APBD: Politisasi Dugaan Korupsi di Garut Disayangkan'. Interview on June 23, 2010 with Police Commissioner Eka Mulyana, deputy kapolres of Garut. Interview on June 24, 2010 with Police Commissioner Hadi Syafriadin, deputy kapolres of Tasikmalaya. Interview on June 22, 2010 with Police Commissioner Ari Wibowo, deputy kapolres of Ciamis. In other research, the Polres leaders also denied that extortion practices had been happening in their office, as long as they knew that in their period of being kapolres or deputy kapolres, there was no case of the type.
13 *Pikiran Rakyat* (November 12, 2003), '500 Polisi Ciamis Siap Mengamankan Jalur Mudik'. *Kabar Priangan* (December 26, 2008), 'Amankan Natal, 567 Polisi Diturunkan'.

122 *Local government perspectives*

14 Interview on November 9, 2009, with Police Commissioner Indarto, deputy kapolres of Cirebon Municipality; interview on June 24, 2010 with Police Commissioner Hadi Syafriadin, deputy kapolres of Tasikmalaya; interview on June 22, 2010 with Police Commissioner Ari Wibowo, deputy kapolres of Ciamis; interview on June 22, 2010 with Eka Mulyana, deputy kapolres of Garut; interview on July 2, 2010 with Subiantoro, deputy kapolres of Cirebon; interview on June 23, 2010 with H. Iing Syam Arifin, vice-bupati of Ciamis; interview on June 22, 2010 with H. Hilman Faridz, Secretary of Garut Government; interview on July 1, 2010 with Dedi Supardi, bupati of Cirebon; interview on July 7, 2010 with Ayi Vivananda, deputy mayor of Bandung Municipality.
15 The data is summarized from the local annual budget (APBD) of the four districts and two municipalities 1998–2008, various interviews, personal communications, and related documents. Particularly in Bandung Municipality, the deputy mayor, Ayi Vivanandam, said that in his territory there is a strict procedure to take money for the support budget from the APBD, as long as they have a proposal that makes sense and are not double-covering the budget from the national government. Interview on July 7, 2010 with Ayi Vivananda, deputy mayor of Bandung Municipality.
16 Interview on November 9, 2009, with Police Commissioner Indarto, deputy kapolres of Cirebon Municipality; interview on June 24, 2010 with Police Commissioner Hadi Syafriadin, deputy kapolres of Tasikmalaya; interview on June 22, 2010 with Police Commissioner Ari Wibowo, deputy kapolres of Ciamis.
17 Interview on November 4, 2009, with Police Inspector General Drs Andi Chaeruddin, Coordinator of Police Expert Staff of the Polri, Jakarta; interview on November 5, 2009, with Police General Commissioner Drs E. Winarto, Head of Human Resources of the Polri; interview on November 9, 2009, with Police Commissioner Indarto, deputy kapolres of Cirebon Municipality; interview on June 24, 2010 with Police Commissioner Hadi Syafriadin, deputy kapolres of Tasikmalaya; interview on June 22, 2010 with Police Commissioner Ari Wibowo, deputy kapolres of Ciamis.
18 For more explanation of local autonomy post-Suharto, see Aspinall and Fealy (eds) (2003); Tornquist (2004); Erb *et al.* (eds) (2005).
19 Interview on June 17, 2010 with Heri Mei Oloan, MP of the Indonesian Democratic Party of Struggle in the West Java DPRD (FPDIP DPRD Jawa Barat); interview on July 2, 2010 with Sandi (pseudonym), Asmana (pseudonym) and Abigail (pseudonym), West Java.
20 Interview on November 8, 2009 with Dr Sugianto, political observer from the Cirebon Islamic University (STAIN); interview on July 22, 2010 with a senior politician in an East Priangan District; personal communication on July 3, 2010 with a senior NCO in Polres Cirebon District Office.
21 Interview on June 25, 2010 with a retired senior mid-ranking army officer, Bandung; personal communication on June 23, 2010 with a mid-ranking army officer in Bandung; interview on June 25, 2010 with a junior mid-ranking army officer, Bandung.
22 See *Radar Tasik* (May 24, 2008), 'Dandim 0612 Sertijab'; interview on June 21, 2010 with a mid-ranking army officer, Tasikmalaya.
23 Interview on June 22, 2010 with Police Commissioner Eka Mulyana, deputy kapolres of Garut. See also interview on June 22, 2010 with Arief Mukti, Head of KNPI, Garut Branch.
24 Interview on July 17, 2010 with Feri (pseudonym), Bandung. See also *Koran Tempo* (October 4, 2004), 'Sebulan Penuh Tanpa Hiburan Malam di Bandung'.
25 *Tribun Jabar* (August 9, 2006), 'TNI-Polisi Baku Tembak'.
26 *Pakuan* (May 30, 2009), 'Pasca Bentrokan, Kodam Siliwangi dan Polda Jabar Adakan Pertemuan'.
27 Interview on June 23, 2010 with H. Iing Syam Arifin, vice-bupati of Ciamis; interview on June 22, 2010 with H. Hilman Faridz, Secretary of Garut Government; interview on July 1, 2010 with Dedi Supardi, bupati of Cirebon; interview on July 7, 2010 with Ayi Vivananda, deputy mayor of Bandung Municipality.

9 Politicization

> Do not ever think that police officers are as a good friend, because they never think we are good friends but profitable for them.
> (A local leader in West Java Province, 2010)

Marenin (1977) and Beltran (2009) confirm that the politicization of police is based on a two-step agenda: the political will from the new regime to manipulate the police as guardians of the regime, and the position of the police being not yet consolidated in the changing regime. In Indonesia, these two steps occurred simultaneously at the national level, where both prerequisite conditions were found and the Polri was trapped for months in the political games of the new regime. However, in the local contexts, that situation was not found. There was a lack of knowledge about law and of experience in politics on the part of local government and DPRD members, and the local Polri officers took advantage of this to enrich themselves illegally. A consequence of this politicization was the rise of internal rivalry inside the Polri.[1]

Local security and political recognition

In addition, the motive within the context of a politicization of police by local governments is more associated with the desire to control the Polres for political purposes and development programmes. The assumption is that by controlling the Polres, the kapolres will voluntarily perform a variety of programmes that support policies that are synergistic with the local government. However, since the relationship between Polres and local government is a coordinative one, carrying out the local government's plan becomes difficult. All the steps taken by the local government are intended to position the kapolres in a transactional relationship.

Based on the interpretation above, the model of police politicization by local government is a closed one, with a number of factors and characteristics differing from those of Marenin (1977) and Beltran (2009), as laid out in the Introduction, and from the model that occurred at the national level, as discussed in Chapters 5 and 6. There are four factors distinguishing the characteristics of politicization in the context of the local compared to national level: the non-subordinative (equal) relationship between Polres and local government; local political and social dynamics; weak bargaining power of local politicians in both local government and DPRD against Polres, especially over issues of law enforcement and corruption; and a desire to enrich themselves.

Based on this explanation, the presence of Polres in local government structures became very important as part of the adjustment of the governmental system for better coordination and cooperation. However, as stated above, although political dynamics at the national level do not have linear implications at the local level, in practice there are similarities in the patterns of conduct of hierarchical institutions, such as the politicization of Polres being controlled by local leaders.[2] In general, this politicization of Polres is divided into two forms: first, the politicization of kapolres; and second, the politicization of Polres performance.

In the first form, the Polri headquarters politicizes the replacement of a kapolres. This change, directly or indirectly, brings debate into local politics as some people may agree or disagree with a proposed appointment. This step also indirectly involves the Polres internally because the change of leader would also mean a change in the formation of some positions inside the Polres.[3]

There are three reasons that a new kapolres appointment might be rejected. The performance of a kapolres could be considered good or bad; if his performance is good then he should be maintained, or if bad replaced. The relations of the kapolres with the public could be also good or bad. Finally, the kapolres may or may not understand the local politics and cultures of the community, with this being a consideration for success or failure in carrying out Polres programmes.[4]

These three reasons were significant in districts with a strong cultural and religious community, such as Cirebon. There was a rejection of the appointment of a new kapolres in Cirebon Municipality based on a religious issue. The new kapolres, Edison Sitorus, was a Christian, replacing Rochiyanto who was a Muslim.[5] However, K.H. Mahfudz Bakri, chairman of the Nahdlatul Ulama (NU, a traditional Muslim organization in Indonesia) in Cirebon Municipality, said that the rejection was not from the Muslim community of Cirebon but was organized by Islamic hardliners such as the Islamic Defenders Front (Front Pembela Hislam), the Indonesian Mujahidin Council (Majelis Mujahidin Indonesia) and Hizbut-Tahrir Indonesia, all of which in Cirebon were considered to be fundamentalist organizations and not representative of Cirebon as a Muslim city (*kota santri*).[6] Cirebon's Kasepuhan Sultan, PRA Arief Natadiningrat, emphasized in an interview with me that, although the people of Cirebon are devout Muslims, they are not radical. His statement was in the same tone as that of the local NU chairman KH Mahfudz Bakri, who told me that the refusal was not from the people of Cirebon.[7]

In addition, there was a biassed attitude of the Cirebon DPRD and the mayor, Subardi, related to this issue. On one side, the replacement of a kapolres is the responsibility of the Polri headquarters as a hierarchical agency, but on the other hand, there was a depressed feeling in the DPRD and local government because they wanted the Polri to hear the aspirations of citizens of Cirebon. Sunaryo, the former chairman of the DPRD who later became deputy mayor during Subardi's second term as mayor, considered that in the context of local autonomy, refusal of anything or anyone who is dropped in from the national level is naturally a local issue, especially given the fact that 92 per cent of the population in Cirebon is Muslim, so the Polri headquarters should hear and understand local aspirations about it.[8]

In other words, the local government as a stakeholder should be invited to communicate, at least before the replacement of the kapolres, on the development situation in the community, which should be addressed wisely by its local government and DPRD. With such a synergistic relationship, formally or informally, between the kapolres and the Polri and local government, a permanent foothold could be guaranteed which would develop well in the interest of keeping peaceful security.

The politicization of the Polres in the first form was also present in the accountability for local government assistance, in the form of grants or other operational support from the local budget (APBD). Over the last few years the Ministry of Internal Affairs and the national government have issued a succession of policies[9] that prohibit local governments from allocating budgets for national hierarchical agencies.[10] A number of districts and municipalities in West Java, including every one of the six areas studied, allocate funds from their budgets, with the amount varying depending on the ability and the local sources of revenue (*pendapatan asli daerah*) of each region. However, these budgeted amounts have to be reported publicly and accounted for by the kapolres.

There are four reasons why the local government asks for a report on this budget from the kapolres. The first is for accountability to the local parliament, as it is known that the budget proposed by the head of the region must obtain the approval of the DPRD as representatives of the people. Such a procedure is definitive because the allocated budget for Polres is part of the local government's annual budget, its APBD.[11]

Second, the philosophy of leadership and accountability in the use of the Polres budget is a form of recognition of the existence of the local head by the Polres. This has an informal but strong psychological effect in making the local government and local head more confident in coordinating and cooperating with Polres and other government agencies.[12]

Third, money for support of the Polres is from the public budget, and so any form of budget support provided to the Polres should be accountable to the DPRD and the public. The account of the Polres budget is made in writing and submitted to local parliament through the bupati or mayor.[13]

Fourth, the report is a form of subordination by local government power of the Polres. Although the Polres has different institutional interests, in practice its presence has the role and function as an institution responsible to local government for *harkamtibmas* (*pemeliharan keamanan dan ketertiban masyarakat* – maintenance of public order and safety) in its scope of internal security. This is directly a part of local government programmes. Therefore, it should be stressed that the Polres is implicitly subordinate to local government, without it having been realized by kapolres.[14]

Indeed, this is reflected in local government wishes to integrate the role and function of the municipal or district Satpol PP with the national police's Polres. This wish is because of the similarity in role and function between the Polres and the Satpol PP. The overlap is limited only by their relative authority in conducting investigations, where Satpol PP personnel must be accompanied by a Polres investigator to bring perpetrators to the nearest police station. Steps to subordinate the Polres under the local government were a part of the initial condition for local governments to gradually assume responsibility for providing a budget allocation to the local Polres from the local budget.[15]

However, the interesting thing was the Polres see accountability only in a form of reporting the use of assistance funding from the government budget as something ordinary and reasonable. There was no feeling of being subordinated by being accountable to the local government in other ways, except in limited cooperation and coordination among several institutions. As it is in the direct line of a national hierarchical agency, a Polres considers that it is responsible to the Polri headquarters through its line Polda and not to local government.

The support from the local budget is only stimulation, and the easiest way to control the kapolres is to meet the various expressed needs of the kapolres or deputy kapolres, so it will facilitate local government leadership to control the Polres in accordance with the government leaders' desired pattern.[16] Former bupati advisor Makmun Gunawan Sidik told me that he often saw what the bupati of Cirebon was doing to systematically control leaders of Polres, both kapolres and deputy kapolres. Almost all the kapolres in Cirebon during Dedi Supardi's period as bupati of Cirebon were relatively driven and controlled by him in various ways, from the fulfillment of personnel needs such as 'coffee money' up to matters of female escorts and other adult entertainment services.[17]

The main powerholder where the Polres is physically located is the local government. Even if there were a feeling of Polres being subordinates of local government this cannot to be blamed on politics, because local government is a main powerholder. This is a consequence of the local autonomy that gives local government authority, especially in districts and municipalities that are relatively wide and large. Both Dedi Supardi, bupati of Cirebon, and Sunaryo, vice-mayor of Cirebon Municipality, realized that their governments need to be recognized as the authority over their areas, including from security organizers. So assuming the position of the Polres as being part of the local government is not wrong, although not justified by law.[18]

'APBD-gate', local inferiors and the police

The politicization of the Polres in the second way occurs in two activities: the handling of political issues, including corruption cases; and the asking of a Polres to stop sensitive cases in the area. A number of local governments saw the intervention of the ruling regime in national government by using the Polda and Polres as part of the Polri in the APBD-gate case. In fact, it is not beyond the control and intervention from the central government, either through the Polri headquarters or other channels such as the Ministry of Internal Affairs.[19]

One of the local leaders in a research area realized that the police were not guaranteed to be good friends for politicians or anyone including local government and DPRD, because, although there might be mutual benefit, a Polres would reject the friendship if the leaders of the Polres were summoned and ordered by the Polri headquarters to arrest people, either local leaders or DPRD members, due to alleged abuses of power and corruption. He also said that more than 65 per cent of the 80 DPRD members who had problems in the APBD-gate affair and several local leaders, bupatis and vice-bupatis or mayors and deputy mayors in West Java were in the same party as he was, the PDIP, an opposition party in the national parliament. The rest were from other parties, including the Golkar, PAN (Partai Amanat National – National Mandate Party), PKB (Partai Kebangkitan Bangsa – National Awakening Party) and PPP parties.[20]

In Cirebon Municipality, the chairman and members of its DPRD were questioned on allegations of budget graft, with possibilities of corruption. This appeared to have involved a systematic effort to misuse, violate and negate a number of regulations, even though the formal accusation was only of administrative and procedural improprieties.[21] In what was labelled 'APBD-gate', Suryana (PDIP), former chairman of the 1999–2004 Cirebon Municipality DPRD, Dahrin Sjahrir (Golkar Party), chairman of the 2004–2009 DPRD and 49 other DPRD members, including Sunaryo, subsequently the current Cirebon deputy mayor, were accused of graft for using the municipality's budget improperly.[22] Up to the time this research was being conducted, the local Polres and prosecutors were still processing the case.

The detention processes of the bupati and the government secretary of Garut, Agus Supriadi and Wowo Wibowo, on charges of misusing the local budget and corruption, were slightly different from those in Cirebon. Many people believed that Agus Supriadi was tripped up because he had created too many enemies during his leadership. Agus, a retired army colonel, was considered unflexible in leading Garut.[23] The pattern of relationship between his local government and the Polres also tended to be formal and positioned the Polres as subordinate within the old approach of the New Order era. So, although the Garut Polres initially investigated the case, the case had only just started before it was passed over to the KPK (Komisi Pemberantasan Korupsi – Corruption Eradication Commission).[24]

Eka Mulyana, deputy kapolres of Garut, acknowledged that the leadership between the Polres and Agus's local government was too formal, including almost no informal elements, as had that implemented by previous bupati before. Eka implicitly agreed that Agus Supriadi was arrested by the Polres and sent to Polda and then the KPK because his subordinates were dissatisfied with his policy and there was public complaint related to his programme. According to the data from the time Agus Supriadi had led Garut as its bupati, there had been several complaints from the public and internally from within the Garut government about irregularities committed by him.[25]

The case of the Garut government secretary, Wowo Wibowo, was more about political disputes among local government employees. Wowo Wibowo was regarded inside the Garut Government as one of Agus Supriadi's men, and they wanted all of these to have to go to jail. Once Agus Supriadi had been arrested by the KPK for allegedly misusing the APBD for his personal interests, the role of the secretary was considered as having been part of the bupati's activities. Political attacks made Wowo Wibowo suffer from stress and depression, until he was considered unable to act as secretary.[26] Hilman Faridz replaced him, although later in the trial process Wowo Wibowo was freed because he was not proven to be involved in the misuse of APBD for personal benefit.[27] Wowo Wibowo was one example of how the Polres of Garut had been being politicized by local political interests.[28]

The question then arose in the public opinion about whether the investigation of corruption cases involving the local government, the DPRD, and contractors were part of the professionalism and independence of the police. The public in Garut questioned this, especially in connection with police extortion activities in handling corruption cases against several members of DPRD and local government officials who, allegedly, had given money to stop these cases, but whose cases had still been brought to the court.[29]

The former bupati, Agus Supriadi, who was directly dealt with by the KPK and whose case was run relatively in accordance with applicable legal norms, was found guilty. However, the cases of Wowo Wibowo and several other Garut local government officials and DPRD members were handled by Polres during their investigation, and the process seemed long-winded and ultimately demoralizing for suspects who were public officials. Some of them were released after they gave money to the crooked police, the public prosecutor and the court to reduce the sentence and be released.

In Tasikmalaya and Ciamis, similar charges were also made against a number of members of these districts' DPRDs and they were arrested for alleged misuse of their budgets and also corruption. A public statement by local leaders asserted that there was a systematic attempt to throw local leaders and members of DPRD into jail. I found that these cases related with that in Cirebon and Garut. During my observations, what the Polres did in arresting the local leaders and DPRD members was systematically following the instructions from the national government through the Polri headquarters, especially in districts or municipalities which were led by an opposition party or had relations with an opposition party as part of a political coalition.[30]

However, the cases occurring in Tasikmalaya and Ciamis did not become national news items as did those in Cirebon and Garut, because there was an agreement between the Polres, the local government, DPRD, and district attorneys to coordinate in the Muspida to keep Ciamis peaceful.[31] This was publicly recognized by an investigator from the Ciamis Polres office who was reported as saying that DPRD members and local government officials had been cooperative and had not complicated the process of investigation except in the case of the vice-bupati, Dedi Sobandi (PDIP).[32]

In Tasikmalaya District there were also a number of cases besides budget graft and corruption of local leaders. These include a case of alleged corruption of the Special Allocation Fund[33] (Dana Alokasi Khusus) for Education that was being handled by the Tasikmalaya Public Attorney, where the head of the Educational, Training and Personnel Agency of Tasikmalaya (Badan Pendidikan, dan Latihan Kepegawaian), Abdul Kodir, was allegedly involved in graft.[34] Other cases of local government contractors and the local DPRD involving bribery were related to the construction of a new building for the Tasikmalaya DPRD, involving Taskmalaya Government Secretariat staff.[35]

However, I found a sense of inferiority in relation to the Polres on the part of local leaders and DPRD members.[36] This feeling is reflected in various statements and attitudes from them about Polres and other national hierarchical agencies with a strong presence in the local areas. The superiority of the Polres compared to the DPRD and local government of course is not entirely true but, in the areas of my research apart from Bandung, this feeling tended to be massive.

This may be because as the capital of West Java Province, in Bandung information is relatively accessible and local government officials are well educated in terms of law and regulations. In addition, there is a commitment of local leaders to open up to the public all kinds of control on the transparency of governance. Such issues, either from members of the internal administration or from the Polres, were almost absent. An exception was in the period 1998–2003, when Bandung was led by Mayor Aa Tarmana, a retired army colonel who tended to implement a military-style leadership, which of course was incompatible with the reform spirit and was not liked by his subordinates. In his period, his administration also kept a distance from the Polres, while asking the police for reports related to deviations and processing them.[37]

In the districts and municipalities, studied efforts to ask the Polres to stop handling sensitive cases followed three patterns. The first was a pattern that was practised upon personal request, by providing money for the case to be discontinued and with no further processing by the Polres. The amount of money involved was around Rp.50–100 million (about AU$5,500–11,000) depending on who had the problem – a person in a higher position having to pay much more than one with a lower position – and on what case was involved.[38] Politicians and government officials who were inexperienced in politics and law, such as from the PDIP, PPP and PKB in Cirebon, usually followed this pattern.[39] Their lack of political experience and legal understanding made some members and former members of a DPRD prefer to bribe crooked police investigators and the kapolres not to follow up an investigation and not to deliver the case to the prosecutors and courts.

Second, the Polres dropping a case could be on the request of local leaders and the DPRD, where there was considered to be a possibility that if the case were continued there could be chaos that ultimately would disrupt security and public order in the area. In this second pattern, the trend occurred in areas that were relatively not large, like Tasikmalaya and Ciamis.[40] So it can be concluded that the various issues and allegations of corruption involving cases that circulated about a number of members of local government and DPRD applied in only the smaller districts such as Ciamis and Taskimalaya.

Third, the stopping of a case can be at the request of central government. This is similar to the second situation, but with it being the national rather than the local government arguing that continuing would carry the consequence of a disruption of public security. In this third model, there are two possibilities that might occur: stopping the case before it has become an issue for public news consumption, or having it taken over by the provincial-level Polda or into the direct control of both the Polri headquarters and KPK. Usually the case will be taken over, as in the case of Agus Supriadi, the former Garut bupati, which was taken over by the KPK.

From the above accounts, we can see that steps and requests made to stop the investigation of corruption cases were caused by three things. First, there are growing opportunities in the era of *reformasi* for Polres, local governments and DPRD. Opportunities are related to the local cultures that developed to utilize and take advantage of local political and economic positions. No wonder, in some cases, that the request for a case termination by suspected individuals or their family became a tool for blackmail of the person or family by crooked Polres officers.[41]

Second, the regulations were not synergistic with the new spirit of local autonomy; there were central government efforts to keep control of political dynamics at the local level, as had happened in the New Order era. These cases as discussed earlier became a bad precedent for the handling of APBD-gate cases involving almost all the leaders and members of DPRD around Indonesia, although later a number of the cases were stopped because it was decided that they were limited to only administrative misuses, while others were wound down and suspended.[42]

Third, political dynamics were marred by the lack of knowledge and limited experience of local leaders and DPRD members in political and legal control. Because of that, the political situation was chaotic due to being trampled on by the narrow concerns of local leaders and DPRD members to keep away from the legal process. This was a strong consequence of the political attacks between local governments and DPRD as part of the new political rights and democratic freedoms.

It must be pointed out that certainly the politicization and decentralization of the Polri has brought implications for its existence as an institution; its authority and political position at the local level are increasing. Nevertheless, it can be suggested that taking benefits from its politicization in handling the corruption cases by the Polres, as discussed in this chapter, is in opposition to the goals of Polri reform.

Notes

1 Internal rivalry within the Polri in local areas will be discussed in Chapter 10.
2 *Garut Pos* (May 15, 2006), 'Kapolres Siap Berantas Korupsi'; *Kabar Priangan* (July 2, 2008), 'Polwil Priangan Harus Dicintai Masyarakat'.
3 See *Tribun Jabar* (March 2, 2006), 'Kapolwil Minta Motor Dikembalikan'; interview on November 8, 2009 with Dr Sugianto, Political Observer from Cirebon Islamic University (STAIN Cirebon).
4 See *Kabar Priangan* (April 22, 2008), 'Polresta Rangkul Tokoh Agama'; *Radar Cirebon* (September 1, 2006), 'Kapolri Pesan Supaya Independen'; interview on November 8, 2009 with PRA. Arief Natadiningrat, Sultan of Kasepuhan, Cirebon; interview on June 23, 2010 with KH. Miftah Fauzi, Islamic Preacher in Tasikmalaya; interview on June 30, 2010 with KH. Mahfudz Bakri, chairman of Nahdlatul Ulama (NU) Cirebon Municipality; interview on June 25, 2010 with Dr Mahi M. Hikmat, Political Observer, Bandung.
5 *Pikiran Rakyat* (October 21, 2006), 'Ulama Tolak Kapolresta Baru (Beragama Kristen)'.
6 Interview on June 30, 2010 with KH. Mahfudz Bakri, chairman of Nahdlatul Ulama (NU) Cirebon Municipality.
7 Interview on November 8, 2009 with PRA. Arief Natadiningrat, Sultan of Kasepuhan, Cirebon.
8 See Pemerintah Kota Cirebon (2008); *Kompas* (April 6, 2010), 'Kota Cirebon Makin Sesak'; *Tribun Jabar* (October 12, 2010), 'Penduduk Kota Cirebon Naik 0,84% Tiap Tahun'.
9 Including the Instruction Paper of the Minister of Internal Affairs No. 15/2004, Government Decree No. 58/2005, Government Decree No. 37/2006, and Ministry of Internal Affairs Decree No. 37/2010.
10 For more explanation of support budgets from local governments to the local police, see Chapter 8.
11 Interview on November 8, 2009, with H. Dahrin Sjahrir, a former chairman of the Cirebon Municipality DPRD from the Golkar Party (FPG DPRD Kota Cirebon); interview on June 22, 2010 with Ade Suryana, MP in the Garut DPRD from the National Mandate Party (FPAN DPRD Garut); interview on June 23, 2010 with Demi Hamzah R. MP in the Tasikmalaya DPRD from the National Mandate Party (FPAN DPRD Tasikmalaya).
12 Interview on July 1, 2010 with Dedi Supardi, bupati of Cirebon. This can be compared with statements from Ronny Lihawa and Chaeruddin Ismail about recognition of the kapolres by the local leader. Interview on November 2, 2009 with Police Inspector General (retired) Drs Ronny Lihawa, Secretary of the Kompolnas; interview on June 13, 2010 with Police General (retired) Dr Chaeruddin Ismail, former deputy and acting chief of the INP.
13 *Radar Cirebon* (June 24, 2006), 'Ajak Ciptakan Situasi Kondusif'; interview on July 7, 2010 with Ayi Vivananda, deputy mayor of Bandung Municipality.
14 What the Cirebon bupati did to the Cirebon District kapolres was one good example of the local government control. Dedi Supardi realized that as bupati, he should take initiatives to ask any hierarchical institution in his territory to report or at least coordinate its roles and function there. He had various ways to control and subordinate the heads of hierarchical agencies, including the Polres, from providing for their private needs and supporting the operational budget to providing pleasure activities.
15 See *Radar Cirebon* (August 30, 2006), 'Jelang Puasa, Razia Besar-besaran'; interview on June 22, 2010 with Suherman, Head of Garut Kesbangpol Linmas; interview on June 23, 2010 with Imam Gadjali, Head of Tasikmalaya Kesbangpol Linmas, and Ali Rochman, Head of Tasikmalaya Satpol PP; interview on June 30, 2010 with Adam Nurdin, Head of Cirebon Municipality Kesbangpol Linmas. Those opinions can be compared with those of Kelana (2010, unpubd).

132 *Local government perspectives*

16 *Kabar Priangan* (November 13, 2008), 'Kapolres Dicatut'; interview on July 26, 2010 with Makmun Gunawan Sidik, a former advisor of bupati Cirebon.
17 *Koran Tempo* (May 3, 2009), 'Oknum Polisi Minta uang Pelicin Rp.3 Juta Agar Berita Acara Perampokan Keluar'; *Tribun Jabar* (September 15, 2010), 'Oknum Polisi Diduga Gelapkan Uang STNK Rp.90 Juta'.
18 Interview on July 1, 2010 with H. Sunaryo, deputy mayor of Cirebon Municipality; interview on July 2, 2010 with Dedi Supardi, bupati of Cirebon.
19 For example, *Kompas* (October 27, 2009), 'Penyidikan Kasus 'APBD Gate' yang Melibatkan Walikota dan 16 Anggota DPRD Cirebon Dihentikan'.
20 Interview on July 2, 2010 with a senior politician of the PDIP in Cirebon District; interview on July 7, with a senior official of Bandung Municipality; *Kabar Priangan* (July 2, 2008), 'Polwil Akan Bentuk Tim Pengawas Khusus: Antisipasi Penyelewengan APBN dan APBD'; *Mitra Dialog* (July 11, 2007), 'Walikota Cirebon Bantah Terima Uang Hasil Korupsi'.
21 Interview on November 8, 2009, with H. Dahrin Sjahrir, a former chairman of the Cirebon Municipality DPRD from the Golkar Party (FPG DPRD Kota Cirebon), and Sri Maryati, a former MP in the Cirebon Municipality DPRD from the Indonesian Democratic Party of Struggle (FPDIP DPRD Kota Cirebon).
22 'APBD-gate' is the name given to a large case of misuse of the local budget by DPRD members, alleged by prosecutors to be corrupt but claimed by the defendants as being because they lacked knowledge of the confusing laws and regulations related to it. *Mitra Dialog* (January 5, 2008), 'Kombes Mochammad Nasser Amir jabat Kapolwil Cirebon'; *Mitra Dialog* (May 16, 2008), 'DP Ancam Balik Lapor Polisi'; *Pikiran Rakyat* (August 4, 2010), 'Sidang APBD-gate Cirebon dinilai Lamban'.
23 Interview on June 22, 2010 with Asep Maher, Coordinator of MAPAG, Garut; interview on June 23, 2010 with Askur (pseudonym); *Tribun Jabar* (July 26, 2006), 'Bupati Bela Anak Buahnya, Dugaan Penyelewengan Dana Bencana Alam'; *Pikiran Rakyat* (July 26, 2006), 'Kerusakan Jalan Membuat Bupati Kesal'.
24 Interview on June 22, 2010 with Asep Maher, Coordinator of MAPAG, Garut; interview on June 22, 2010 with Moch. Mukti Arip, chairman of Indonesian Youth National Committee, Garut Branch (KNPI Garut). See also *Tribun Jabar* (August 12, 2006), 'Berkas Korupsi Pasar Diteliti'; *Tribun Jabar* (August 14, 2006), 'GGW Minta Bantuan KPK, Jawaban Bupati Sulit Dimengerti'; *Kabar Priangan* (October 4, 2008), 'Tersangka Kasus "Mamin" Dilarikan ke RSUD'.
25 The roles of the Polres in arresting the Garut bupati and government secretary were unique and tended to obtain benefits for its institution or crooked investigators among its personnel. See *Kompas* (July 11, 2007), 'Bupati Garut Didesak Mundur, Agus Supriadi: Kalau Tidak Puas Silakan Bawa ke PTUN'; *Kabar Priangan* (July 2, 2008), 'Polres Buka Kembali Kasus Tipikor Lama'.
26 When I asked members of his family about interviewing him, they told me that he was still depressed and could not chat with other people, especially in relation to that case.
27 Interview on June 22, 2010 with Ade Suryana, MP in the Garut Parliament from the National Mandate Party (FPAN DPRD Garut); *Tribun Jabar* (August 15, 2006), 'Ketua Gapensi Garut Jadi Tersangka'; *Kabar Priangan* (July 14, 2008), '20 Anggota DPRD Garut Dipanggil Polda Jabar?'
28 *Kabar Priangan* (May 16, 2008), 'Wowo Wibowo dan Barman Diadukan ke Polda'.
29 Interview on June 22, 2010 with a former member of Garut District DPRD; interview on June 22 with Asep Maher, Coordinator of MAPAG, Garut; *Pikiran Rakyat* (July 19, 2009), 'Semua Mantan Anggota Dewan Diduga Terseret APBD-gate; 15 Mantan Pangar Segera Ke Pengadilan'.
30 *Radar Tasik* (June 28, 2008), 'Koalisi Merah Putih Mencuat'; *Pikiran Rakyat* (April 9, 2009), 'Engkon Komara Dilantik jadi Bupati Ciamis'; *Radar Tasik* (October 20, 2010), 'Ahmad Saleh Tak Ingin Kalah Dua Kali'; interview on June 22, 2010 with a

former member of the Garut District DPRD; interview on July 2 with a former member of the Cirebon District DPRD.

31 *Pikiran Rakyat* (May 24, 2004), 'Pemeriksaan Dugaan Korupsi DPRD Ciamis Hampir Tuntas'; *Pikiran Rakyat* (February 4, 2005), 'Kepala Perpustakaan Ciamis Dituntut 4 Tahun; Sidang Kasus Korupsi DPRD Ciamis Senilai 5,2 Milyar'; interview on June 23, 2010 with Imam Gazali, Head of Tasikmalaya Kesbangpol Linmas; interview on June 24, 2010 with H. Iing Syam Arifin, vice-bupati of Ciamis; interview on June 23, 2010 with Ahmad Irfan Alawi, MP in the Ciamis DPRD from the PKB (FPKB DPRD Ciamis); interview on June 24, 2010 with Gandjar M. Yusuf, MP in the Ciamis DPRD from the Golkar Party (FPG DPRD Ciamis).

32 *Kabar Priangan* (April 30, 2008), 'Dua Kapolsek Dicopot'; *Kabar Priangan* (July 22, 2008), 'Polisi Masih Mencari Jati Diri'.

33 These are funds allocated from the national government to local governments for specific purposes, rather than the General Allocation Funds (Dana Alokasi Umum, DAU) which are not tied to specified projects.

34 *Kabar Priangan* (July 1, 2008), 'Dua Kepala Sekolah SD Diperiksa'; *Pikiran Rakyat* (January 5, 2010), 'Tersangka Korupsi Dicalonkan Jadi Sekda'.

35 *Kompas* (February 11, 2010), 'Proyek Pembangunan Gedung DPRD Tasikmalaya: Kejaksaan Selidiki Dugaan Penyuapan'; *Kabar Priangan* (May 16, 2008), 'DAK di Priangan Timur Bocor 30 Persen'.

36 Interview on November 8, 2009, with Cecep Suhardiman, MP in the Cirebon Municipality DPRD from the Democratic Party (FPD DPRD Kota Cirebon); interview on June 22, 2010 with Ade Suryana, MP in the Garut DPRD from the National Mandate Party (FPAN DPRD Garut); interview on June 23, 2010 with Ade Sugianto, MP and deputy chairman in the Tasikmalaya DPRD from the Indonesian Democratic Party of Struggle (FPDI); interview on June 24, 2010 with Gandjar M. Yusuf, MP and deputy chairman of the Ciamis DPRD from the Golkar Party (FPG); interview on July 2, 2010 with Mustopha, MP in the Cirebon DPRD from the Indonesian Democratic Party of Struggle (FPDIP DPRD Cirebon); interview on July 21, 2010 with Tedy Rusmawan, MP in the Bandung Municipality DPRD from the Prosperity and Justice Party (FPKS DPRD Kota Bandung).

37 *Gatra* (June 23, 2001), 'Demo Buruh dan BBM: Bandung Lautan Aksi'; *Pikiran Rakyat* (May 2, 2003), 'Polda Jabar Usut Soal Dana Kaveling'.

38 Personal communications on June 17, 18, 19, 20 and 21, 2010 with former members of the DPRD in East Priangan Districts and Cirebon Municipality. Some former DPRD members said the crooked police asked for higher than Rp.100 million. The situation would be one of trading, bargaining and haggling for as low as you can, then paying.

39 *Pikiran Rakyat* (October 16, 2003), 'Penipuan KTP Sulit Diproses'; *Pikiran Rakyat* (October 24, 2003), 'Polda tak Akan Bisa Proses Kasus KKN Tanpa Dukungan warga'.

40 *Pikiran Rakyat* (June 14, 2004), 'Hari Ini Anggota DPRD Dipanggil Kembali Kejaksaan'; *Pikiran Rakyat* (June 17, 2004), 'Anggota DPRD Garut Kembalikan Uang APBD'.

41 Interview on July 2, 2010 with Dedi Hariyadi, Executive Director of Bandung Institute of Governance Studies (BIGS). Interview on June 21, 2010 with Budhiana Kartawijaya, chief editor of the Bandung newspaper *Pikiran Rakyat*.

42 *Berita Kota* (July 30, 2010), 'Air Mata Isteri APBD Gate'; *Republika* (August 2, 2010), 'Kasus APBD Muncul Karena Konspirasi'.

Part V
Local police perspectives

10 Internal conflicts and the effect of extortion

> The effect of disassociation the Polri from ABRI for us in local police was too hard and complicated to promote our ranks and to get better positions because those needed to be paid.
> (A middle-ranking officer in West Java Police Office, 2010)

As discussed in Chapters 5 and 6, the disassociation of the Polri from the ABRI had broad consequences for the existence of the Polri at national and local levels. Politicization and intervention, as well as various other implications associated with the disassociation at the national level, made the Polri's position very vulnerable to political exploitation by post-Suharto regimes. In the local context, as discussed in Chapter 9, the politicization of Polres contrasts with what happened at the national level. At the local level, the Polres are more confident and tended to act as superior to the local governments and DPRD. The Polres even implemented their power in the field of internal security to utilize their personnel and organization in carrying out extortion practices.

Disassociation of the Polri from the ABRI also had implications for internal Polri activity and its role in maintaining internal security. In addition, although the Polri budget continues to have significant increases, the amount made available for allocation down through its system is still far from ideal for operations and the prosperity of its personnel. The effect of a low budget and welfare is irregularities and illegal practices, which are justified under the pretext of budget shortfalls both through formal endowments from local governments and informal approaches from kapolres for additional payments in extortion and other activities involving brokers, fixers, and other accomplices.

This chapter will discuss internal conflicts and rivalry among police at the local level in the six districts and municipalities studied, including their effects based on the various groups at the national level.[1]

Kickbacks in police recruitment and education

After disassociation from the ABRI, there was an increase in internal conflict and rivalry inside the Polri based on two main issues: access to higher ranks and strategic positions, and access to sufficient funding resources to be able to operate effectively. These became major issues in the Polri at all levels throughout Indonesia, in some ways even outweighing the various advantages of the new independence that came from the dissociation. Within the West Java Polda there were various conflicts, which will be discussed below.

In the New Order era, when the Polri was still part of the military, the same two issues had become enough of a problem that the Polri was not able to perform its role and functions as well as it otherwise could. When the Polri had handled a case, there could be problems with objectivity because of intervention from the military and the usual lack of budget resources for initiating the case as soon as possible. This meant that the Polri had no power to control every case because the ABRI headquarters monitored them.

The second issue, that of access by police to promotion or preferred assignments, also arose during the New Order but in a different way to the problem post-disassociation.[2] During the New Order era, it was part of the government's scheme to control the dynamics of the community by assigning Polri officers and military Babinsa as part of the ABRI territorial command. No wonder, then, that attempts to get position or career advantage were made by the Polri officers who had close relations with local military units, as they would get a good recommendation.[3]

Inside the *reformasi* Polri, the various processes of selection for positions might look normal, but are not purely choices made by its formal internal mechanism. In fact, according to Monica Tanuhandaru, a former police reform programme coordinator of the International Organization of Migration (IOM), to be assessed by the evaluation team before being listed by the Wanjakti at the Polri headquarters, Polda and Polres, a police officer must pay a lot of money to get a higher rank or position. An indication of the size of the payments required is given in Table 10.1.[4]

Even this would not guarantee the desired result, with that depending on the amount of bribery money; because almost all appointments involve competition between candidates, there must be some competition between their payments unless the payments are simple rentier or rent-seeking ones in which a payment must be made to ensure a request is passed on to the next stage of selection. At the Polri headquarters there is an Assessment Centre, outside the Wanjakti, which conducts assessments of candidates before they are selected and listed by the Wanjakti for levels such as Kapolda or in the headquarters, and also for leaders at the Polres level.[5] It is known that this closed internal mechanism caused many Polri officers try to get an advantage, whether for a rapid career track or in asking for a specific title and position.[6]

The dominant authority of the Polri headquarters and Polda in promotion and appointment had made the opportunity for deviation greater, from the start of the process to the final submission of the names of those appointed. The president controls only the two very top positions of chief and deputy chief of the Polri. All other positions below those two are directly under the control of the Polri chief and the Wanjakti.[7] They both finally use what the applicants' superiors said in their reviews of the applicants' performances.[8]

Table 10.1 Kickbacks in police recruitment and education in West Java Polda post-disassociation

Current rank	Next rank and school required for it	Amount (Rp. million)
Police brigadier (low rank)	Brigadier NCO grade (SPN, Pusdik, SPPBP, SEPOLWAN)	25–75[1]
Candidate officer	Inspector (SECAPA)	50–100[2]
Police officer	Inspector (Akpol, SIPSS)	50–300[3]
Senior inspector	Captain/adjutant commissioner (PTIK, SELAPA)	50–200[4]
Commissioner	Commissioner (SESPIM)	150–300[5]
Senior commissioner	Adjutant chief commissioner/chief commissioner (SESPATI)	200–500[6]
Special training	Private/senior NCO grade and low-level officer (Admin, Sebasa, Reskrim, Intelkam, Lantas, Brimob, Polair)	10–50[7]

Notes
1 Personal communications on July 8, 2010 with an NCO's brigadier in West Java Polda, Bandung; on July 21 with a parent of an NCO's brigadier recruited in Bandung; interview on July 10, 2010 with a senior Polwan officer, Jakarta.
2 Personal communications on July 20, 2010 with a senior NCO's brigadier in West Java Polda, Bandung; on November 8, 2009 with a junior police officer in Cirebon Municipality Polres; on June 30, 2010 with a junior officer in Cirebon District Polres.
3 Personal communications on February 15, 2010 with a fixer, Bandung; on July 19, 2010 with a parent of an Akpol trainee recruited in Bandung; on July 20, 2010 with a junior police officer in West Java Polda; on July 27, with a junior officer in Bandung Municipality Polres.
4 Personal communications on November 9, 2009 with a student of the PTIK, Jakarta; on December 12, 2009 with a student of SELAPA; group discussion on November 23, 2009 with several Masters students of the PTIK, Jakarta; the money provided by the student would including payment to a ghost writer for daily assignments, group work, and the final BA thesis.
5 Personal communications on June 15, 2010 with a student of SESPIM, Bandung; on June 16, 21 and 26, 2010 with a senior non-police staff member of SESPIM who connects students with persons who were willing to be ghost writers, Bandung; on July 8, 2010 with a middle-rank officer, Bandung. The money provided by the student would include payment to a ghost-writer for daily assignments, group work, and a final report.
6 Personal communications on November 11, 2009 with a student of SESPATI, Bandung; on June 21 with a senior officer in the West Java Polda, Bandung; personal communications on June 16, 21 and 26, 2010 with a senior non-police staff member of SESPIM who connects students with persons who were willing to be ghost writers, Bandung.
7 Personal communications on June 24, 2010 with an NCO's brigadier in Ciamis District Polres Office; on June 22, 2010 with a traffic NCO's brigadier in Garut District Polres Office; communication on July 22, 2010 with a senior NCO's brigadier in West Java Polda, Bandung; on July 24, with a junior officer of Polwan, in Bandung Municipality Polres Office.

A Polri officer already with the rank of commissioner (major in the military) would have to spend around Rp.250 million (AU$28,000) from the start when they submit their names in their application to enrol at SESPIM until they graduate from it (see Table 10.1). The assumption was that the bribe money would be replaced once they have graduated from the SESPIM and become a kapolres or take another prestigious position.[9] In each case the payments include that for the hiring of ghost-writers who could actually write the scientific papers required by administrative staff of the PTIK, the SELAPA, the SESPIM and the SESPATI.[10]

Kickbacks for promotion and position

There are four models of recruitment and assignment at the Polri headquarters post-disassociation from the ABRI. The first is through assessment by leaders. This model should always be that used inside the Polri, and be part of the formal recruitment conducted by the Polri leaders to fill all positions and offices as well as for tours of duty.

It is noticeable that those Polri officers who are under supervision of the INP headquarters have a normal career path without any problems. Remarkable officers will reach higher ranks and positions in a short time. A deputy kapolres in Cirebon Municipality was one of the best-graduated officers and was given two opportunities at the same time, to study at the SESPIM and to study in a doctoral programme at a leading private university in Bandung. On the other hand, the deputy kapolres in Cirebon, Garut, Tasikmalaya and Ciamis districts have had different experiences. They had taken the test for continuing education in the SESPIM twice in a row, but failed.

The second model is the so-called 'salutation from the windows' (*memberi hormat dari jendela*). Many Polri officers will come early in the morning before their leaders arrive and give a salute when the leader comes, to mark their presence and respect in the memory of the head. This model is a slightly different version of 'licking the boss's boots', in the form of greetings and salutations through the windows of the room.

A third model is by lobbying high-ranking officers in the Polri headquarters. This model, although infrequent, still exists and is conducted as part of a final shortcut when other ways to gain promotion have failed. One of the officers who managed to get out of this situation was a mid-ranking officer recruited from the university who had become stuck in the West Java Polda, but later became a head of the police administration unit (Kepala Urusan Administrasi, Kaurmin) in the Polri headquarters and was promoted from police adjutant commissioner (AKP) to full police commissioner (Komisaris Polisi, Kompol).[11] He had realized that if he used the normal avenues, it would be impossible to get a higher position and rank.

The fourth model for obtaining promotion is through access to political power and money. This model is likely to apply in the cases of the more crooked Polri officers who are less worthy in their ability and track records.[12] They take shortcuts using political power and money. A bad thing was that this model is considered as a way to get access to political power. It arose, as did the two previous models, when the normal way to get the higher positions was difficult. However, as in economic transactions, the rise in demand to get jobs and titles was responded to by many Polri officers in the personnel bureaus at all levels from headquarters down to the Polres, with transactions involving recommendations and appointments among the internal positions and ranks of the Polri.[13]

In the West Java Polda, the transactions for rank and position were common and prolonged. Although it was not obvious and visible, based on research and observations made during fieldwork there were a number of cases that involved almost all the personnel bureau staff, directly or indirectly.

There are three sub-patterns of transaction over rank and position in the West Java police. The first is by pre-payment. This pattern has really become one of the elements in the personnel bureau's efforts to dredge money from a number of police officers who had been recruited as university graduates, had passed through the Police Academy (Akademi Kepolisian, Akpol), but then had got stuck in their careers and ranks. They tended to spend Rp.10–25 million (AU$1,150–2,800). The problem then is that these Polri officers are usually reluctant and shy about asking for the promotions and positions that had been promised. This pattern is usually conducted by new players who do not know either the inside situation or the transactions for ranks and promotions.

The second pattern is by post-payment. A number of the Polri officers and non-Academy graduates have been accustomed to give tributes and kickbacks for progress in their careers and ranks (see Table 10.2). These are usually experienced players: Polri officers who had been accustomed to give some money as a gesture of thanks to staff in the personnel bureau. This pattern of corruption in assignments was dominated by police officers that had graduated from the Akpol, with very few others attempting it. One of these was a kapolres who serves in one of the six districts and municipalities studied. He had been recruited as a university graduate, and had survived for more than three years in his position as a kapolres against various manoeuvres for his position.[14]

The third pattern is a combination of the two patterns described above. It was not widely used because it was not often needed when those involved already know each other and the applicant was already guaranteed by someone, so there was no need to deposit some money as an advance. However, when there were doubts about the guarantee of the officer, then the crooked personnel bureau officer would not hesitate to ask the applying officer for a deposit. Usually this happened when they did not know one another well.

Internal conflict: the police ATMS group, the Akpol group and the religious police group

The system of appointments has several consequences, among which are rivalry and conflict in the Polri; the level of welfare inside the Polri; programme achievement based on performance; and coordination with other relevant agencies. The first consequence is that the pattern of relationships in the Polri leads to rivalry and conflict between officers. Three types of rivalry emerge from this: between officers who have graduated from the Academy, but in different classes or cohorts; between Academy and non-Academy police graduates; and between units.[15]

Obviously, these rivalries develop not solely due to problems in gaining higher titles and ranks, but also because of the egos of officers who graduated from the Academy or those who have been assigned to units that have relatively easy access to illegal financial benefits, which are identified as 'police ATMs' or 'walking ATMs'.[16] The feeling of being treated as second-class in the Polri became a common feeling among non-Academy graduated officers, because in

Table 10.2 Kickbacks for promotion and position in West Java Polda post-disassociation

Title	Rank	Level	Amount (Rp. million)
Investigator and traffic policeman[22]	Police NCO brigadier	Polsek and Polres	10–50[1]
Head of investigation	First inspector	Polsek	25–100[2]
Kapolsek	First inspector or adjutant commissioner	Polsek	50–150[3]
Head of unit	Commissioner or adjutant	Polres	50–300[4]
Deputy kapolres	Commissioner or adjutant chief commissioner	Polres	100–300[5]
Kapolres	Adjutant chief commissioner or chief commissioner	Polres	300–750[6]
Director of a directorate, head of a bureau in Polda	Adjutant chief commissioner or chief commissioner	Polda	200–400[7]

Notes
1 Personal communications on April 12, 2010 with a senior NCO brigadier, a traffic police officer of Bandung Municipality Polres; on April 23, 2010 with an NCO brigadier of West Java Polda; on July 1, 2010 with a senior NCO brigadier, an investigator of Reskrim of Cirebon District Polres.
2 Personal communication on April 25, 2010 with a first-rank officer of a Polsek in Bandung Municipality Polres; on June 22 with a first-rank officer of Garut District Polres; on June 23, 2010 with a first-rank officer of Tasikmalaya District Polres; on June 24, 2010 with a first-rank officer of Ciamis District Polres.
3 Personal communication on May 2, 2010 with a first-rank officer who had already paid Rp. 25 million to crooked police officers in the Personnel Bureau in Bandung Municipality Polres Office six months previously, for a prestigious position as a Kapolsek, before I met him and discussed it; the Personnel Bureau had not yet informed him any position.
4 Personal communication on November 8, 2009 with mid-rank officers of Cirebon Municipality Polres and Cirebon District Polres; on May 11, 2010 with a mid-rank officer of West Java Polda; on June 2, 2010 with a mid-rank officer of Bandung Municipality Polres.
5 Personal communications on June 11, 2010 with a student of SESPIM, Bandung; on June 12, 2010 with a mid-rank officer in West Java Polda; on July 15, 2010 with a mid-rank officer in the Polri Headquarters, Jakarta.
6 Personal communications on April 2, 2010 with a student of SESPATI, Bandung; on November 4, 2009 with two senior mid-rank officers of the Polri Headquarters, Jakarta; on July 22, 2010 with a mid-rank officer of West Java Polda, Bandung.
7 Personal communications on November 25, 2009 with a senior mid-rank officer of West Java Polda; on July 20, 2010 with another senior mid-rank officer of West Java Polda; on July 23, 2010 with a senior mid-rank officer of West Java Polda; on August 1, 2010 with a high-rank officer of the Polri Headquarters, Jakarta.

practice, although their quality and capability are considered equal, access to reach higher positions leans towards the Academy graduates, and this occurs at almost all levels.

These interpretations are strong and widespread among non-Academy graduated officers, and must be understood as a consequence of the existing mechanisms. In an interview with me, Dr Hadiman, lecturer at the PTIK and a retired two-star police general, emphasized that not all Academy graduated officers are better than non-Academy graduated – in a few cases, vice versa.[17] He had served as the Kapolda of North Sumatra, having graduated as a medical doctor who chose a career as a Brimob officer, using the non-Academy avenue of university graduate recruitment.

A 'bad cop' (*polisi nakal*) is a policeman who can be bribed and asked for a negotiation in '8–6' code,[18] while a 'good cop' (*polisi baik*) tends to be more religious and keep a distance from the deviation from procedures. When I was carrying out my observations, one Academy graduate officer who was known to be against bribery complained that he was concerned and uncomfortable with the pattern of settlement in a case where a bupati in the northern region of West Java had been caught using drugs but was released by this officer's superior because the suspect had paid more than Rp.250 million in order to stop his case being proceeded with.

Another interesting fact is that the group of 'good cops' were conducting some of their activities in the form of routine study at the police mosque in the office complex of the West Java Polda. They pointed out that the routine was part of a Jama'ah Tabliq network with a strong link to the Polri headquarters. A number of Polri generals, for example the former head of the East Java Polda, Anton Bahrul Alam, are members of this Islamic group, which is based in India.[19] Unlike some other Islamic groups, Jama'ah Tabliq was focused on cleansing the soul and was not radical, so that some Polri officers or personnel joined with them.[20]

Another group of rivalries in the Polri was 'academic' and 'non-academic'. The difference between them was reflected in the learning orientation among police officers and in the intellectual level of these officers. The rivalry between non-academic and academic police was widespread whether or not related to the Polri's roles and functions.[21] The academic police groups usually prefer an advanced education or study at higher level to taking less prestigious positions and spending money to get it.

Part of the problem is a growing opinion among the public that after the disassociation from the ABRI, all the Polri officers have become economically prosperous. In many cases this opinion was applied to members of the Polri who were, in fact, disadvantaged and had become less comfortable. This prosperity gap eventually built up a less than good atmosphere within the Polri at all levels, from precinct police to district police, provincial police, all the way up to the headquarters.

The public expect the Polri to accelerate the programme and improve performance. Various models of job assignment and positions to directly carry out programmes got stuck, because the achievement of police programmes and performance improvements in the Polsek and Polres are based on the fast-changing dynamic of society. The programmes in Polres were dependent on the deputy kapolres because internally the deputy holds the key to the success or failure of programmes carried out by a Polres.

In contrast, another example of internal competition over control and influence that ended with conflict was between an earlier Cirebon District kapolres, Syamsul Bahri, and his deputy, Nurhadi. Their competition had led to Nurhadi having to leave, because of an alleged fraud case involving luxury cars. In

Nurhadi's version, Syamsul Bahri had victimized him because, in the Polres hierarchy, all policies related to a Polres have to be known by its kapolres. Nurhadi claimed that he had thought that it was impossible that Syamsul Bahri did not know that this case had been happening.[22]

The complaint on the rapid turnover of kapolres as they were continually replaced came also from local leaders. The main reason for this concern was because the rapid periodic replacement of the police heads disrupted the programme. For example, Dedi Supardi, Cirebon bupati for six years, complained that during his period in office, the Cirebon District Polres had experienced seven changes of kapolres. Similarly, Ayi Vivananda, in his fourth year as vice-mayor of Bandung, had already experienced more than four changes of the local kapolres.

One of the intentions of the Polri's model of vertical mobility had been to position it to be able to settle various rivalries and conflicts which would interfere in its functioning. Over the past ten years, the settlement of conflicts and rivalry in the West Java Polda and its subsidiary districts and municipalities had worked in three ways.

The first was by a leadership approach. This method was relatively informal and recognized by leaders, both in the Polda and the various Polres, as being relatively powerful. Based on friendly approaches, the atmosphere of rivalry and conflict would weaken, not emerge, and not interrupt the performance in the field. However, in some cases, the level of conflict and rivalry within the Polda caused a conflict in the Polda and Polres that was relatively difficult to resolve.

The second approach was to transfer to other areas Polri officers who were having problems or conflicts in factional or other groups.[23] With this reassignment method, the Polri was hoping to break a string of conflicts and rivalry between two groups and focus on its tasks and function. However, a problem that arose was that these transfers were often conducted in favour of members of groups that were able to provide 'compensation' to personnel or human resources bureau staff, while other groups tended to wait and hope that a transfer would bring them to the positions they desired.

The third, and usually the last, choice in the settlement of conflict and rivalry is a dismissal. However, this solution is very rarely used unless the members of the Polri have made serious violations, such as committing a crime or illicit drug use. In the context of conflict and rivalry, a dismissal would only be carried out if there had been disturbances to the performance of a number of units and Polri members. Thus, this policy has never been practised in handling internal conflict and rivalry.

This chapter has argued that the Polres are relatively well positioned in relation to the local military units and local government at the level of formal roles, so that the models of relationships between those institutions are different to those at the national level. It has argued that the internal conflicts and rivalry among police at the local level are because of the limited accesses to economic sources and vertical mobility to get higher positions and promotions.

The effect of a low budget on the welfare of the police is irregularities and illegal practices which are justified under the pretext of budget shortfalls. These range from formal endowments from local governments and informal approaches from kapolres for additional payments to extortion and other criminal activities involving parties outside the police to smooth the illegal activities or deviant practices that enrich Polres personnel in preparation for the 'fees' they will need to cover for their possible future appointments to police schools, promotion, and new assignments in the Polri.

Notes

1 For basic information on the six districts and municipalities, see Chapter 7.
2 For more on the impacts of disassociation on internal mechanisms of the Polri at national level, see Chapter 5.
3 Djamin (2007), pp. 205–210; Zachrie and Wiwanto (eds) (2010), pp. 297–301; Hendrowinoto *et al.* (2010), pp. 48–64. See also Chapter 4.
4 Interview on June 16, 2010 with Monica Tanuhandaru, former coordinator of the programme of police reform of the IOM, Jakarta. See also *Okezone News* (2010), 'Banyak Perwira Polri Kurang Berkualitas', available at: http://news.okezone.com/read/2010/10/12/339/381526/banyak-perwira-polri-kurang-berkualitas (November 3, 2010); personal communication on January 5, 2010 with a senior high-ranking officer, Jakarta; personal communication on September 10, 2010 with another high-ranking officer, Jakarta.
5 Especially for Polres leaders and below, the Wanjakti is involved in selecting or listing candidates put forward by the HRD and the Propam with the Bureau of Personnel in Polda, with final selection approved by the Wanjakti and signed by the chief of the INP.
6 Interview on November 4, 2009 with Police Inspector General Drs Andi Chaeruddin, Coordinator of the Expert Staffs for the Chief of the Polri; interview on November 5, 2009 with Police Commissioner General Drs E. Winarto, Head of Human Resources of the Polri Headquarters; personal communication on July 7, 2010 with Dr La Ode Husein, member of the Kompolnas.
7 For more information on the composition of the Wanjakti, see Chapter 5.
8 In Polda and Polres, the persons who are dominant in selecting and reviewing the applicants before their names are sent to the Polri Headquarters are the deputy Kapolda, the deputy kapolres and the head of the Personnel Bureau.
9 After graduating from the SESPIM, an officer will be able to become a kapolres or take a similar prestigious position. It would then be easy to get enough money to pay back what they had spent for their education.
10 Information elicited from a group discussion with several graduate students of Police Studies at the PTIK-UI, November 23, 2009; interview on July 15, 2010 with a senior non-police administration official in SESPIM, Bandung; written communication with a student of SELAPA Polri, December 12, 2009; interview on June 1, 2010 with Police General Drs Sutarman, Head of SELAPA Polri, Ciputat, Jakarta; interview on June 12, 2010 with Police Inspector General Drs Paulus Purwoko, Head of SESPIM Polri, Lembang, West Java.
11 Interview on June 28, 2010 with a mid-ranking officer of the Polri, Jakarta.
12 From the opinions of some informants, it appears that the proportion of crooked police in the Polri is quite large, more than 10 per cent of all of the members of the Polri. For example, see *Vivanews* (2011), 'Anak Buah Kombes WW Jadi Tersangka Pemerasan', available at: http://us.metro.vivanews.com/news/read/57078-anak_buah_kombes_ww_jadi_tersangka_pemerasan (March 4, 2011).

13 *Pikiran Rakyat* (August 1, 2003), 'Tagihan Rp.28 M Dikirim ke Polda'; *Kabar Priangan* (December 2, 2008), 'Kapolda, Anggota Polri Jangan Membebani Masyarakat'.
14 There were very few positions in the Polri for officers who were not Akpol graduates. If they had positions, they were supposed to be in non-operational areas like the administration office. Interview on June 18, 2010 with Police Inspector General (retired) Dr Hadiman, a PTIK Lecturer; he graduated from the University of Indonesia in 1965 as a medical doctor and later joined the Brimob. He had a good career as a non-Akpol graduate. Before he retired, Dr Hadiman led North Sumatra Police as a Kapolda.
15 In the Polri headquarters there is an additional background of rivalry and conflict based on ethnicity, such as Javanese versus Sundanese, Bataknese, Makassarese, Balinese, and also, to some extent, around religion, such as Muslim and non-Muslim.
16 In the Polri, the Crime and Investigation Units (Reskrim) and the Traffic Police Units (Lantas) at all levels are very important in supporting the Polri operations due to the limited state budget. *Kabar Priangan* (August 22, 2008), 'Puluhan Kendaraan Terjaring Operasi'; *Kabar Priangan* (August 5, 2008), 'Nama Kapolres Garut Dicatut untuk Menipu'.
17 Interview on June 18, 2010 with Police Inspector (retired) Dr Hadiman, a lecturer at the PTIK.
18 '8–6 code' is the Polri official code for clear negotiation of any cases between the Polri officers and members of the public.
19 *Koran Tempo* (October 30, 2009), 'Kapolda Jawa Timur Anton Bachrul Alam Diganti'. Anton Bachrul Alam is now the Polri Head of Human Relations (Kadiv Humas).
20 For more discussion on Jam'ah Tabliq, see *Majalah Shyariah* (August 7, 2004), 'Membongkar Kedok Jamaah Tabliqh'; Juandi, Erik (2009, unpubd).
21 *Pikiran Rakyat* (August 20, 2003), 'Polda Gelar Penataran Terpadu Bagi Wartawan'; *Pikiran Rakyat* (August 21, 2003), 'Manajemen Informasi tak Baik, Rugikan Polri'.
22 This will be discussed in the next sections of this chapter.
23 See Hasbullah and Rauf (2010); Suwarni (2009).

11 The police budget and extortion

> When we support the local police office with our money, it means that the police will protect and secure our business, or at least they do not disturb our property and its activities.
> (A businessman who runs a couple of nightclubs in West Java, 2010)

Innovations by heads of local police

It takes innovation and creativity from the kapolres to anticipate funding shortfalls from the state budget. A number of kapolres reported to me that there are three ways to try to meet their needs and use the budget optimally.

The first of these is to make cross-subsidies in the existing budget.[1] As an illustration, the Polres in Bandung, Garut, Tasikmalaya, Ciamis, Cirebon District and Cirebon Municipality have different regional geographic and demographic characteristics.[2] However, their budgets from the Polri headquarters through the provincial West Java Polda are the same, based on an assumption of the possibility of an intensification of police operations in a number of existing police districts due to rampant crime.

In development, there are three types of Polsek under a Polres: Polsek type B1, type B2, and pre-Polsek. Type B1 police receive money beyond the regular budget, excluding salaries and office stationery needs, Rp.28 million per year; police of type B2 receive around Rp.22 million per year; and the pre-Polsek, in a new expanded sub-district police office set up as part of a new sub-district or a development of a police post in response to demographic and geographic changes, Rp.12 million per year. The amount for Polri operational costs is Rp.90–150 million per year for the Polres in West Java, where the budget has been mostly absorbed for the Reskrim operation.[3] However, except for Bandung Municipality, which is a Polres type A1, all districts and municipalities are type B1. So the budget that is received by Polres Bandung Municipality is much higher than those of other districts and municipalities, but still not more than Rp.150 million per year.

Based on geographical characteristics that are different for different types of Polsek, a re-allocation of the budget can be done by cross-subsidies; for example, the budgets for Polsek type B2 and pre-Polsek will usually not be used up completely, because their local crime level is not as high as those for type B1 sub-district police. So some of the budgets designated for pre-Polsek and type B2 Polsek will be used for operations at type B1 Polsek, with reference to the activities that are reported based on their data.[4]

The second way of meeting budget needs is to use the operational support funds (Dukop) for Polsek, Polres and Polda. These amount to Rp.1 million per month for a Polsek, Rp.30 million per month for a Polres, and Rp.90–150 million per month for the Polda. The use of this Dukop budget actually shows that police leaders at all levels must always be ready for when their staff and subordinates require funding beyond the operations budget. The interesting thing about the Dukop is that the budget must be used and does not need to be returned if it is not.[5]

The third way to ensure that budget needs are met is to accept donations from people involved in criminal cases. The principle established is that Polri, including Polres investigators, 'do not ask, but do accept when given'.[6] Some kapolres have dismissed this claim, arguing that the donations are destined for case handling and can be resolved with careful consideration, both from the investigators and the kapolres.[7] Usually, investigators say that the Polres has a limited budget, so the policy is to follow up cases involving sensitive issues, especially relating to stability and public order as a first priority, so the 'donations' are to avoid the donors' case being deferred or not started.[8]

This phenomenon can lead to the assumption that what is done is also part of an effort to cover the budgets needed for investigations that are not adequately provided for by the state budget. Although recognized as such by a number of leaders in Polres, the situation also tends to enrich them.[9] WDS, an investigator in a Polres within the research area, confirmed that the donations from the public related to case handling were not only on the initiative of investigators alone, but also on initiatives from members of the public or lawyers.[10]

The three participation schemes: community, friend, and mafias

Beyond these three ways, there are other activities that support the operational budget and personnel of the Polri, in the form of what is called 'participation': 'community participation' (Parmas), 'friend's participation' (Parman), and 'criminal or mafia participation' (Parmin). For an indication of the amounts involved in these, see Table 11.1. In their current form the three 'participatory assistance schemes' are vulnerable to misuse, because there are no accountability reports to the public.[11] This tends to open spaces for irregularities and corruption committed by leaders of Polsek, Polres and Polda because the schemes are not open and transfer donated money directly to the accounts of the leaders and not the institutions.[12]

From community participation, Parmas, there is a kind of comfort for community figures who gave money to the Polri in hope that the Polri will help them if they experience legal problems. This is where they believe a mutual benefit

Table 11.1 The contributions of the participation schemes to operational Polres budgets in West Java Polda post-disassociation

Type of participation	Sources	Amounts (Rp. million)
Community participation (Parmas)	Public, local business, small entrepreneurs	1–100[1]
Friends participation (Parman)	Night club and adult night entertainments	100–250[2]
Criminal or mafia participation (Parmin)	Gambling, prostitution, pimping and other criminal activities	300–500[3]

Notes
1 Interview on June 23, 2010 with a businessman in East Priangan; personal communication on June 24, 2010 with mid-rank officers of Garut, Tasikmalaya and Ciamis Polres.
2 Interview on June 15, 2010 with Neta S. Pane, a coordinator of IPW, Jakarta; interview on July 10, 2010 with Ferry (pseudonym), Bandung; West Java Police Watch (2008).
3 Interview on June 15, 2010 with Neta S. Pane, a coordinator of IPW, Jakarta; interview on July 10, 2010 with Ferry (pseudonym), Bandung; interview on July 2, 2011 with Febby (pseudonym), Cirebon.

has been established between local police leaders and community members who contribute and provide assistance, either in money or goods.[13] A local businessman in the areas of research revealed that each year he spent at least Rp.50 million per year to help Polres operations, and when business travel assistance and support to his local Polsek were included, the amount he spent could reach Rp.100 million per year.[14] The rewards for these donations were that the businessman, and his family and companies, were safe in their operations.

The participation by friends, Parman, is practised as a form of support from 'friends' to a kapolres to keep his operation running. 'Friends' of the police are usually obtained because of a potential mutually beneficial relationship. Usually, 'friends' of the kapolres are the owners or managers of adult night entertainment such as karaoke, massage parlours, bars or nightclubs. The relationship is a guarantee that such all night amusement activities are guaranteed and backed by local police leaders. The support ranges from Rp.100 million to Rp.250 million per year and depends on the size of the cities and districts.[15]

Criminal participation, Parmin, is conducted similarly to the Parman, but the difference is in the protected object. The Parman targets are legal activities and the Parmin are illegal, with the payments coming from the controlling managers of gambling, prostitution, pimping and other criminal activities.[16] The figure is almost certainly more than Rp.300 million per year in each of the districts and municipalities, except for Bandung Municipality, where the Parmin support to Polres is claimed to be more than Rp.500 million per year. According to Neta S. Pane, the police support budget from criminal activities in big cities is very big money, from around Rp.500 million up to Rp.2.5 billion.[17]

The illegal activities being protected were not limited to 'night businesses'. Febby (pseudonym), a businessman involved in 'illegal excavation type C' (Galian C) in Cirebon, stated that the transport of sand and soil without permission, which would likely damage the environment, has been protected. The money paid to Polsek and Polres to keep the trucks moving varied between Rp.3 million and Rp.5 million per day, depending on how many trucks were being used and the material transported.[18]

Meanwhile, aid from backing the gambling locations, prostitution and other related activities is closed information, but continues to flow every week or month.[19] Ferry (pseudonym), who acts as a connector between crooked police in Bandung and a number of nightclub owners, told a newspaper that the amount of money flowing from just one manager of gambling and prostitution into the pockets of police every month was at least Rp.20 million.[20] In Bandung there were more than 30 such places, which suggests that at least Rp.500 million per month was being spread to local police personnel and leaders.[21]

To date, no police leaders in Polsek, Polres or Polda have been arrested on accusation of the use of money from unofficial sources.[22] Instead, they have gained personal benefits to enrich themselves. But also in this context, the Polri as an institution and the personnel from Polri headquarters down to Polsek hvae been enabled to play their roles as law enforcers in the midst of budget constraints and an understanding of public law. This is where the real stakes for the Polri have come in, because the organization has been able to make its foundation more settled compared to when it was only a part of the armed forces. However, the public image of the Polri is like 'a dirty buffalo that walks slowly in law enforcement in Indonesia' (*Kerbau Kotor yang lamban dalam Penegakan Hukum di Indonesia*).[23]

Local budget support, mutual benefit and personnel welfare

Institutionally, local governments' support for their district police is more than just an institutional relationship; they also have shared interests in guaranteeing security and order in their territories. The Polres as an institution in charge of security can take initiatives in proposing a variety of needs and desired budget supports to local government which increases but doesn't double its budget from the state.

In contrast to the informal and largely non-legal budget assistance provided through the non-government sources used by the various levels of the Polri, the various types of assistance provided by the local government budgets in the form of operational support are susceptible to criminal graft by kapolres or Kapolda. In 2008, when Susno Duadji became Kapolda of West Java, he was suspected of graft in the West Java gubernatorial election of Rp.4 billion for personal gain.[24] In Cirebon District in 2007 there were cases of embezzlement over luxury cars involving Nurhadi, deputy kapolres. In his dissatisfaction, Nurhadi, who felt victimized by his kapolres, revealed all financial transactions and the alleged irregularities committed, such as weekly money deposits from the traffic unit of Rp.150 million used for personal gain by the kapolres.[25]

The flow of supportive operational budget funding from the local government also opens opportunities for kapolres to use it for personal gain. From 1999 to

2008 annual aids and operational grants from each local government have ranged between Rp.75 million and Rp.3 billion, with their disbursements in two patterns. The first was the proposal basis, in which the Polres was asked to make use of the budget from the local government. According to Bandung's deputy mayor, Ayi Vivananda, ever since he had been in that position, the budget absorption by Polres Bandung was never more than 75 per cent of the total amount allocated to it, so these funds must be returned to the Bandung government's Department of Finance.

The second pattern pays over a fixed fraction of the total annual grants and operation budget in regular instalments, such as every three or six months. In Ciamis, for example, the 2008 budget for its Polres was Rp.200 million, paid over to the kapolres at Rp.50 million every three months. In Cirebon Municipality, the total grant of Rp.300 million was also paid to its Polres in quarterly instalments. Similarly, when I was interviewing the Cirebon District bupati, Dedi Supardi, in the middle of the year, he mentioned that half of the Rp.1 billion that his government had granted to the Cirebon District Polres had still to be paid over.[26]

Kapolres provided three justifications for having these grants from their local government paid into a personal account, or to a Polres account but later transferred to a kapolres account. First, the funds are used to cover the shortage of operational funds and the Dukop of the Polres. With an average of Rp.30 million per month (AU$3,350), some kapolres claimed they did not have enough to cover the needs of the operational budget for all operations of their Polres.[27]

Second, it was done to replace a number of personal budgets used to cover the operational budget, where the existing budget and the Dukop are inadequate. In this context, the kapolres was forced to use his personal budget for operational purposes and then replace the amounts from various assistance payments from several agencies and organizations.

Third, the budget was used to provide welfare to members of other police units so, in that sense, the supplemented 'personal' budget is not being fully used by the kapolres for personal interests, but also for the welfare of his Polres personnel. However, based on my observations, it was not visibly obvious that some Polres provided better welfare than they had before. Another observation was in the Polres Bandung Municipality office. An administrative staff member, a senior NCO, had received some money from a person who needed driving licenses for himself and for his relatives. I asked the staff member why he was still breaking the law. He answered that only their leader becomes rich and prosperous; he and other staff members, especially the back office ones, were forced to be 'brokers' of driving licenses, because the welfare improvement promised by their leaders was not being realized.[28]

The fixer, the broker and the police

Based on the previous discussion in this chapter and that in Chapter 6, it can be recognized that the irregularities and unlawful practices that occur among police

152 Local police perspectives

at the local level are not much different from what happens at the national level. In general, practices of extortion and other illegal activities have the same motives: economic access and vertical mobility through both national and local levels.

Extortion and other illegal practices in generaly do not involve a potential payer acting alone, but often involve parties who directly or indirectly, internally or externally, facilitate, utilize, seek and ultimately make their livelihoods from assisting these practices. These third parties develop beneficial relationships between kapolres and the other parties concerned, such as local entrepreneurs and members of local political elites, as happened in my research area of six West Java districts and municipalities. For some of the payments involved see Table 11.2.

The 'fixer' in the context of law enforcement in Indonesia, particularly related to the Polres, is someone who is considered able to solve problems related to the police roles and functions, including through individuals such as leaders in the Polres who have influence in decision-making. The 'broker' has a similar role definition; the only difference is in the scope of their work. The fixer does more things related to big cases such as corruption, or abuse of power by leaders. The broker works on smaller cases related to the service, role, and function of police such as driving licences; vehicle registration or vehicle ownership documents;

Table 11.2 Tariffs for brokers in six Polres in West Java Polda post-disassociation

Service	Amount (Rp. thousands)
Creating/extending driving licence	125–750[1]
Extending registration and ownership papers (BPKB)[2]	300–1,000[3]
Clearing tickets and releasing impounded cars[4]	250–750[5]
Settling minor cases[6]	500–2,000[7]

Notes
1 Personal communications on March 5, 2010 with a brigadier NCO of Bandung Municipality Polres Office; on March 7, 2010 with Asep (pseudonym), a person who used a broker to issue and make driving licenses; on June 26, 2010 with a senior brigadier NCO of Bandung Municipality Polres Office.
2 Usually, a broker would take a fee of at least 25 per cent from the price. However, some brokers sometimes also asked prices from 'consumers' of more than 300 per cent of the price to arrange the issue of vehicle registration or vehicle ownership documents.
3 Personal communications on June 22, 2010 with Dede (pseudonym), a broker in Garut District Polres Office; on July 3, 2010 with Ronny (pseduonym), a broker in Cirebon District Polres Office; on July 3, 2010 with Mulkan (pseudonym), a broker user in Cirebon District Polres Office.
4 Depending on the vehicle type; for more expensive or luxurious vehicles, the fee for the broker would be higher than normal fees.
5 Personal communications on November 10, 2009 with Kamal (pseudonym), a broker in Cirebon Municipality Polres Office; on June 24, 2010 with Badru (pseudonym), a broker in Tasikmalaya District Polres Office.
6 Usually, a broker will take a fee of around 20 per cent from the deal price between a crooked police officer and a member of the public who has had a problem with the police.
7 Personal communications on July 3, 2010 with Ronny (pseudonym), a broker in Cirebon District Polres Office; on June 26, 2010 with a senior brigadier NCO of Bandung Municipality Polres Office; on November 10, 2009 with Kamal (pseudonym), a broker in Cirebon Municipality Polres Office; on June 24, 2010 with Badru (pseudonym), a broker in Tasikmalaya District Polres Office.

traffic fine tickets; and the settlement of minor cases such as village brawling and drug use, usually cases that have not yet been taken over by investigators.

Since the scope is smaller, players in the brokering business are more varied compared to the fixers, who are derived from the internal police, both personnel and civil servants, at the Polres offices, including retired policemen. Many of the external broker influences are from people who have good relationships with leaders and senior officers of the police. The number of fixers is not as many as the brokers at a Polres office. Fixers and brokers are known as 'Markus' (*Makelar Kasus*) or case brokers, pointing out personnel capable of making various efforts for the benefit of clients. The presence of Markus is more focused on the process of handling the legal matters of cases.[29]

The interesting thing about fixers and brokers is that they have unlimited access to the Polres, either internally or externally to it. Some of them even have desks and act as police officials, particularly in the Reskrim unit and the Lantas (traffic) unit. There is also a broker in the cafeteria, or in parking areas, or others who work part-time as hawkers near the Polres office, such as a broker for a special driving license, vehicle registration or vehicle ownership certificates. For some of the payments involved see Table 11.3.

Some fixers have a permanent desk, as they come to the Polres office daily, or at least a temporary desk prepared when they come to the Reskrim or Lantas units. Farhan, a fixer in the Bandung Municipality Polres, told me that accessing information makes the work easier. This person comes into the Polres at least two or three times a week to finish a client's case and to maintain good relations with the police officers in the Polres. Every time he comes to the Polres, there is a ritual of providing kickbacks (*menyangoni*) or just treats for the staff and Polres officers to keep his easy access to them when working on a case.[30]

Alfian, a police brigadier NCO, is also a broker in the Bandung Municipality Polres office. He told me that the fees earned from arranging driving licences had to be divided among his traffic unit office colleagues, and with other

Table 11.3 Prices of fixers for some services in six Polres in West Java Polda post-disassociation

Service	Amount (Rp. million)
Case trading in investigation unit	50–350[1]
Recruitment for police rookies and officers	50–300
Dealing with luxury cars	25–75
Arranging a meeting between local entrepreneur, politicians and Kapolres	10–30
Solving cases related to legal affairs	50–250

Note
1 Personal communication on June 15 and 18 and February 3, 2010, with Farhan (pseudonym), a fixer in Bandung Municipality; interview on June 20, 2010 with Askur (pseudonym), a fixer in Tasikmalaya and Ciamis Districts; personal communications on June 23, 2010 with Abdullah (pseudonym), a fixer in District Garut, and on June 30, 2010 with Alinurdin (pseudonym), a fixer in both Cirebon District and Municipality. These are also the sources for the other 'service fees'.

sections, including the head of the Lantas unit and also the deputy and kapolres through the head of the Lantas unit.[42] Alfian stated that if he is lucky, he may get Rp.5,000,000 per day, far beyond his monthly salary of Rp.1,500,000, assuming that the amount is a net income after the required division and passing on of the kickbacks.

The East Priangan districts of Garut, Tasikmalaya, and Ciamis have far fewer people than live in Cirebon District, Cirebon Municipality or Bandung Municipality. Their Polres kickbacks from providing driver's licences or vehicle registrations are therefore much less. A noodle peddler at one of these East Priangan Polres offices was enthusiastic when I asked him how to get a driving licence without the test and driving exam. He said that he could help and there were people in the office that could help the process faster. The fee would be between Rp.1 million and Rp.3 million for a driver's licence for a person who does not have local ID card.

In Tasikmalaya and Ciamis, there is a fixer who commutes between the two districts to complete and clean up various issues in the Ciamis and Tasikmalaya Polres.[32] The same thing was done by a fixer in Cirebon, who used to solve various problems in the Polres of both Cirebon District and Municipality.[33] This fixer is a person within the close circles of the two Polres and also has access to decision-makers in the provincial Polda and the Polri headquarters, who are usually old players and former members of the police.

The fixer Askur (pseudonym) also reported that one difficulty in handling cases as a fixer was negotiation with kapolres, who could always suddenly change tack. There were some kapolres who initially refused the proposed kickback, but with an intensive approach including asking the previous kapolres to lobby his current successor, they would look again at the matter. Nevertheless Askur admitted that many new kapolres assigned were initially assertive in their rejection only to increase their bargaining position in front of the fixer and of his subordinates in the Polres Reskrim unit. Finally they would look for money anyway.

Alinurdin, a fixer in Cirebon District and Municipality, was less successful in dealing with an APBD-gate case as delivered to him by a suspect from the PDIP. The suspect considered the previous fixer was trying to extort from him with his claims of needing more funds to be used as 'communication money' with the kapolres and the municipality attorney. It turned out that the case was processed to the courts. According to Alinurdin, another fixer in Cirebon, the suspect had chosen the wrong fixer. Therefore, the communication with the Cirebon Municipality Polres, municipality attorney, and even the municipality court was not good.

In Bandung Municipality, Farhan gets an income of up to hundreds of millions. One political case he handled was the alleged defamation of several Golkar Party members of the Bandung DPRD, the chairman of the Siliwangi Young Generation (AMS) and his colleagues in a youth organization under the wing of the Third Regional Military Command of Siliwangi (Siliwangi III Kodam), by a number of students and youth activists in the coalition of the

Society Against Crooked Politicians (Masyarakat Melawan Politisi Busuk – MAMPUS). Students and activists had some evidence that Bandung legislators had received bribes for building permits for the Hotel Planet.[34] Farhan saw the situation and arranged a bridge meeting between these offended legislators and Johnny Hidayat, chairman of AMS Bandung, with MAMPUS. There was finally a peaceful solution between MAMPUS in Bandung and the legislators. The Bandung Municipality Polres also approved the peace move in order to maintain security in Bandung because Johnny Hidayat, as chairman of the AMS, could have called on radical members who would fight against the students and youth activists.

Based on the above discussion, it appears there are similarities between the fixer and broker patterns in a number of the Polres. There are three patterns: being requested by the service user; being requested by service providers to service users; and offering services to clients and public.

In the first pattern, the fixer and broker are both known by the service user so the transactions between them and the service user are running simultaneously. The broker or fixer will respond to the desire and purpose of service users in a systemic process. In this first pattern, trust is the bonding factor between broker, fixer and service users. The fixer is more concentrated on keeping a good reputation in resolving problems of lawsuits. This pattern is found in almost all Polres in the six districts and municipalities.

Meanwhile, the second pattern is more of a mutual and beneficial relationship between fixer, broker and internal Polres. There are three possibilities why internal Polres staff ask a broker and fixer to work on the case: the need of personal kickbacks and operations; the suspect having already been targeted by Polres, the case involves rich people and it will be easy to exploit for Polres or personal kickbacks; or Polres requires intermediaries to express their demands, but not through lawyers.

In the third pattern, fixer and broker are relatively new and do not yet have a good reputation in handling cases. The third pattern is also in the context of handling political cases, with many people claiming to be fixers who are able to solve problems quickly and easily. However, since suspects have already spent a lot of money, old fixers such as Alinurdin do not ask for excessive fees. This, according to Alinurdin, is a cleaning process against fake fixers and brought back the good reputation of fixers in Cirebon, both District and Municipality; even the former member from the PDIP finally gave the money to Alinurdin in appreciation because he had taken over their case from the fake fixer and made the trial process easy.[35]

This chapter has described the role of third parties positioned as fixers and brokers who arrange mutually beneficial relationships between the Polri at the local level and parties with their own interests in the services and roles that the Polri can provide to them.

This chapter also claims that the corruption and extortion practices in the Polri at the local level post-disassociation have been increasing and widespread in all roles and functions of the Polri. Public supports for the Polri were being used not only for operational budgets, but also to personally enrich the officers and personnel themselves. However, the budget support of the Polri by various members of the public were considered by them to be in their own interest as they need to have their business or properties secured and protected by the Polri, as an institution or by its individual members.

Notes

1 Interview on June 22, 2010 with Eka Mulyana, deputy kapolres of Garut; interview on June 24, 2010 with Police Commissioner Ari Wibowo, deputy kapolres of Ciamis. See also *Tribun Jabar* (February 2, 2006), 'Kapolwil Minta Motor Dikembalikan'; *Tribun Jabar* (September 17, 2006), 'Kapolwil Ingatkan Kapolres Garut'.
2 *Pikiran Rakyat* (February 25, 2003), 'Polwiltabes Bandung Tidak Jadi Dihapus, Strukturnya Termasuk Polres Tipe A.1'. How kapolres cover a Polres budget in such districts and municipalities will be discussed further in a later section of this chapter.
3 Interview on June 22, 2010 with Eka Mulyana, deputy kapolres of Garut; interview on June 24, 2010 with Police Commissioner Ari Wibowo, deputy kapolres of Ciamis. Bandung Municipality Polres is a Type A1, which makes its budget different from those of the other districts and municipalities which are for fieldwork.
4 Interview on June 22, 2010 with Eka Mulyana, deputy kapolres of Garut; interview on June 24, 2010 with Police Commissioner Ari Wibowo, deputy kapolres of Ciamis.
5 Interview on November 9, 2009, with Indarto, deputy kapolres of Cirebon Municipality; interview on June 22, 2010 with Eka Mulyana, deputy kapolres of Garut; interview on June 24, 2010 with Police Commissioner Ari Wibowo, deputy kapolres of Ciamis.
6 Interview on June 13, 2010 with Police General (retired) Dr Chaeruddin Ismail, Bandung.
7 For example see *Pikiran Rakyat* (August 4, 2003), 'Polres Kuningan "Kandangkan" 24 Sepeda Motor dan 2 Mobil'; *Pikiran Rakyat* (August 7, 2003), 'Mahasiswa ITB "Bedah" Kinerja Kepolisian'.
8 Based on my observations and personal communications with several investigators in the Reskrim Units in all six Polres in my researched areas. They told me that with their limited budgets, the Polres had priority cases to be solved, such as drugs and terrorism, so that if the people needed their case to be solved quickly, the investigators just told them that Polres had a limited budget, and usually someone would give money to the investigator and ask that their case be solved sooner.
9 For example, *Pikiran Rakyat* (December 12, 2003), 'Ketua Kopas Dipanggil Polisi'. Compare this with *Pikiran Rakyat* (January 18, 2003), 'Hilangkan Jual Beli Kasus'; *Priangan* (July 23, 2008), 'Kapolres Tindak Polisi Nakal'.
10 *Pikiran Rakyat* (September 9, 2003), 'Polda Sita 941 Bungkus Roko Tanpa Pita Cukai'. Personal communication on July 2, 2010 with Karmin (pseudonym).
11 Public participation in budget support to Polres is never made accountable to the public. For more discussion on the public participation in support of the police in Japan, see Bayley (1978).
12 Interview on June 15, 2010 with Neta S. Pane, IPW Coordinator; Pane has argued that the Parmas is a form of illegal income for Polri officers, personally enriching them.
13 Interview on July 2, 2010 with Ferry (pseudonym); *Pikiran Rakyat* (August 31, 2003), 'Paguyuban Pengusaha Danai Ruang Tahanan'.
14 Interview on June 23, 2010 with a businessman in East Priangan; interview on July 2, 2010 with Ferry (pseudonym); for example, *Kabar Priangan* (July 3, 2008), 'LPPI dan Polwil Garut Gelar Pameran'.
15 Neta S. Pane was strongly certain that the Parman support is very much bigger than this. In Bandung, for example, Pane and his institution have surveyed and found that

Parman support was more that Rp.500 million per year (AU$55,560) and close to almost Rp.1 billion per year (AU$120,000). Interview on June 15, 2010 with Neta S. Pane, Coordinator of the IPW.

16 *Pikiran Rakyat* (January 23, 2003), 'Polres Ciduk 20 Preman, Ketahuan Sedang Mengutip "Uang Jago"'; *Kabar Priangan* (August 12, 2008), 'Pelaku Judi Digrebek Polisi'.
17 Interview on July 10, 2010 with Ferry (pseudonym). *Kabar Priangan* (April 28, 2008), 'Delapan Penjudi Diamankan Polisi'; *Kabar Priangan* (April 29, 2008), 'Lagi, 8 Penjudi Ditangkap'.
18 Interview on July 2, 2010 with Febby (pseudonym). In comparison with this see *Kabar Priangan* (April 24, 2008), 'Tiga Pengoplos BBM Ditangkap'; *Kabar Priangan* (April 28, 2008) 'Delapan Penjudi Diamankan Polisi'. Galian C is the exploitation of sand, stones and soil in some areas. These activities are illegal and damage the environment.
19 *Pikiran Rakyat* (February 5, 2003), 'Polda Jabar Pecat 12 Personel Polri'; *Pikiran Rakyat* (February 5, 2003) 'Dua Perwira Polda Diperiksa Provos'.
20 *Pikiran Rakyat* (September 3, 2003), 'Hotel-hotel Diduga Banyak Menunggak Pajak, Polda Jabar Harus Tangani Kasus Pajak'.
21 *Pikiran Rakyat* (September 5, 2003), '41 Polisi Dipecat tak Hormat'; *Pikiran Rakyat* (September 20, 2003), '40 Pengunjung Kena Razia Operasi Antik'.
22 *Seputar Indonesia* (December 16, 2006), 'Kapolresta Desak Perda No. 7 Direvisi'; *Kabar Priangan* (March 19, 2008), 'Ratusan Kendaraan Dirazia'.
23 Muradi (2009b), Chapter 7. Almost identical statements were made by Adrianus Meliala and Neta S. Pane when I interviewed them.
24 *Kompas* (September 29, 2010), 'Susno Didakwa Korupsi Rp.8.4 Miliar'. See also *Vivanews* (2010), 'Susno Disebut Nikmati Rp.4 Miliar Dana Pilkada', available at: http://korupsi.vivanews.com/news/read/180374-susno-disebut-nikmati-rp4-miliar-dana-pilkada (September 29, 2010). See *Kompas* (December 10, 2010), 'Kapolri Perintahkan Buka Kasus Susno'.
25 *Detiknews* (2010), 'Kejar-kejaran Warnai Penangkapan Eks Wakapolres Cirebon', available at: http://us.detiknews.com/index.php/detik.read/tahun/2007/bulan/10/tgl/06/time/040919/idnews/838658/idkanal/10 (September 29, 2010).
26 Besides supporting the daily operations of the Polres, the budget from the local government is also used to bribe superiors for promotion and education by Polres leaders; some use the money to enrich themselves, and some use it for pleasure activities such as gambling and sex.
27 The operational budget of Polres and the Dukop from INP Headquarters does not include salaries for personnel and officers of Polres; these are funded separately, with salaries being paid regularly every month directly into the bank account of each Polres personnel and officer. See previous sections of this chapter.
28 Personal communication on June 26, 2010 with a Senior NCOs Brigadier of the Bandung Municipality Polres; *Kabar Priangan* (June 6, 2008), 'Berdiri 2 Tahun, Primkopol Polreskab Untung 2 Kali Lipat'; *Kabar Priangan* (October 24, 2008), 'Wakapolwil, "Jumlah Polisi Harus Ditambah dan Kesejateraannya Ditingkatkan"'.
29 For more discussion of Markus in the Polri Headquarters, see Chapter 6.
30 Personal communication on June 15 and 18 and February 3, 2010 with Farhan (pseudonym).
31 Personal communication on March 5, 2010 with a brigadier NCO of Bandung Municipality Polres Office.
32 Interview on June 20, 2010 with Askur (pseudonym), a fixer in Tasikmalaya and Ciamis.
33 Personal communication on June 30, 2010 with Alinurdin (pseudonym), a fixer in Cirebon, both District and Municipality.
34 *Kompas* (October 25, 2008), 'Caleg Ramai-ramai Lapor Polisi'.
35 Interview on July 2, 2010 with Mustopha, a PDIP Member of Cirebon District DPRD.

Conclusion

Disassociation and reform – the position and relationships of the police in post-Suharto Indonesia

> The images of the Polri post-disassociation from the ABRI are like a dirty buffalo that walks slowly in law enforcement in Indonesia.
>
> (Meliala 2009)

This conclusion summarizes the analyses, findings and implications of the study of the Polri at both local and national levels during and since its disassociation from the Indonesian military, after what had been a long-term military regime.

The book has examined the role of the Polri in the fall of this regime with the emergence of the widespread movement for democratization and decentralization. Importantly, this movement included pressures for the disassociation of the police from the military and a new role for the Polri as the professional state institution for internal security, law and order.

In particular this book was intended to answer four questions: How was the disassociation of the Polri from ABRI carried out? What role has the Polri had in the processes of regime change? What general influences has the implementation of the *reformasi* policy of decentralization had on the post-disassociation relations between the Polri, national and local governments and the military? What internal Polri changes have occurred as results of the new disassociated, decentralized system over its first decade?

The national perspective

The police and the armed forces pre-disassociation

The Polri was powerless in deciding about its role and functions in law enforcement and internal security, as these decisions were controlled by policies within ABRI; the selection of police leaders at all levels was dependent on the mechanism of the ABRI Wanjakti and reliant on the blessing and policies of President Suharto and the Ministry of Security and Defence Affairs. At lower levels, the approval and recommendation for replacement of police leaders had to be from the local military commander.

Its subordinate relationship in the structure of the ABRI made Polri unable to perform a role and function as a professional and independent organization in law enforcement to uphold internal security. Intervention and cooptation inside the Polri made by the New Order regime were worse than those during the Sukarno presidency. During that period the leaders of Polri and the P3RI (Persatuan Pegawai Polisi Republik Indonesia – Indonesian Republic Police Officials Union) as a political support organization still kept some independence in the face of politicization by various elements, including steps to reposition the Polri in the fixed structure and as a tool of political power.

The end of armed forces control

As was shown in Chapter 2, the control and cooptation of the Polri by the ABRI started to slacken during the economic and political crisis that marked the fall of President Suharto's New Order regime. The loosening military control over the Polri provided for a political momentum in its top leadership not accepting being used as a scapegoat in the Trisakti case, which had triggered riots in several major cities in Indonesia before Suharto stepped down. However, these efforts towards some independence made by the Polri chief at that time, Dibyo Widodo, did not receive enough internal support, and he was sacked by General Wiranto, the commander of ABRI and minister of security and defence affairs, and replaced with Roesmanhadi, a subordinate member of Wiranto's own staff.

At first, during the Indonesia-wide turmoil under the temporary Habibie presidency, ABRI rejected suggestions of dismantling itself by disassociating the Polri from its integrated structure. However, Wiranto established his uncontested control and it was decided that ABRI would support the demands for democratic reform, the military and police would separate and both would become professional institutions with specified, limited roles and functions. These hurdles were considered to have been achieved and, in less than the two years, in 2000 under the Wahid Presidency, the Polri was moved to be directly under the president's office and out of the ministry, which was now restricted and renamed as the Ministry of Defence.

The Polri position on regime change

Potential moves from within the Polri to consolidate and to reject ABRI control had been weakened by opportunism and factions that compromised solidarity in supporting the reaction by Dibyo Widodo and Hamami Nata against what they saw as scapegoating by ABRI.

As a consequence of its subordinated position in ABRI, the Polri leadership lacked experience and confidence in negotiating its own interests with members of political elites and was thus not able to use the early political momentum of the *reformasi*. Moreover, due to its decades of structural entrapment within ABRI, the Polri had a history of having been unable to follow up and solve cases as it had been restrained by ABRI's concerns about 'security and political stability' and had also been involved in many acts of brutality. This had contributed to a poor image and opinions among the general public, inseparable from its mistrust and antagonism about the ABRI overall.

Political reform and a reluctant participant

This study suggests five factors behind why the Polri can be considered to have been a reluctant participant in the political reform in Indonesia: a paranoid attitude to Polri-related change; a tendency to wait and see before taking advantage of the political situation; the use of another person's hand to achieve its objectives; a waiting to see the will of the ABRI, as its policy-making Polri supervisor; and an inability to follow the political dynamics.

The desire of the leadership in the Polri to conduct political acceleration also appeared in their attempts to use civil society to support their interests. Actually, these attempts were to keep the respect of some officials in the ABRI in recognizing and continuing discourses about the Polri reform after the fall of the New Order regime. It became a prominent strategy for the Polri in its efforts as an institution that encouraged and supported the political changes after Suharto fell, to help strengthen the political reform movement.

The disassociation of the Polri from the ABRI

As discussed in the Introduction, five models of police disassociation from the military have been described: through a political decision and decree; in a peace agreement between a government and rebels; from pressure from the masses and civil society; by a referendum or plebiscite; or in the issuing of new constitution which separates them. In the Indonesian context, this research found that the disassociation of the Polri from the ABRI was a combination of two models: by a political decree and from widespread demand from civil society.

The presence of mass public insistence urged the new regime to disassociate the Polri from ABRI. The willingness of the military to remove the Polri from rest of its own structure was due to public pressure and diverted public attention from the issue of revocation of the previous dual function of ABRI and its territorial command system. The new regime of Habibie and the ABRI leaders identified the Polri as being an integral part of the previous regime, and acted on this in utilizing the political momentum of the movement for *reformasi*.

The disassociation had four characteristics at the national level: it was advocated and supported by ABRI; it had a positive response from the new *reformasi* regime; there had been a strengthening of public discourse about it being a prerequisite of a professionalization of both the military and the police; and there had been strong public pressure for this. None of these involved much contribution from the Polri itself. The INP failed to take much advantage of the political momentum of either the fall of Suharto's New Order or the strengthening of the discourse of disassociation. However, in the end it drew only benefits from the political situation, including for internal personal opportunities, although it was still vulnerable to political interference in terms of interventions from the ruling regime.

The struggle for control: the military, president and parliament

As explained in Chapters 3 and 4, the end of military control over the Polri after 38 years did not mean the Polri was completely free from intervention and cooptation from other institutions. Although the Polri clearly stated that the disassociation from the ABRI gave it the momentum to be an independent and professional police, in practice the efforts of several institutions, especially the president and parliament as well as the military, continued to attempt to control the Polri for their personal interests. This began with President Wahid's steps, as he wanted to control the Polri to protect his precarious power.

This book found that the struggle to control the Polri post-disassociation arose from the three institutions: the military, the president and parliament. The motive was clear in the appointment of Chaeruddin Ismail as deputy chief and then as acting chief of the Polri, replacing the current chief Bimantoro, to secure his political policies against threats from the parliament after being rebuffed in this by the military, in spite of his offers of benefits, and then by Bimantoro. The military's motive was the desire to control the Polri again because, post-disassociation, military access to economic resources, formal and informal, was almost entirely switched to the Polri.

As was shown in Chapter 3, after Wahid was sacked from his presidency by the parliament, the president still controlled the Polri as it was under the presidential office. Moreover, although the parliament had the final decision on appointing a new Polri chief as it had the right to choose from the list of those submitted to it by the president, this was manipulated by the successive presidents, first Megawati and since then Yudhoyono, submitting only one name.

Public expectations of the Polri

The Polri post-disassociation was faced with public expectations of better roles and functions of the police, because the position of Polri was back directly under the executive authority, the president. However, over time, the Polri was seen to be committing irregularities and corrupt practices, such as trading cases, using supplementary budgets from local government for private interests, and extortion in the name of law enforcement. The public, especially those who had trouble with the law and police, tended to be used as objects of exploitation and were taken advantage of by arguments that the police operating budget was limited and required support from people who wanted to have their cases resolved.

The public also felt that post-disassociation the Polri did not show an improved performance. There were increasingly widespread practices of fraud, extortion and corruption relating to the police provision of public services in law enforcement and internal security and also in selecting cases that won the favour of power and wealth. The public saw the poor law enforcement and ineffectiveness of the police in providing service to the public. All services related to the role and functions of Polri were lowered in their quality by crooked police officers who took advantage under the pretext of inadequate budgets for police operations and welfare.

From military control to military influence: relations between the Polri and the military at national level

This book found different models of relationship between the Polri and the military at national and local levels, as will be explained below. Particularly at the national level there is a psychological bond that has not really worn off, and every step taken by the police tries to not offend or to avoid association with the military. At the local level, the police have a different approach to the relationship with the military. In addition, because the local military and police are led by a younger generation, the relationships at local level tend to be better than at national level: a more equal relationship.

The Polri has made good progress to reducing violent approaches in their roles and function between 1998 and 2008, as reported in Chapter 4. This is happening because of the Polri's internal determination to kick out military cultures from its organization by changing the educational curriculum and also changing rank names to use civilian terms. The military have tried to subordinate the Polri with disability issues within the roles and functions of the Polri in combating terrorism and corruption.

The relationship between the Polri and the military post-disassociation creates an interesting situation, characterized by the disassociation having been made but the institutions' cultures still being linked to each other, as was shown in Chapters 2 and 3. However, it also has similarities with the different relations of the Polri with national and local government. As described in the Introduction, there are four models of the relationship between the police and the military post-disassociation: control of the police by the military; military influence over the police; an equivalence relationship; and a professional relationship.

Free from the crocodile's lair but plunged into the lion's den: relations between the Polri and the government at the national level

As argued in the Introduction, relatively similar models of the relationships between the police and government can be applied in analysing these in the context of developing countries, in countries undergoing a transition to democracy, and in developed countries including those with well-established democracies. The major issues that distinguishes them are the level of politicization of the police and political intervention, with professional police in developed countries always under political authority, but not politicized. When government interests politicize the police in a country, it is assumed that they are not yet professional.

As described in the Introduction, there are four models of the relationship between the police and the government: professional; quasi-professional; equivalence; and interventions. This research found two different models at the national level and the local level in Indonesia. At the national level, it is one of interventions, where the Polri is vulnerable to intervention and the political interests of government. This reduced the bargaining power of the police with the government after the Polri was disassociated from the ABRI.

This book has also shown that a national police under civilian political authorities can be implemented in Indonesia, but that it is not yet free from politicization by government and the police have a tendency to take advantage for personal benefit and enrichment. The relationship between the Polri and the national government actually reflects a situation where the Polri as an institution has its role and functions within the field of internal security, and therefore could not be separated from the central government as the maker of national policies, of which the Polri is one of its implementers. At national level, the Polri has a weak position in relation to the government and parliament (DPR and MPR) and tends to be controlled, while at the local level, the Polri has a strong position in relation to the local government and parliament (DPRD), and is superior to other local institutions.

The relationship model that developed between the Polri and the central government led to other forms of intervention and the Polri was in a weak position against the government's efforts to utilize it as a representative of the ruling regime. The relationship model between national government and the Polri was likely to lead to a politicization of the police, with some degree of influence into it based on the desire of the ruling regime to exploit all the potentials of state institutions for its political purposes. There was a dilemma faced by the Polri; on one side there was an eagerness to escape from the shadow of the military by being disassociated from the ABRI, but on the other side, putting the Polri under the president's office was a rational choice in the midst of political change.

There have been three patterns of intervention in the Polri undertaken by central government: changing in leaders of the Polri; setting the budget for the Polri; and requiring Polri support for the ruling regime.

The interests of presidents ensured that, in the middle of discourses on the importance of professionalism and independence for the Polri, there was a strong spirit that encouraged presidents to intervene and control the Polri in various ways. By controlling the Polri's chief, presidents and the ruling regime would be able to make the Polri adhere to policies created by and aligned with the political will of the ruling regime.

Another issue raised post-Suharto about the pattern of government intervention in the Polri concerned the raising of the Polri budget. One of the reasons why Wiranto and Habibie kept the Polri under the minister of security and defence affairs during the transition period was because the government was not yet able to allocate enough funding for the Polri to be an independent institution. This was then used by President Habibie to raise the issue of the budget and welfare of the Polri.

164   Conclusion

The third pattern of intervention was to drag the Polri into publicly supporting the government. This step was carried out as part of the reflection on the transition to democracy in a country that had been ruled by the military. The tendency of civilian leaders, democratically elected, was to want to utilize the military and police as political shields to protect their power. Among all four post-Suharto presidents, the most obvious attempt to reinforce the Polri partisanship in government occurred in the period of President Wahid.

However, this book found five characteristics that reinforced these three patterns of intervention: a feeling of acceptance among post-Suharto presidents; a restriction on police independence in law enforcement; a strengthening of the Polri's internal conflict; a Polri attitude that tended to follow the will of the regime; and a political marginalization of the Polri.

As a result of intervention and politicization by the government, efforts to build the Polri as an independent and professional police were interrupted at both national and local level. Even after a decade, efforts to make the Polri focus on law enforcement seemed to still result in playing selected cases and avoiding handling cases related to the regime. This step ultimately positioned the Polri in a poor circumstance, where the desire to develop the focus of the Polri on law enforcement was blocked.

The fourth characteristic of the relationship between the Polri and the national government was a strengthening of internal conflict in the Polri. There were two attitudes within the Polri related to politicization by the government: against the practice, or accepting it as a political reality since the Polri was an institution under the president's office. The first attitude occurred only in the time of President Wahid, when the chief of the Polri, Bimantoro, rejected the attempted politicization of the Polri based on procedural reasons but violating the rule. Moreover, most of the Polri chiefs also felt that the support of the ruling regime was part of a politics of reciprocity and led to political favour, because they had been inaugurated as Polri chiefs.

The last characteristic of government intervention to the Polri was that its internal configuration tended to change following the ruling regime. This was one effect of the strengthening internal conflicts in the Polri. It was slightly different from the military, with the Polri staff tending to divide themselves into groups based on how the regime intervened. In the army, division and factions were based on political ideology, such as a nationalist faction or a Muslim faction, while the Polri tendency in its internal political configuring was more on the basis of attitude towards intervention and politicization by government.

Local perspectives

Rivalries and clashes: post-disassociation relations between the Polri and the military in local areas

The relationships between the Polri and the military in the six local areas studied tend to be more dynamic than those at the national level. This book found that the relationships built from the military influence led to equality. The relationship between the leaders of Polres and local military, the Kodim (Komando Distrik Militer – Military District Command), the Korem (Komando Resort Militer – Military Sub-regional Command) or the combat battalions was one in which the continuing military influence led to an equal relationship which had the negative effect of neither having enough authority over the other to prevent clashes between personnel of the Polres and the Kodim or the combat battalions, mostly over informal economic access and control and also competitive and combative *esprit de corps*, as was described in Parts IV and V.

In the six local areas there are three patterns that affect the relationship between the Polres and the local military: the relationship between the Polres and local leaders; operational assistance and other grants from local government; and the control of informal sources of income.

The first pattern relates to changes in the status of the Polri at the national and local level. The disassociation of the Polri from the military had consequential effects on the pattern of relations between the two agencies. The pattern of interaction between the Polres and local government was not only in official forums but also in informal forums about security and public order in such areas. Harmonious and mutual relationships in these, directly or indirectly, affected the relationship between the Polres and the Kodim or the Korem. In Bandung and Cirebon Municipalities, this pattern involved a strong influence on the relationship between the Polres and local military.

In contrast, in the more rural districts, especially in Ciamis District, their relationship was not good, with the Polres personnel being provoked into clashes with the local military. In the Garut, Tasikmalaya and Cirebon Districts, this pattern was much weaker but the Polres were still pressured from the local military especially over sensitive security issues, although overall the Polres in these districts had tried to be equal in relation to the local military.

The fund and operation grants from local budgets for the Polres could reach two times higher than those allocated for the Korem or Kodim, as was shown in Chapters 7 and 8. The differences in grants and operational assistance result in jealousy from the local military, given the fact that in the New Order era, local government assistance for the Polres used to be through the local military. This pattern has had a strong influence on the relationship between the Polres and local military in Bandung and Cirebon Municipalities and in Cirebon District due to the local governments' understanding of the situation, explaining to the local military and trying to support the personal needs of local military, as happened in both Cirebon Municipality and District.

However, in the East Priangan districts of Garut, Tasikmalaya and Ciamis, the pattern was just of an influence on the relationship between the Polres and local military because the local governments were still trying support the local military in what they wanted, even though less so than their Polres. This situation was not good because the local military, especially lower ranks and personnel, had felt that it was not fair. The situation in the three East Priangan districts was reported to be like 'fire under the husk'; although on top they looked fine and peaceful, especially in Garut and Tasikmalaya, jealousy had risen inside the local military due to the different standard of facilities given to the Polres.

The third pattern of influence on local Polri–military relations was in control over informal incomes. As was shown in Chapter 8, there was a change in control and management of informal financial sources from the local military to the Polres. This has emphasized that the authority of the Polres at local level is strong. Strengthening the Polres' existence concerns how to position them as a stakeholder in security, law and order. Therefore, the initiative of their respective leaders must be to share the power of control over informal financial sources, as was found in Cirebon, both Municipality and District.

In the East Priangan Districts of Garut, Tasikmalaya and Ciamis the competition to control informal incomes did not appear due to those areas having few night amusements, so there was no pattern to influence the relationship between the Polres and local military. In those districts, informal incomes came only from local business companies, which shared their support in similar amounts between the Polres and local military as 'public participation', in return having their businesses protected from extortion and other crimes.

Also, in the six local areas studied, three characteristics were found that reinforced the relationship between the Polres and the Korem or Kodim: the relationship between their leaders; acknowledging the limits to their respective roles and functions; and the rise of their *esprit de corps*.

First, the characteristics of the relationship between the Polres and the local military were influenced by the relationship of their leaders in all the areas except for in Ciamis. As was shown in Chapter 7, the leaders' relationship was influential, especially when it came from a closeness in Military Academy generations that would made their relationships easier in terms of equality and professionalism as they carried out their duties and functions.

Second, courteous recognition or acknowledgment of the existence of the Polres by the local military leader was important as a form of respect that marked the different roles and functions between those agencies. This was found in Bandung and Cirebon Municipalities and in Garut, Tasikmalaya and Cirebon Districts. However, in Ciamis, the local military leader was not adequately acknowledging the existence of the Polres.

The third characteristic influencing the relationship between the Polres and the local military was the rise of their *esprit de corps*. The high number of post-disassociation clashes between personnel of the Polri and the Military has marked this. Actually, a unit's *esprit de corps* reflects a good spirit, but can have a negative impact on practices, one obvious one being physical clashes between police and military units.

On the other hand, in some cases the *esprit de corps* unfortunately had become a negative spirit with the Polres personnel becoming arrogant, considering themselves as the only institution that understood the law and taking advantage of it, as was found in Bandung Municipality and Ciamis District. In those local areas, the ego and pride of the institutions collided with their roles and functions as security agencies.

Personal negotiations for mutual benefit: relations between the Polri and local government

This book found that, in the six areas studied, the model of the relationship between police and government was of equivalence leading to quasi-professional. This is because local politicians, both in the government and the DPRD, lacked knowledge about various legal instruments. There was a tendency to make contradictory policies and legal issues at the national level also apply at the local level. Because of this, the Polres tended to easily accelerate law enforcement, handling cases but using them for extortion and asking for kickbacks on the pretext of supporting operational costs and enriching themselves.

This book also argues that there was a synergistic relationship between the Polri's role and government's political interests at the national level, acting through the Polri headquarters to use the local Polres to arrest local politicians who had engaged in political abuses and opposes the national government. As was shown in Part IV, Polres were utilized as representatives in a variety of ways to ensnare a number of local leaders and members or former members of DPRD who did not support the government's policies at the national level, or who were members of a political coalition that tended to not abide by political agreements to support the current government.

The characteristic model of the relationship between the Polres and local government is in contrast to what happened at the national level. Unlike politicization at the national level, the politicization of the Polri in the six local areas studied was focused on the relationship between kapolres and leaders in the local government and DPRD. This was because the Polri and local government have no line of subordination between each other, and were not even in a common administrative hierarchy. Therefore the relationship between kapolres and local government was one of independence in an equality model leading to a quasi-professional one.

It was found in the six areas studied that the model of the relationship between the Polres and decentralized local government tended to be profitable for the Polres as an institution and for its individual members. These profits came in four patterns: reporting uses of budget to local government; rotation of kapolres; relationship between kapolres and local leaders; and 'case trading' in cases of corruption and political irregularities.

The first pattern exploited the existence of budget support from local budget and accountability for Polres operations. Although there were restrictions from central government through the Ministry of Internal Affairs, in reality, the support is still going. As was shown in Part IV, the desire of local government to support Polres operations is based on political motives including attempting to reposition the Polres under the coordination and political control of local government by providing grants and other funding to Polres but requiring their use be accounted for to the local government. This was not contradictory to the essence of the *dekonsentrasi* programme, which included adjustment of the Polres in the context of the overall decentralization policy in the sense that, in the six areas studied, whatever was done by kapolres did not conflict with the policy of *dekonsentrasi* or disturb the existence of the Polri in those areas.

There were two ways the Polres got support funding from local government: first, from the local government initiatives to invite the Polres to present its programme to local government which would then decide how much it would grant in terms of its own programme; second, from a Polres initiative to send its programme proposal to local government with a request for specified funding. Examples of the first model were found in Garut, Tasikmalaya, Ciamis, and Cirebon Districts, and of the second in Bandung and Cirebon Municipalities. There was also additional, more informal, support from local government providing Polres leaders with such things as 'coffee money' or personal accommodation when they were summoned by the Kapolda or had other out-of-town meetings. This happened often in the four districts but less in the two municipalities, as the Polres there had financial support from other sources such as night amusements or local business companies.

The second pattern in benefits from local government to Polres involved the replacement of kapolres. Even though this was under the authority of the Polri headquarters, the process may have affected the relationship between local government and the Polres. Besides the issues of community acceptance of a new kapolres, the pattern of relationships between local government and the Polres could be affected.

The third pattern was in the effect that replacing a kapolres had on his keeping a good relationship with the local government head in maintaining supports for the Polres programme hand in hand with the local government's programme. One point in this context was that kapolres and local government never knew when a kapolres would be replaced and reassigned. The pattern of reassignment and recruitment by the Polri headquarters and Polda are still based on the military system; the replacement system in the Polri generally did not provide reasons for when or why staff would be replaced or appointed.

Interestingly, different patterns and situations were found in the six local areas studied. In Bandung Municipality the changeovers did not influence the relationship between the Polres and local government, as open media and information access made the relationship between the Polres and local government tend to be professional. In Ciamis and Garut Districts the pattern was of neutrality, because the bupati and DPRD had assumed and understood that the replacing of kapolres or deputy is the right of the Polri headquarters and Polda, with the local government's role just one of coordinating programmes to secure its authority with the Polres chiefs.

In Cirebon District, the pattern did influence the relationship between the institutions. As was shown in Chapter 7, the bupati of Cirebon had complained about kapolres being replaced too often, but he had formulated a plan to control and coordinate with every kapolres in his territory. In Cirebon Municipality, the changeover pattern had a strong influence on the relationship between police and local government. The mayor and DPRD needed to be involved, or at least the

INP headquarters would ask them about what the public and local government wanted in terms of Polres leaders.

The fourth pattern in the relationship was about the handling of issues of corruption and political irregularities. In some contexts these gave opportunities for the Polres to gain profits, both institutional and personal. The Polres handled cases based on policy made by the Polri, but on the other hand, they mixed this up with national government interests demanding the trial process for graft and corruption cases involving DPRD members or local leaders, especially politicians from opposition parties.

The relationship was different in Garut District and Cirebon Municipality, where the cases had been shown off to the public and covered by national and local media. This happened because the relationships between the local government and Polres in the past had not gone well, and this continued while the Polres were handling the cases of APBD-gate, corruption and misuse of authority. Meanwhile, in Bandung Municipality there was not an influence on the relationship between the Polres and local government; each institution had been focusing in its own roles and functions, and stayed away from being involved due to media coverage and public access.

Studying these four patterns of politicization of the Polres provides a different perspective on what happened at the national level, in terms of the patterns and political bargaining of the various Polres. This reflects a strengthening of the Polri at the national level, especially on matters related to the roles and functions of the Polri in issues of corruption and political irregularities that made the political bargaining power of the Polres at local level more powerful than the Polri at the national level. To a certain degree, the Polres also control the local political situation for the institutional and personal benefit of the Polres, where the relationship between local leader and the Polres becomes a main issue in the relationship between the Polres and local government being based on equality and quasi-professionalism.

Related to the above context, there were seven characteristics of the relationships found between the Polres and the local government in local areas: adjustment to the decentralization of the Polri; Polres taking economic advantage; 'trading in cases'; character of local government; changes in local government attitude; internal configuration of the Polres; emerging of Polres internal conflict.

First, the adjustment to the decentralizing of the Polres caused the relationship between the Polres and local government to be taken more seriously by the Polri headquarters, based on the policies of *dekonsentrasi* and 'local boys for local jobs'. While the latter policy had been designed to apply to low-ranking policemen, in practice the policy had been also applied for Polri officers, with some modifications that allowed the officers from a different area to serve in strategic positions as district kapolres or sub-district kapolsek. This characteristic was found in all six local areas.

Adjustments were also made in the character of the Polres in order to facilitate personnel and kapolres to identify problems particular to the region, and so the Polres could more easily understand the characteristics of the area and coordination with local leaders would also be easier.

The two policies issued by the Polri headquarters – *dekonsentrasi* and 'local boys for local jobs' – were responses to two challenges faced by the Polres. First, government policies related to decentralization made the Polres as a hierarchical nation-wide institution align better with local political dynamics, where local government had been transformed into 'small kings' that could have caused complications for the Polres. Second, leaders and personnel of the Polres would hopefully build synergies between the Polres and social dynamics at local level. The desire to assign to the Polres officers who understand the dynamics at the local level was part of the reason for the 'local boys for local jobs' policy.

Second, in the context of the relationship between the Polres and local government, the Polres had taken profitable advantage of the relationship economically and politically. The profit was based on the awareness of the Polres that allowed kapolres to use the *dekonsentrasi* policy in the region to build independent relationships with local government. Based on this approach, many police officers were choosing strategic positions at the Polres rather than in the Polda or the Polri headquarters.

This characteristic was strong in Cirebon Municipality and all of the four districts, because there had been mutual benefits between their local governments and their Polres. In Cirebon, both District and Municipality, and in East Priangan District, Garut, Tasikmalaya, and Ciamis, the local government support budget provided annually had been taken from the APBD for the Polres in various ways. A different situation was happened in Bandung, where even the local government had been allocating budget in their APBD for the Polres, but it was hard for the Polres of Bandung Municipality to get their budget due to procedure in Bandung Municipality government. If the Polres needed the support budget, the Polres had to send the proposal to the local government, and if the proposal did not make sense, the local government would reject its proposal.

Third, the relationship between the Polres and local government was also based on a number of legal cases involving institutions and individuals. The 'trades in cases' were obvious deviant acts and were often based on two issues, corruption and political irregularities. The trading over cases involving local government figures was made possible by the Polres being above the local government structurally by having legal powers to arrest and prosecute, and culturally by having greater understanding of the laws that could be related to the cases.

Fourth, the relationship between the Polres and local government was influenced by the leadership characteristics of local leaders. If the local leader was a flexible person and understood the socio-political dynamics, kapolres could easily interact and attempt to maintain good relations through a variety of approaches. As was found in the six areas, two main types of characters appeared in local government leadership: flexible leadership and formal-militaristic leadership. The first type of local leaders tended to recognize the presence and significance of the Polres in their area and take formal or informal steps to embrace the leaders of the Polres.

In Bandung Municipality and the Garut and Cirebon Districts, this characteristic was strong. The first two were led by former army colonels, and in the third, the bupati strongly dominated the relationship between Polres and local government. In the other three areas, this characteristic was less apparent. In Cirebon Municipality, the vice-mayor was a former army colonel but the authority was still in the hands of the mayor, a politician of the PDIP (Partai Demokrasi Indonesia Perjuangan – Indonesian Democratic Party of Struggle).

Fifth, by definition the decentralization era was marked by strengthening local power and legitimacy. However, the local feeling of power and ruling the area usually did not last long, as it was undermined by an increasing number of local heads and members of DPRD being arrested in APBD-gate and corruption cases and for abuse of authority, with their cases being handled by the Polres, the local representative of a national agency. In this context, there was a change of attitudes in local leaders, who had felt powerful, suddenly becoming inferior in front of kapolres. The feeling of inferiority was based on poor knowledge and lack of capability in terms of legislative process and law. So the Polres carried out investigations into various alleged cases while at the same time frequently negotiating transactions to gain financial benefits.

In Bandung and Cirebon Municipalities and also Cirebon District, this characteristic was less apparent due to the local leaders having been able to control the Polres in various ways previously. The strong leadership of local government was very influential in changes of attitude towards them, especially in relation to their Polres. However, the opposite happened in the three East Priangan Districts, where this characteristic was clear; the changes in attitude happened there because the local governments had a lack of knowledge about the law and less political experience.

Sixth, the changes in attitude also marked the dynamics of local government and the internal configuration of the Polres. The political bargaining of the Polres had some impact on their internal dynamics. Some kapolres gave a fair part of the support funding from local government to Polres personnel in the form of welfare support. However, some kapolres had taken money from local government and done 'case trading' for their own interests. This triggered internal conflict between a kapolres and his deputy, or between Polres units such as the Reskrim unit and the Lantas unit and others such as Brimob and Polres administrative personnel.

This characteristic was strongly present in all of the six local areas. The internal tensions happened especially in the lower levels and units. Not every kapolres was involved. Particularly in Cirebon Municipality, Cirebon District and Bandung Municipality, dissatisfaction was rising among the lower levels due to their leaders never sharing the income from extortion activities.

Seventh, the strengthening of the position of the Polres had built internal conflict. In addition, a conflict based on the need for kickbacks to gain promotions and titles that occurred at the level of Polda led to conflict in the Polres because of differences in access to extra economic benefits. This was based on how kapolres managed and improved the welfare of their personnel. If kapolres had more interest in their own personal benefit, then they were more likely to be rejected and conflict would rise in their Polres.

This characteristic was also found to be strong in all six local areas. The differences were only in the actual extortion practices, with every single Polres having its own ways to collect money for their personnel to pay for the process of promotions and higher ranks through the Polda personnel bureau in West Java Polda. For example, in the Bandung Municipality Polres, the personnel tended to act for themselves rather than use brokers to collect the money from extortion activities, while in the Cirebon District Polres the senior brigadier NCOs as investigators chose to tell the people who report their cases to the Polres that his office had only a limited budget, so if you needed the case solved quickly, it would need money to cover the operational budget.

Budgets, corruption and extortion practices

This book found that the Polres in six local areas studied had been innovative and creative to anticipate budget shortfalls from their state budget through gaining additional funding from several other sources, which can be divided into six categories: support budgets from local governments; cross-subsidies in their existing budgets; use of their operational support funds (Dukop); accepting donations from people involved with crime cases; three types of funding participation from the public (Parman, Parmin, and Parmas); and practicing extortion, with or without third parties such as fixers or brokers. This book also found that the inadequate budget for the state and the welfare concerns of the local personnel were being used to justify the irregularities and illegal practices, both formal and informal: additional payments, extortion and other criminal or deviant activities involving parties outside the police such as brokers, fixers and other accomplices.

This book found that the third-party role of fixers and brokers had increased post-disassociation, to enable the newly available mutually beneficial relationships between the Polri at the local level and parties with their own interests in the services and roles that the Polri could provide to them. One of the indicators for the acceptance of these third parties was they had wide access inside the Polres and were being used as alternative approaches for the public who needed special service from the Polres related to its roles and functions. This book found that, post-disassociation, corruption and extortion practices in the Polri in the local areas studied had been increasing and spreading across all roles and functions of the Polri.

Disassociation and police reforms: the case of Indonesia

In this book, the process of disassociation of the Polri from the military and from its position in the post-Suharto era have advanced the prospects for independence and professionalism. This has been important as part of the government's and the public's *reformasi* agenda of a process of democratic transition, with the

Polri disassociation from the ABRI and freedom from political interference from the military and the government at national and local levels believed to be two preconditions of democratic and professional policing. However, this book has updated the study of police and politics in Indonesia. This book had two perspectives, national and local, related to the police and politics in post-Suharto Indonesia, so that it represents a more specific and comprehensive study compared with previous works.

Moreover, this book has shown that the characteristics of the relationship between the Polri and the government at national and local level ultimately also affect the interaction between the Polri and the military. This is a confirmation that at the national level, the Polri was often used by the regime to protect its power and occasionally experienced psychological pressure from the military. The decentralization policy and the politicization of the Polri was a tremendous shock experienced by leaders of Polres, who were given large and wide authority, not only formal but also informal. There were some negative effects of this internally, with an increase of internal conflict over problems of access to new economic advantages and to promotions, and the need to pay internal bribes and kickbacks.

This book also found that the Polri disassociation from the ABRI has had serious effects, both at national and local levels. At the national level, there have been policies and steps to reduce military involvement in some strategic policies, such as counter-terrorism and specific military roles in state defence. At the local level, one effect was the Korem or Kodim commanders being unhappy and feeling they now had different and lesser rights compared to the Polres on grants and aid for their operational support from local government.

This book has suggested the usefulness of a more extensive exploration of the police and politics in Indonesia. It has described the complexity of the process of disassociation of the Polri from the military as part of the democratization process and its impacts at local and national level between 1998 and 2008. In addition, the study examined previously proposed models of disassociation and the form and degree of political support for that process, with two of them fitting the Indonesian case.

More studies will definitely be needed. As explained earlier, this study was not intended to be a representative sample of Indonesia's whole geographical diversity. Each local area has its own characteristics related to leadership and relationship models and accesses to resources, and there could be characteristics of local police that are different from those in the sample of local areas of this study. This should be further explored, with this study's approach of detailed research into local areas replicated in other countries. The study can also become a basis for further similar research related to the police, politics and the military relationship in post-Suharto Indonesia as *reformasi* and other developments continue beyond the ten-year period covered in this book.

In spite of other local differences this applied in all the six areas, as did their police not having enough resources from the central government to adequately carry out all the responsibilities they had been given, so having to rely on the local government to support them. These common characteristics probably apply to all areas of Indonesia, but the extent to which they are modified or replaced by other local factors can be found out only by further studies elsewhere. It was found that West Java appears to be recognized within the Polri as a temporary stage for ambitious mid-ranking officers intending to seek further training and promotions. At the national level, this book has analysed the nature, pattern, characteristics and models of the relationship between Polri, the government and the military during the first decade of Indonesia's transition to democracy, and demonstrates how they differed from what has been found in other countries.

Bibliography

A Books

Abdul Gani-Knapp, Retnowati (2007). *Soeharto: The Life and Legacy of Indonesia's Second President.* Singapore: Marshal Cavendish.

Abdussalam and Zen Zanibar (1998). *Refleksi Keterpaduan Penyelidikan dan Peradilan dalam Penanganan Perkara.* Jakarta: Dinas Hukum Mabes Polri.

Aditjondro, George Junus (2006). *Korupsi Kepresidenan: Reproduksi Oligarki Berkaki Tiga: Istana, Tangsi, dan Partai Penguasa.* Yogyakarta: LkiS.

Ake, C. (1981). *The Political Economy of Africa.* Harlow Essex: Longman.

Alderson, John (1998). *Principled Policing: Protecting the Public with Integrity.* Winchester: Waterside Press.

Anderson, B.R.O.G. (1972). *Java in a Time of Revolution: Occupation and Resistance 1944–1946.* Ithaca: Cornell University Press.

Anwar, Dewi Fortuna (2002). *Gus Dur Versus Militer: Studi Tentang Hubungan Sipil-Militer di Era Transisi.* Jakarta: Gramedia Widiasarana Indonesia.

Anwar, Rosihan, K.H. Ramadhan and Ray Rizal (1997). *Kemal Idris: Bertarung Dalam Revolusi.* Jakarta: Sinar Harapan.

Aspinall, Edward, and Greg Fealy (eds) (2003). *Local Power and Politics in Indonesia: Decentralization and Democratization.* Singapore: ISEAS.

Azhari, Aidul Fitriciada (ed.) (2003). *Kesaksian di Tengah Badai: Dari Catatan Jenderal Purnawirawan Wiranto.* Jakarta: IDE Indonesia.

Badrun, Ubeidillah (2006). *Radikalisasi Gerakan Mahasiswa: Kasus HMI MPO.* Jakarta: Media Raushanfekr.

Bailey, John and Lucia Dammert (eds) (2006). *Public Security and Police Reform in the Americas.* Pittsburgh: University of Pittsburgh Press.

Baker, Richard W. (1999). *Indonesia: the Challenge of Change.* Singapore: ISEAS.

Bayley, David H. (2001). *Democratising the Police Abroad: What to Do and How To Do it.* Washington, DC: Department of Justice.

Beltran, Adriana (2009). *Protect and Serve? The Status of Police in Central America.* Washington, DC: WOLA.

Bhakti, Ikrar Nusa (2000). *Militer dan Politik Kekerasan Orde Baru: Soeharto Berada Dibelakang Peristiwa 27 Juli?* Jakarta: LIPI.

Bhakti, Ikrar Nusa (2004). *Relasi TNI dan Polri Dalam Penanganan Keamanan Dalam Negeri, 2000–2004.* Jakarta: LIPI-P2I.

Bienen, Henry (ed.) (1968). The *Military Intervenes: Case Study in Political Development.* New York: New York University Press.

Bittner, E. (1997). *The Functions of the Police in Modern Society*. Cambridge: Gunn & Hain.

Bruce, David, and Rachel Neild (2005). *The Police that We Want: A Handbook for Oversight of the Police in South Africa*. Johannesburg: Centre for the Study of Violence and Reconciliation, Open Society Foundation for South Africa, Open Society Justice Initiative.

Budiyarso, Edy (2009). *Melawan Skenario Makar: Tragedi 8 Perwira Menengah Polri di Balik Kejatuhan Presiden Gus Dur 2001*. Jakarta: Pensil-324.

Cahyono, Heru (1998). *Pangkopkamtib Jenderal Soemitro dan Peristiwa15 Januari 1974*. Jakarta: Pustaka Sinar Harapan.

Chrisnandi, Yudi and M.T. Arifin (2005). *Reformasi TNI: Persfektif Baru Hubungan Sipil-Militer di Indonesia*. Jakarta: LP3ES.

Cohen, J. and E. Baker (1991), 'US Foreign Policy and Human Rights in South Korea', in Shaw, W. (ed.). *Human Rights in Korea: Historical and Policy Persective*. Boston: Harvard University Press.

Conboy, Ken (2004). *Intel: Inside Indonesia Intelligence Service*. Jakarta: Equinox Publishing.

Cramer, James (1964). *The World's Police*. London: Cassell and Co.

Critchley, T.A. (1976). *A History of the Police in England and Wales, 1000–1966*. London: Constable.

Cribb, Robert (1992). *Historical Dictionary of Indonesia*. Metuchen, NJ: Scarecrow.

Crouch, Harold (1978). *The Army and Politics in Indonesia*. Ithaca and London: Cornell Uniersity Press.

de Fransisco, Gonzalo (2006) 'Armed Conflict and Public Security in Colombia', in Bailey and Dammert (eds). *Public Security and Police Reform in the Americas*. Pittsburgh: University of Pittsburgh Press.

Departemen Pertahanan dan Keamanan (1966). *Doktrin HANKAMNAS dan doktrin perdjuangan ABRI 'Catur Dharma Eka Karma': Hasil seminar HANKAM ke-i tanggal 12 Nopember s/d 21 Nopember 1966 di Djakarta*. Djakarta: Departemen Pertahanan dan Keamanan.

Diamond, Larry (1999). *Developing Democracy: Toward Consolidation*. Baltimore: Johns Hopkins University Press.

Djamin, Awaluddin (1995). *Pengalaman Seorang Perwira Polri: Awaluddin Djamin*. Jakarta: Pustaka Sinar Harapan.

Djamin, Awaluddin (2001). *Agenda Reformasi Polri: Pasca Sidang Istimewa MPR 2001*. Jakarta: PTIK Press.

Djamin, Awaluddin (2007). *Kedudukan Kepolisian RI dalam Sistem Ketatanegaraan: Dulu, Kini, dan Esok*. Jakarta: PTIK Pers.

Djatmika, Wik (2007). *Di Bawah Panji-panji Tribrata*. Jakarta: PTIK Press.

Djojoadisurjo, Ahmad Soebardjo (1978). *Kesadaran Nasional: Sebuah Otobiografi*. Jakarta: Gunung Agung.

Dwipayana, G. and K.H. Ramadhan (1989). *Soeharto, Pikiran, Ucapan, dan Tindakan Saya*. Jakarta: Citra Lamtoro Gung Persada.

Edwards, Charles (2005). *Changing Policing Theories for 21st Century Societies*. Annandale: The Federation Press.

Elson, Robert Edward (2001). *Suharto: Political Biography*. Cambridge: Cambridge University Press.

Erb, Maribeth, Priyambudi Sulistiyanto and Carole Faucher (eds) (2005). *Regionalism in Post Suharto Indonesia*. London and New York: RoutledgeCurzon.

Feith, Herbert (1957). *The Indonesian Elections of 1955*. Cornell University: SEAP.
Findlay, Mark (2004). *Introducing Policing: Challenges for Police and Australian Communities*. New York: Oxford University Press.
Findlay, Mark, S. Eggers and J. Sutton (eds) (1983). *Issues in Criminal Justice Administration*. Sidney: Allen & Unwin.
Finer, S.E. (1962). *The Man on Horseback: The Role of the Military in Politics*. London: Printer Publishers.
Goldstein, Herman (1990). *Problem Oriented Policing*. New York: McGraw-Hill.
Gunseikanbu (1943). *Orang Indonesia Jang Terkemoeka di Jawa*. Djakarta: Gunseikanbu.
Habibie, Bacharuddin Jusuf (2006). *Detik-detik yang Menentukan: Jalan Panjang Indonesia Menuju Demokrasi*. Jakarta: The Habibie Center.
Hadiman (1998). *Sosok Raden Said Soekanto Tjokrodiatmodjo: Melalui Spiritual Membangun Polisi yang professional*. Jakarta: Mabes Polri.
Hadiman and Suparmin (1985). *Kepolisian RI Sejak Proklamasi-1950*. Jakarta: GPM.
Handoyo, Aris (2003). *Managemen Securiti: Dasar-dasar Pengamanan dan Usaha Jasa Keamanan*. Jakarta: Elex Media Computindo.
Haramain, A. Malik (2004). *Gus Dur, Militer dan Politik*. Yogyakarta: LkiS.
Hardilani, Ahmad Hadi, Eki Agus Setiono and Bagoes Satrijanto (2003). *Maklumat Presiden RI 23 Juli 2001: Meluruskan Arah Perjuangan Reformasi dan Merajut Kembali Merah Putih yang Terkoyak*. Jakarta: ILUNI Jakarta.
Harsono, Irawati (2004). *Jejak Langkah RPK (Ruang Pelayanan Khusus)*. Jakarta: LBPP Derap Warapsari-Partnership.
Hasbullah, Abdullatif and Syarifuddin Rauf (2010). *Rapor Merah Polisi: Catatan Advokasi Dr Jazuni, SH, MH*. Jakarta: IPW.
Haseman, John B. and Eduardo Lachica (2009). *The US-Indonesia Security Relationship: The Next Steps*. Washington, DC: USINDO.
Hasibuan, Imran, Baskara Trisila and Heru Nugroho (2004). *Biografi Widodo Budidarmo: Semua Karena Kuasa dan KasihNya*. Jakarta: Praja Bhakti Nusantara.
Hasrullah (2001). *Megawati Dalam Tangkapan Pers*. Yogyakarta: LkiS.
Hendrowinoto, Nurinwa Ki. S. *et al.* (2007a). *Jenderal Polisi R. Soejipto Danoekoessoemo: Kapolri ke 3 Periode Tahun 1964–1965*. Jakarta: Panitia Penulisan Ensiklopedi Kapolri.
Hendrowinoto, Nurinwa Ki. S. *et al.* (2007b). *Jenderal Polisi Drs Hoegeng Iman Santoso: Kapolri ke 5 Periode Tahun 1965–1971*. Jakarta: Panitia Penulisan Ensiklopedi Kapolri.
Hendrowinoto, Nurinwa Ki. S. *et al.* (2007c). *Jenderal Polisi Anton Soedjarwo: Kapolri ke 9 Periode Tahun 1982–1986*. Jakarta: Panitia Penulisan Ensiklopedi Kapolri.
Hendrowinoto, Nurinwa Ki. S. *et al.* (2007d). *Jenderal Polisi Drs Moch Sanoesi: Kapolri ke 10 Periode Tahun 1986–1991*. Jakarta: Panitia Penulisan Ensiklopedi Kapolri.
Hendrowinoto, Nurinwa Ki. S. *et al.* (2007e). *Jenderal Polisi Drs Kunarto, MBA: Kapolri ke 11 Periode Tahun 1991–1993*. Jakarta: Panitia Penulisan Ensiklopedi Kapolri.
Hendrowinoto, Nurinwa Ki. S. *et al.* (2007f). *Jenderal Polisi Drs Banurusman Astrosoemitro: Kapolri ke 12 Periode Tahun 1993–1996*. Jakarta: Panitia Penulisan Ensiklopedi Kapolri.
Hendrowinoto, Nurinwa Ki. S. *et al.* (2010). *Polri Mengisi Republik*. Jakarta: PTIK.
Hill, Helen M. (2002). *Stirrings of Nationalism in East Timor: Fretilin 1974–1978: The Origins, Ideologies and Strategies of a Nationalist Movement*. Otford: Otford Press.
Hogg, R. (1983), 'Perspective on the Criminal Justice System' in Mark Findlay, S. Eggers and J. Sutton (eds). *Issues in Criminal Justice Administration*. Sidney: Allen & Unwin.

Hinton, Mercedes S. (2006). *The State on the Streets: Police and Politics in Argentina and Brazil*. Colorado: Lynne Reinner Publishers.
Honna, Jun (2004). *Military Politics and Democratization in Indonesia*. London: Routledge/Curzon.
Ismail, Chaeruddin (2001). *Reposisi Polri dan Otonomi Daerah*. Lembang: Sespim Polri.
James, Ann and John Raine (1998). *The New Politics of Criminal Justice*. London: Longman.
Jamin, M. (1946). *Tan Malaka: Bapak Republik Indonesia*. Djakarta: Moerba Berdjoeang.
Jenkins, David (1984). *Suharto and His Generals: Indonesian Military Politics, 1975–1983*. New York: Cornell University SEAP Program.
Jones, Sidney et al. (2004). *Reforming the Indonesian Police Mobile Brigade (BRIMOB)*. Jakarta: Partnership for Governance Reform in Indonesia.
Kahin, Audrey (1999). *Rebellion to Integration: West Sumatra and Indonesia Polity*. Amsterdam: University of Amsterdam Press.
Karnavian, Tito et al. (2008). *Indonesian Top Secret: Membongkar Konflik Poso*. Jakarta: Gramedia.
Kincaid, Douglas A. and Eduardo Gamarra (1994), 'Police-Military Relations', in L. Erik Kjonnerud (ed.). *Hemispheric Security in Transition: Adjusting to the Post-1995 Environment*. Washington, DC: National Defense University.
Kontras (2007). *Kilas Balik Kondisi HAM 2006: Hak Asasi Manusia Belum Menjadi Etika dan Peradaban Politik*. Jakarta: Kontras.
Kunarto (1997). *Tri Brata Catur Prasetya: Sejarah-Perspektif dan Prospeknya*. Jakarta: Cipta Manunggal.
Kunarto (ed.) (2002). *Merenungi Satu Realitas: Polri Dalam Cobaan*. Jakarta: Cipta Manunggal.
Kustiati, Retno and Fenty Effendi (2004). *Agum Gumelar – Jenderal Bersenjata Nurani*. Jakarta: Pustaka Sinar Harapan.
Lebang, Tomi (2006). *Berbekal Seribu Akal Pemerintahan Dengan Logika: Sari Pati Pidato Wakil Presiden Jusuf Kalla*. Jakarta: Gramedia.
Ledge, J.D. (2003). *Sukarno: A Political Biography*. Singapore: Stamford.
Lev, Daniel (2009). *The Transition to Guided Democracy: Indonesian Politics 1957–1959*. Singapore: Equinox Publishing.
Liang, His-Huey (1992). *The Rise of Modern Police and the European State System from Metternich to the Second War*. New York: Cambridge University Press.
Linz, Juan J. and Alfred Stepan (1996). *Problems of Democratic Transitions and Consolidation: Southern Europe, South America, and Post-Communist Europe*. Baltimore: John Hopkins University Press.
Lobe, Jim and Anne Manuel (1987). *Police Aid and Political Will: US Policy in El Salvador (1962–1987)*. Washington, DC: WOLA.
Lubis, Nina Herlina et al. (2000). *Sejarah Kota-kota Lama di Jawa Barat*. Jatinangor: Alqaprint.
Luhulima, James (2001). *Hari-hari Terpanjang Menjelang Mundurnya Presiden Soeharto dan Beberapa Peristiwa Terkait*. Jakarta: Kompas.
Mabes Polri (1959). *Manifesto Kepolisian*. Djakarta: Mabes Polri.
Mabes Polri (1965). *Program Perjuangan Takari*. Jakarta: Mabes Polri.
Mabes Polri (1987). *Biografi Jenderal Polisi R.S. Soekanto Tjokrodiatmodjo*. Jakarta: Sub-Direktorat Sejarah Direktorat Personil Markas Besar Polri.
Mabes Polri (1999a). *Reformasi Menuju Polri Yang Profesional*. Jakarta: Mabes Polri.

Mabes Polri (1999b). *Sejarah Kepolisian di Indonesia*. Jakarta: Mabes Polri.
Mabes Polri (2004). *Kajian Grand Strategi Polri Menuju 2025*. Jakarta: Mabes Polri.
Mabes Polri (2008). *Derap Langkah Polri Ditengah Dinamika Bangsa*. Jakarta: Mabes Polri.
Mabes Polri (2009). *Akselerasi Transformasi Polri Melalui Program Reformasi Birokrasi: Paparan Tim Kerja Reformasi Birokrasi Nasional Kepada Tim Kerja Reformasi Birokrasi Nasional*. Jakarta: Mabes Polri.
Mabes Polri (2010). *Kebijakan Operasional Polri 2010 untuk Mewujudkan Pelayanan Prima*. Jakarta: Mabes Polri.
Marshall, Geoffrey (1965). *Police and Government*. London: Butler & Tanner.
McCullough, Lesley (2000). *Trifungsi: The Role of Indonesian Military in Business*. Jakarta: ICG.
Mietzner, Marcus (2009). *Military Politics, Islam, and the State in Indonesia: From Turbulent Transition to Democratic Consolidation*. Singapore: ISEAS.
Misol, Lisa (2006). *Too High a Price: The Human Rights Cost of Indonesian Military's Activity*. Jakarta: Human Rights Watch.
Morris, Kenneth E (2010). *Unfinished Revolution: Daniel Ortega and Nicaragua's Struggle for Liberation*. Chicago: Lawrence Hill Books.
Muhammad, Farouk and Hermawan Sulistyo (eds) (2006). *Buku Putih Bom Bali: Peristiwa dan Pengungkapan*. Jakarta: Pensil 324.
Muradi (2004). *Pergerakan Politik Kaum Marxis di Indonesia: Kiprah Sjahrir dan Tan Malaka Dalam Pergerakan Nasional*. Jakarta: CEDESS.
Muradi (2005). *Berpijak Di Atas Bara: Kegamangan Politik TNI Pada Masa Transisi*. Bandung: University of Padjadjaran Press.
Muradi (2007). *Community Policing Sebagai Upaya Mewujudkan Polri yang Profesional dan Demokratik*. Jakarta: INFID – The RIDEP Institute.
Muradi (2008). *Evaluasi Kinerja TSTB TNI Dalam Pengambilalihan Bisnis TNI*. Jakarta: INFID.
Muradi (2009a). *Mau Kemana Brimob Polri?*. Bandung: Pustaka Sutra.
Muradi (2009b). *Penantian Panjang Reformasi Polisi*. Yogyakarta: Tiara Wacana.
Muradi (2009c). *Quo Vadis Brimob Polri? Menuju Polisi Paramiliter Profesional dan Demokratis*. Bandung: Pustaka Sutra.
Muradi (2010a). *Polri, Politik, dan Korupsi*. Bandung: PSKN UNPAD.
Muradi (2010b). *Polmas dan Profesionalisme Polri*. Bandung: LCKI – PSKN UNPAD.
Muradi (2011). *Dinamika Politik Pertahanan dan Keamanan di Indonesia*. Bandung: Widya Padjadjaran.
Muradi et al. (2007). *Metamorfosis Bisnis Militer: Sebaran Bisnis TNI Pasca UU TNI Diterbitkan*. Jakarta: The RIDEP Institution-FES.
Nasution, A.H. (1956). *Tentara Nasional Indonesia*. Jakarta: Jajasan Pustaka Militer.
Nasution, A.H. (1982). *Memenuhi Panggilan Tugas: Jilid I*. Jakarta: CV Haji Masagung.
Oudang, M. (1952). *Perkembangan Kepolisian di Indonesia*. Jakarta: Mahabrata.
Pane, Neta S. (2009). *Jangan Bosan Kritik Polisi*. Jakarta: Indonesia Satu.
Patebang, Edi (2000). *Konflik Etnis di Sambas*. Jakarta: ISAI.
Peluso, Nancy Lee (1992). *Rich Forests, Poor People: Resource Control and Resistance in Java*. Berkeley, CA: University of California Press.
Pemerintah Kota Cirebon (2008). *Profil Kota Cirebon Dalam Angka*. Pemerintah Kota Cirebon.
Poeze, Harry A. (1988). *Tan Malaka: Pergulatan Menuju Republik, Volume 1*. Jakarta: Grafiti Pers.

Poeze, Harry A. (1999). *Tan Malaka: Pergulatan Menuju Republik, Volume 2, 1925–1945*. Jakarta: Grafiti Press.
Poeze, Harry A. (2008). *Tan Malaka, Gerakan Kiri dan Revolusi Indonesia, Jilid I: Agustus 1945–Maret 1946*. Jakarta: YOI.
Pour, Julius (1993). *Profil Prajurit Negarawan*. Jakarta: Yayasan Kejuangan Panglima Besar Sudirman.
Pour, Julius (ed.) (1997). *Sudomo: Mengatasi Gelombang Kehidupan*. Jakarta: Gramedia.
Pour, Julius (2007). *Benny: Tragedi Seorang Loyalis*. Jakarta: Kata Hasta Pustaka.
Prihatono, Hari J. and Jessica Evangeline (2008). *Police Reform: Taking the Heart and Mind*. Jakarta: Pro Patria.
Rabasa, Angel and John Haseman (2002). *The Military and Democracy in Indonesia: Challenges, Politics, and Power*. Santa Monica, CA: RAND.
Ramage, Douglas E. (1995). *Politics in Indonesia: Democracy, Islam, and the Ideology of Tolerance*. London: Routledge.
Reid, Anthony (1974). *The Indonesian National Revolution 1945–1950*. Howthorn, Victoria: Longman.
Rinakit, Sukardi (2005). *The Indonesian Military After the New Order*. Singapore: ISEAS–NIAS Press.
Sage, Lazuardi Adi (2003). *Polisi, Politik dan Kontroversi*. Jakarta: Jakarta Citra.
Santoso, Aris *et al.* (1997). *Peristiwa 27 Juli*. Jakarta: ISAI-AJI.
Santoso, Aris *et al.* (2009). *Hoegeng: Oase Menyejukkan Ditengah Prilaku Koruptif Para Pemimpin Bangsa*. Yogyakarta: Bentang.
Sebastian, Leonard C. (2006). *Realpolitik: Indonesia's Use of Military Force*. Singapore: ISEAS.
Seskoad (1967). *Catur Dharma Eka Karma II: Second Army Seminar 1966*. Bandung: Seskoad.
Simanjuntak, P.N.H. (2003). *Kabinet-Kabinet Republik Indonesia: Dari Awal Kemerdekaan Sampai Reformasi*, Jakarta: Djambatan.
Sibarani, Santhy M. *et al.* (2001). *Antara Kekuasaan dan Profesionalisme*. Jakarta: Dharmapena.
Skolnick, J.H. (1966). *Justice Without Trial: Law Enforcement in Democratic Society*. New York: Wiley.
Soeriatmadja, Soeparno (1971). *Sejarah Kepolisian Tentang Pendahuluan dan Zaman Klasik*. Jakarta: PTIK.
Stepan, Alfred (1976). *Authoritarian Brazil*. New Haven and London: Yale University Press.
Suaedy, Ahmad *et al.* (2010). *Politisasi Agama dan Konflik Komunal: Beberapa Isu Penting di Indonesia*. Jakarta: the Wahid Institute.
Sumarkidjo, Atmadji (2006). *Jenderal M. Jusuf: Panglima Para Prajurit*. Jakarta: Kata Hasta Pustaka.
Sundhaussen, Ulf (1982). *Road to Power: Indonesian Military Politics 1945–1967*. Oxford: Oxford University Press.
Suprananto, Agung (2005). *Reformasi Manajemen Keuangan Polri*. Jakarta: Partnership.
Suryadi, Cecep (2002). *Benturan Ideologi: Arus Deras Gerakan Mahasiswa 1998*. Pekan Baru: Bahana Press.
Suryadinata, Leo (2002). *Elections and Politics in Indonesia*. Singapore: ISEAS.
Sutanto, Hermawan Sulistiyo and Tjuk Sugiarso (2005). *Polmas: Falsafa baru Pemolosian*. Jakarta: Pensil 324.
Suwarni (2009). *Reformasi Kepolisian: Studi Atas Budaya Organisasi dan Pola Komunikasi*. Yogyakarta: UII Press.

Syam, Firdaus (2008). *Berhentinya Soeharto: Fakta dan Kesaksian Harmoko.* Jakarta: Gria Media Prima.
Tabah, Anton (1991). *Menatap Dengan Hati, Polisi Indonesia.* Jakarta: Gramedia.
Tacconi, Luca (ed.) (2007). *Illegal Logging: Law Enforcement, Livelihoods and the Timber Trade.* London: Earthscan.
Tanumidjaja, Memet (1971). *Sedjarah Perkembangan Angkatan Kepolisian.* Jakarta: Departemen Pertahanan dan Keamanan-Pusat Sedjarah ABRI.
Tornquist, Olle (ed.) (2004). *Politicising Democracy: The New Local Politics and Democratization.* New York: Palgrave Macmillan.
Travis, Jeremy (1998). *Policing in Transition.* Budapest: Justice and Public Order.
Trijono, Lambang (2001). *Keluar Dari Kemelut Konflik: Refleksi Pengalaman Praktis untuk Perdamaian Maluku.* Yogyakarta: Pustaka Pelajar.
Turan, Achmad *et al.* (2000). *Jenderal Polisi RS. Soekanto: Bapak Kepolisian Negara Republik Indonesia.* Jakarta: YBB Polri Pusat – Karya Jaya.
Wardaya, Baskara T. *et al.* (2007). *Menguak Misteri Kekuasaan Soeharto.* Yogyakarta: Galang Press.
Welch, Claude E., Jr. (1976). *Civilian Control of the Military: Theory and Cases from Development Countries.* New York: State University of New York.
Wenas, S.Y. (2006). *Korp Brimob Polri dalam Aktualisasi.* PTIK Press.
West Java Police Watch (2008). *Data Bantuan Masyarakat kepada Polda Jawa Barat 2001–2007.* Bandung: WJPW.
Widjajanto, Andi (ed.) (2005). *Reformasi Intelijen Indonesia.* Jakarta: Pacivis UI.
Widoyoko, Danang *et al.* (2002). *Bisnis Militer Mencari Legitimasi.* Jakarta: ICW.
Wilson, Chris (2008). *Ethno-religious Violence in Indonesia: From Soil to God.* London: Routledge.
Wilson, Donald W. (1989). *The Long Journey from Turmoil to Self-sufficiency.* Jakarta: Yayasan Persada Nusantara.
Wiradihardja, Agus (1971). *Sedjarah Lahirnya Pandji-pandji Kepolisian RI.* Jakarta: Mabes Polri.
Wiwoho, B., and Banjar Chaeruddin (1990). *Memoar Jenderal Yoga.* Jakarta: Bina Rena Pariwara.
YLBHI (1994). *Laporan Pendahuluan Kasus Pembunuhan Marsinah.* Jakarta: Tim Pencari Fakta YLBHI.
Yunanto, S., Moch Nurhasim and Iskhak Fatonie (2005). *Evaluasi Kolektif Reformasi Sektor Keamanan di Indonesia: TNI and Polri.* Jakarta: The RIDEP Institute–FES.
Zachrie, Ridwan Jasin and B. Cavara Wiwanto (eds) (2010). *Memoar Jasin Sang Polisi Pejuang: Meluruskan Sejarah Kelahiran Polisi Indonesia.* Jakarta: Gramedia Pustaka Utama.

B Journal articles

Aditjondro, J. George (2005), 'Setelah Gemuruh Wera Sulewana Dibungkam: Dampak Pembangunan PLTA Poso & Jaringan Sutet Di Sulawesi'. *Position Paper* No. 03, Yayasan Tanah Merdeka, Palu. Central Sulawesi.
Barker, Joshua (1998), 'State of Fear: Controlling the Criminal Contagion in Suharto's New Order'. *Indonesia*, Vol. 66, October.
Bayley, David H. (1971), 'The Police and Political Change in Comparative Perspective'. *Law and Society Review*, August.

Bayley, David H. (1978), 'The Future of Social Control in Japan', *Pacific Affairs*, Vol. 51, No. 1.

Bayley, David H. (1992), 'Comparative Organization of the Police in English-Speaking Countries'. *Crime and Justice*, Vol. 15: *Modern Policing*.

Buzan, Barry (1997), 'Rethinking Security after the Cold War'. *Cooperation and Conflict*, Vol. 32, No. 1.

Carter, H. Marshal, and Otwin Marenin (1977), 'The Police in the Community Perceptions of a Government Agency in Action in Nigeria'. *African Law Studies*, No. 15.

Decalo, Samuel (1973), 'Military Coups and Military Regimes in Africa'. *The Journal of Modern African Studies*, Vol. 11, No. 1.

Hills, Alice (1996), 'Towards a Critique of Policing and National Development in Africa'. *The Journal of Modern African Studies*, Vol. 34, No. 2.

Hunter, Wendy (1998), 'Negotiating Civil-Military Relations in Post-Authoritarian Argentina and Chile'. *International Studies Quarterly*, Vol. 42, No. 2.

Jenkins, David (2009), 'Soeharto and the Japanese Occupation'. *Indonesia*, Vol. 88.

Kalmanowiecki, Laura (2000), 'Origins and Application of Political Policing in Argentina'. *Latin Americas Perspectives*, Vol. 27, No. 2, Special Issue: *Violence, Coercion, and Rights in the Americas*.

Kincaid, Douglas A. (2000), 'Demilitarization and Security in El Salvador and Guatemala Convergent of Success and Crisis'. *Journal of Interamerican Studies and World Affairs*, Vol. 42, No. 4.

Loader, Ian (1997), 'Policing and the Social: Questions of Symbolic Power'. *The British Journal of Sociology*, Vol. 48, No. 1.

Marenin, Otwin (1982), 'Policing African States: Toward a Critique'. *Comparative Politics*, Vol. 14, No. 4.

Marenin, Otwin (1986), 'United States Aid to African Police Forces: The Experience and Impact of the Public Safety Assistance Programme'. *African Affairs*, Vol. 85, No. 341.

McCulloch, Lesley (2002), 'The Silent Force of the Conflict in Aceh'. Paper presented at Asia Studies Association, Australia.

Meliala, Adrianus (2009), 'Police as Military: Indonesia's Experience'. Available at: www.emeraldinsight.com/Insight/ViewContentServlet?Filename=Published/Emerald-FullTextArticle/Articles/1810240309.html.

Meyer, Maureen and Roger Atwood (2007), 'Reforming the Ranks: Drug-Related Violence and the Need for Police Reform in Mexico'. *Position Paper*. Washington: WOLA, June 29.

Moon, Byongook (2004), 'The Politicization of Police in South Korea: A Critical Review'. *Policing: An International Journal of Police Strategies and Management*, Vol. 27, No. 1.

Mueller, Gerhard O.W., Wilhelm Kruger and Thomas Buergenthal (1960), 'The Meeting of Two Police Ideas: Anglo-German Experiments in West Germany'. *The Journal of Criminal Law, Criminology, and Police Science*, Vol. 51, No. 2.

Muradi (2006*i*), 'Mereduksi Budaya Militerisme Dalam Pendidikan Polri'. *Journal of SESPIM*.

Muradi (2006*ii*), 'Tantangan Dalam Reformasi Sektor Pertahanan dan Keamanan Indonesia'. *Journal of Pacis*, Department of International Relations, Catholic University of Parahyangan, Bandung.

Muradi (2007*i*), 'Brimob Polri dan Kamdagri'. *Journal of SESPIM*.

Muradi (2007*ii*), 'Penantian yang Panjang: Reformasi Polri Menuju Perpolisian Demokratik'. *Journal of Governance, Research Institution of University of Padjadjaran*, Vol. 7, No. 2.

Muradi (2007*iii*), 'TNI dan Polri: Analisis Tentang Penataan Kelembagaan Politik dalam SSR di Indonesia'. *Journal of UNPAD-UKM SKIM 2007*.

Muradi (2008), 'Peranan Densus 88 AT Dalam Pengamanan Pemilu dan Pilkada'. *Journal of SESPIM*.

Muradi (2009*i*), 'Densus 88 AT: The Role and the Problem of Coordination on Counter-terrorism in Indonesia'. *Journal of Politic and Law*, Vol. 2, No. 3.

Muradi (2009*ii*), 'Indonesia's Police Force: Decentralization for Better Welfare'. Available at: www.rsis.edu.sg/publications/commentaries.asp?selYear=2008&selTheme=6.

Muradi (2009*iii*), 'Praktik-praktik Defense Offset di Indonesia'. *Journal of Analysis CSIS*.

Muradi (2009*iv*), 'TNI dan Polri Pasca Pemisahan: Analisis Tentang Penataan Kelembagaan Politik Dalam Reformasi Sektor Keamanan di Indonesia'. *Journal of University of Al Azhar*.

Muradi (2010), 'Polisi, Militer dan Politik: Model Pemisahan Kepolisian dari Militer'. *Jurnal Administrasi Negara UNPAD*.

O'Connor, James (1975), 'Productive and Unproductive Labor'. *Politics and Society*, Vol. 5.

Potholm, Christian P. (1969), 'The Multiple Roles of the Police as Seen in the African Context'. *The Journal of Developing Areas*, Vol. 3.

Rodrigues, Corinne Davis (2006), 'Civil Democracy, Perceived Risk, and Insecurity in Brazil: An Extension of the Systemic Social Control Model'. *Annals of the American Academy of Political and Social Science*, Vol. 605.

Sato, Shigaru (1996), 'The Pangreh Praja in Java under Japanese Military Rule'. *KITLV Journals*, Vol. 152, No. 4.

Seligson, Mitchell A. (2002), 'The Impact of Corruption on Regime Legitimacy: A Comparative Study of Four Latin American Countries'. *The Journal of Politics*, Vol. 64, No. 2.

Silvestri, Michael (2000), 'The Sinn Fein of India: Irish Nationalism and the Policing of Revolutionary Terrorism in Bengal'. *The Journal of British Studies*, Vol. 39, No. 4.

Skogan, Wesley G. (2008), 'Why Reforms Fails'. *Policing and Society*. Vol. 1.

Sulistiyanto, Priyambudi (2007), 'Politics of Justice and Reconciliation in Post-Soeharto Indonesia'. *Journal of Contemporary Asia*, Vol. 37, No. 1.

Tanner, Murray Scot (2000), 'Review: Will the State Bring You Back in? Policing and Democratization'. *Comparative Politics*, Vol. 33, No. 1.

Ulfelder, Jay (2005), 'Contentious Collective Action and the Breakdown of Authoritarian Regimes'. *International Political Science*, Vol. 26, No. 3.

Van der Kroef, Justus M. (1957), 'Instability in Indonesia'. *Far Eastern Survey*, Vol. 26, No. 4.

Wakeman Jr., Frederic (1988), 'Policing Modern Shanghai'. *The China Quarterly*, No. 115.

C Unpublished works

Jansen, David (2010). *Networked of Security in Indonesia: The Case of Police in Yogyakarta*. Doctoral thesis, ANU, Canberra.

Juandi, Erik (2009). *Interaksi Sosial Dakwah Jama'ah Tabliqh Dengan Masyarakat Sekitar*. BA thesis, Sriwijaya University.

Karisma, Tiara (2010). *Makna dan Reputasi FKPM Karang Pamulang Melalui Persfektif Masyarakat Karang Pamulang Kota Bandung*. BA thesis, FIKOM UNPAD, Bandung.

Kelana, Momo (2010), 'Pelaksanaan Tugas Satpol PP Dalam Persfektif Penyelenggaraan Fungsi Kepolisian di Indonesia: Bahan Masukan Guna Penyiapan Keputusan Bersama Kapolri dan Mendagri Tentang Pembinaan Tekhnis Profesi Satuan Polisi Pamong Praja'.

Muradi (2007), 'A Longing Journey: Police Reform toward Democratic Policing'. Paper prepared for International Student Scientific Meeting, UK.

Muradi (2008). *The Reform of the Mobile Brigade of Indonesia's National Police and Democratization*. MA thesis.

D Laws and regulations

Chief of Information Letter No. Pol.: SE/09/VII/2001 on authority of press releases in the INP (Surat Edaran Kapolri No. Pol.: SE/VII/2001 tentang Kewenangan Memberikan Pernyataan kepada Media di Lingkungan Polri).

Chief of the INP Decree No. Pol.: Kep/4/2010 on the INP educational system (Surat Keputusan Kapolri No. Pol.: Kep/4/2010 tentang Sistem Pendidikan Polri).

Chief of the INP Decree No. Pol.: Kep/5/I/2005 on the procedure of using state funding in the INP (Surat Keputusan Kapolri No. Pol.: Kep/5/I/2005 tentang Prosedur penggunaan Keuangan Negara di Lingkungan Polri).

Chief of the INP Decree No. Pol.: Skep/01/2001 on the new ranks of the INP (Surat Keputusan Kapolri No. Pol.: Skep/01/2001 tentang Kepangkatan Baru di Polri).

Chief of the INP Decree No. Pol.: Skep/30/VI/2002 on the establishment of the INP 88 special anti-terror detachment (Surat Keputusan Kapolri No. Pol.: Skep/30/VI/2002 tentang Pembentukan Detasemen Khusus 88 Anti Teror, Densus 88 AT). Law Anti-Terror No. 15/2003).

Chief of the INP Decree No. Pol.: Skep/737/X/2005 on the implementation of community policing (Surat Keputusan Kapolri No. Pol.: Skep/737/X/2005 tentang Implementasi Program Perpolisian Masyarakat).

Government Decree No. 29/2001 on INP salaries (Peraturan Pemerintah RI No. 29/2001 tentang Gaji di Lingkungan Polri).

Government Decree No. 58/2005 on the restriction of budget support for vertical institutions from the APBD (Peraturan Pemerintah RI No. 58/2005 tentang Larangan Memberikan Bantuan Anggaran Kepada Instansi Vertikal).

Government Decree No. 37/2006 on the restriction of budget support for vertical institution from the APBD (Peraturan Pemerintah RI No. 37/2006 tentang Larangan Memberikan Bantuan Anggaran Kepada Instansi Vertikal).

Joint Agreement between Chief of the INP and Minister of Finance No. 14/KMK.06/2005 on the changed basis of financial management (Perjanjian Kerja sama antara Kapolri dengan Menteri Keuangan No. 14/KMK.06/2005 tentan Perubahan basis Penyaluran dan Pengelolaan Keuangan).

Korps Brimob Polri (1992). *Pembinaan Korps Brimob*. Jakarta: Brimob Polri.

Korp Brimob Polri (2003). *Pendayagunaan Satuan Brimob Polri dalam Rangka Operasi Kepolisian Khususnya di Daerah Rawan GPK*. Juklak/OIR/III/2003.

Korp Brimob Polri (2005). *Upaya Peningkatan Pelayanan Publik Sesuai Dengan Standar Pelayanan Korps Brimob Polri*. Jakarta: Brimob Polri.

Law No. 13/1961 of the Republic of Indonesia on the Indonesian Police Force (UU RI No. 13/1961 tentang Angkatan Kepolisian Republik Indonesia).

Law No. 5/1974 of the Republic of Indonesia on local government (*UU RI No. 5 Tahun 1974 tentang Penyelenggaraan Pemerintahan di Daerah*).

Law No. 8/1981 of the Republic of Indonesia on the Indonesian Code of Criminal Procedure (UU RI No. 8/1981 tentang Kitab Undang-undag Hukum Acara Pidana, KUHAP).
Law No. 20/1982 of the Republic of Indonesia on defence and state security (UU RI No. 20/1982 tentang Pertahanan dan Keamanan Negara).
Law 1/1988 of the Republic of Indonesian on the amendment of Law No. 20/1982 on defence and state security (UU RI No. 1/1988 tentang Perubahan UU No. 20/1982 tentang Pertahanan dan Keamanan Negara).
Law No. 28/1997 of the Repubic of Indonesia on the Indonesian National Police (UU RI No. 28/1997 tentang Polri).
Law No. 22/1999 of the Republic of Indonesia on local autonomy (UU RI No. 22 Tahun 1999 tentang Otonomi Daerah).
Law No. 16/2001 of the Republic of Indonesia on foundations (UU RI No. 16/2001 tentang Yayasan).
Law No. 2/2002 of the Republic of Indonesia on the Indonesian National Police (UU RI No. 2 Tahun 2002 tentang Polri).
Law No. 3/2002 of the Republic of Indonesia on state defence (UU RI No. 3 Tahun 2002 tentang Pertahanan Negara).
Law No. 15/2003 of the Republic of Indonesia on anti-terror (UU RI No. 15/2003 tentang Pemberantasan Tindak Pidana Terorisme).
Law No. 32/2004 of the Republic of Indonesia on local government (UU RI No. 32 Tahun 2004 tentang Pemerintahan Daerah).
Mabes Polri. 1983. Keputusan Kapolri No. Pol. Kep/552/XI/1983. Tentang Likuidasi Satuan Brimob dan Redislokasi Kompi-kompi BS Brimob.
Mabes Polri. 1993. Himpunan Petunjuk Lapangan Polri bagi Satuan Brimob.
Mabes Polri. 1994. Pendayagunaan Brimob. Petunjuk Pelaksana Kapolri No. Juklak/08/V/1994.
Mabes Polri. 1999. *Reformasi Menuju Polri yang Profesional*. Jakarta: Mabes Polri.
Mabes Polri. 2002. Kep Kapolri No. Pol: Kep/27/IX/2002 Tanggal 20 September 2002 tentang Reformasi Brimob Polri.
Mabes Polri. 2004. *Kajian Grand Strategi Polri Menuju 2025*. Jakarta: Mabes Polri.
Ministry of Internal Affairs Decree No. 37/2010 on the restriction of budget support for vertical institutions from the APBD (Peraturan Menteri Dalam Negeri RI RI No. 37/2010 tentang Larangan Memberikan Bantuan Anggaran Kepada Instansi Vertikal).
MPR Decree No. VI/MPR/2000 on the disassociation of the INP from the ABRI (Ketetapan MPR RI No. VI/MPR/2000 tentang Pemisahan Polri dari ABRI).
MPR Decree No. VII/MPR/2000 on the roles the INP and the ABRI after disassociation (Ketetapan MPR RI No. VII/MPR/2000 tentang Peran Polri dan Peran ABRI Paska Pemisahan).
Presidential Decree No. RI. 131/ABRI/1968 on the inauguration of Hoegeng Imam Santoso and Tengku Abdulaziz as Chief and deputy Chief of the INP (Keputusan Presiden No. RI. 131/ABRI/1968 tentang Pengangkatan Hoegeng Iman Santoso dan Tengku Abdul Aziz Sebagai Kapolri dan Wakapolri).
Presidential Decree No. 52/1969 on the INP title change from Commander of the INP back into Chief of the INP (Keputusan Presiden No. 52/1969 tentang Perubahan nama Jabatan pimpinan Polri, dari Panglima Angkatan Kepolisian RI Menjadi Kepala Polri).
Presidential Decree No. 40/Polri/2001 on dismissing S. Bimantoro as chief of the INP (Keputusan Presiden RI No. 40/Polri/2001 tentang Pemberhentian S. Bimantoro dari Jabatan Kapolri).

Presidential Decree No. 41/Polri/2001 on the non-activation of S. Bimantoro as chief of the INP and his replacement by the acting of chief of the INP, Chaeruddin Ismail (Keputusan Presiden RI No. 41/Polri/2001 tentang Penonaktifan S. Bimantoro dari Jabatan Kapolri dan digantikan oleh Pelaksana Tugas Kapolri, Chaeruddin Ismail).

Presidential Decree No. 49/Polri/2001 on the dismissing of S. Bimantoro as chief of the INP (Keputusan Presiden RI No. 49/Polri/2001 tentang Pemberhentian S. Bimantoro dari Jabatan Kapolri).

Presidential Decree No. 77/Polri/2001 on the inauguration of Chaeruddin Ismail as acting chief of the INP (Keputusan Presiden RI No. 77/Polri/2001 tentang Pengangkatan Chaeruddin Ismail Wakapolri dan Pelaksana Tugas Sementara Kapolri).

Presidential Decree No. 70/2002 on the INP organization system (Keputusan Presiden RI No. 70/2002 tentang Struktur Organisasi Polri).

Presidential Decree No. 55/2006 on the etablishment of the National Police Commision (Kompolnas) (Keputusan Presiden RI No. 55/2006 tentang Pembentukan Komisi Kepolisian Nasional republik Indonesia).

Presidential Decree No. 28/2007 on financial support for INP officers (Keputusan Presiden No. 28/2007 tentang Tunjangan Jabatan bagi anggota Polri).

Presidential Decree No. 63/2008 on the implementation of the Law on foundations (Keputusan Presiden RI No. 63/2008 tentang Implementasi UU Yayasan).

Regulation of West Java Province No. 9/2008 on long-term development planning for West Java Province, 2005–2025 (Perda Provinsi Jawa Barat No. 9/2008 tentang Rencana Pembangunan Jangka Panjang Daerah Provinsi Jawa Barat 2005–2025).

Regulation of West Java Province No. 2/2009 on medium-term development planning for West Java Province, 2008–2013 (Perda Provinsi Jawa Barat No. 2/2009 tentang Rencana Pembangunan jangka Menengah Daerah Provinsi Jawa Barat 2008–2013).

Index

Page numbers in *italics* denote tables, those in **bold** denote figures.

ABRI (Indonesian armed forces) *see* military
Agum Gumelar 60, 61
Agus Supriadi 118, 127–8
Ahmad Syabbuddin Alwy 107
Ahwil Luthan 60
Ake, C. 4
Akpol (police academy) 28, *45*, 68, 70–1, 83, 141–2
Alfian (a broker) 153–4
Alinurdin (a fixer) 154, 155
Allies (post Second World War) 20–1
Amir Sjarifuddin 22
anti-terror capabilities 71, 86, 87–8
Anti-Terror Special Detachment (Densus 88 AT) 71, 86, 87–8
APBD (local annual budget) *see* budget
APBD-gate 86, 118, 126–7, 130; *see also* budget
Ari Wibowo 109
armed forces *see* military
Askur (a fixer) 154
Ayi Vivananda 144, 151

Bailey, John 5
Baker, E. 12
Bakorstranas 38
Bandung Municipality: budget 118, 119, 122n15, 147, 149, 150, 151, 168, 170; community policing 111; corruption 119, 129, *139*, *142*, 149, 150, 153–5, 169, 172; description of 108; fixers and brokers 153–5; kapolres, change of 168; and local developers 121n8; local leadership 171; military and Polres 109, 119, 165, 166; politicization in 129; promotion in *142*; protection business 119

Banurusman Astrosemitro 39, *45*
Bayley, David H. 5, 8, 11, 12
Beltran, Adriana 8–10, 12–13, 14, 123
Bimantoro, S. *45*, 56–63, 81–4, 161
Blue Book of the Polri 1, 42, 55, 67, 72
Book of the Indonesian Code of Criminal Procedure (KUHAP) 37
BPI (Central Intelligence Board) 28, 29
bribery 129, 138–9, 143, 155
Brimob 21, 22, 44, *45*, 72
brokers (makelar) 93, 95, 97–9, 152–6, *152*, 172
Bruce, David 5
Brunei-gate 57
budget: amounts 37, 69–70, 86, 147–8, 149–50, 151; APBD-gate 86, 118, 126–7, 130; and central government 163; and corruption 86, 94, 96, 118, 126–8, 130; cross-subsidies 147–8; Dukop (Operational Support Fund) 94, 96, 148, 151; and financial management 70; innovations 147–50, 172; and local government 118–19, 125–6, 150–1, 168–9, 171; meeting budgetary need 147–50; participation schemes 67–8, 148–50, *149*; shortfall 119, 137, 147–8, 150–1, 172; *see also* corruption; *individual districts and municipalities*
Budhiana Kartawijaya 109
Bulog-gate 57
business activities, police 99–102, *100*

calo *see* brokers
career paths 138–41
cartels 94
Carter, H. 12–13

case brokers (*makelar kasus*) 93, 95, 97–9, 152–6, *152*, 172
Catur Prasetya 67
Central Intelligence Board (BPI) 28, 29
Chaeruddin Ismail 58–63, 81, 93, 161
Ciamis District: budget 118, 128, 147, *149*, 151, 168, 170; community policing 111–12; corruption 128, 129–30, 154, description of 108; fixers and brokers 154; kapolres 117, 168; military and Polres 109, 165–6; politicization 128, 129–30
Cirebon District: budget 118, 147, 150, 151, 166, 168, 170; community policing 111–12, corruption 150, *152*, *153*, 154, 155, 172; description of 108–9; fixers and brokers *152*, *153*, 154, 155; internal conflict 143–4; kapolres 117, 126, 131n14, 143–4, 168–9; local leadership 171; military and Polres 109, 110, 165, 166; politicization 126; promotion in 140, *142*
Cirebon Municipality: budget 118, 127, 147, 151, 166, 168, 170; corruption 119–20, 127, 149–50, *152*, *153*, 154, 155, 169; dekonsentrasi 170; description of 109; fixers and brokers *152*, *153*, 154, 155; kapolres 124–5, 140, 170; local leadership 171; military and Polres 109, 119–20, 165, 166; politicization 124–5; promotion in 140; protection business 119–20, 149–50; role of Polri 112
civil society *see* public
closed politicization 13
Cohen, J. 12
combatant paradigm of the police 19–23
combined politicization 13
Command for Restoration of Security and Order (Kopkamtib) 36, 38
Committee of Ten 26, 33n54
communists 22, 26, 27, 28, 29
community participation (Parmas) 148–50, *149*
community policing model 69, 87, 88
community policing programme 111
companies, police 99–102, *100*
cooperatives 99–102
corruption: bribery 129, 138–9, 143, 155; brokers (makelar) 93, 95, 97–9, 152–6, *152*, 172; and business activities, police 99–102, *100*; categories of 94, 95; characteristics of 93–7, *95*; under Da'i Bachtiar and Sutanto 86, 87, 88; and decentralization 96; dropping of cases 129–30; in early years 36–7; external 94–7; extortion 36, *95*, 97, *100*, 102, 119, 137–45, 147–56; fixers 95, 152–6, 172; graft 127, 129, 150; internal 94–6; and internal conflict 96; justification for 172; kickbacks 95, 137–41, *139*, *142*, 153, 154, 171; KPK (Corruption Eradication Committee) 127, 128; levels of 96; at local level 96, 111, 118, 119–20, 127–30, *139*, *142*, 149–50, *152*, *153*, 153–5, 169, 172; models of 95, 97; participation schemes 148–50, *149*; patterns of 93–7, *95*; and promotion 138–41, *142*, 171–2; protection business 102, 119, 149–50; in recruitment process 138–41, *139*; and third parties 93, 95, 96–9, 152–6, 172; Wahid, President 57
Corruption Eradication Committee (KPK) 127, 128
counterterrorism 71, 86, 87–8
criminal investigation unit (Reskrim) 44, 45, 119, 153
criminal participation (Parmin) 148–50, *149*
Critchley, T.A. 4
cross-subsidies, budgetary 147–8

Dada Rosada 108
Da'i Bachtiar *43*, 44, *45*, 84–7
Dammert, Lucia 5
Dedi Supardi 110, 117, 126, 144, 151
dekonsentrasi (semi-autonomy) 88, 92n47, 96, 112, 167–8, 169, 170–1
democracy, transition to 5–14
democratic policing 5–6, 8
Densus 88 AT (Anti-Terror Special Detachment) 71, 86, 87–8
developing countries, and the police **6**, 6–14
Dibyo Widodo 39–40, 41, *45*, 159
disciplinary system 71
Djamin, Awaloedin 37, *43*, 44, *45*, *100*
DKP (Officers' Honour Board) 61, 82, 89n15
donations, towards the budget 148–9
Dukop (Operational Support Fund) 94, 96, 148, 151
Dutch police model 19–20

education, police 138–9, 141–3; police academy (Akpol) 28, *45*, 68, 70–1, 83, 141–2; University (PTIK) *45*, 70–1, 142–3

Edwards, Charles 4
Eka Mulyana 127
esprit de corps 166
ethics, code of 38, 67, 71
extortion 36, *95*, 97, *100*, 102, 119, 137–45, 147–56

Farhan (a fixer) 153, 154–5
finances *see* budget; corruption
Findlay, Mark 4
fixers 95, 152–6, 172
Forum of Local Leaders (Muspida) 109–10
friendship participation (Parman) 148–50, *149*
funding for Polri *see* budget

Garut District: budget 118, 127–8, 147, *149*, 168, 170; community policing 111–12; corruption 118, 127–8, *142*, *152*, *153*, 154, 169; description of 108; fixers and brokers *152*, *153*, 154; kapolres 127, 168; local leadership 171; military and Polres 109, 119, 165–6; politicization 127–8; promotion in 140, *142*
General Supervision Inspectorate (Irwasum) 73
Golkar Party 108, 109
good cop/bad cop 143
graduates, rivalries 141–3
graft 127, 129, 150
Grand Strategy of Polri development 72, 87
Group of Eight 60, 81–3
Guided Democracy Era (1959–65) 26–9
Gus Dur *see* Wahid, President

Habibie, President 40, 159, 160, 163
Hadiman, Dr. 142
Harkamtibmas (maintenance of public order and safety) 118, 125
Hasan, Mohammad 36, *45*
Hatta, Vice-President 20, 21
Hills, Alice 5, 7–8, 10–11, 12–13
Hindromartono 22
Hinton, Mercedes 9–11
historical context 19–30, 35–46
Hoegeng (Hugeng) Iman Santoso 35, *43*, 44, *45*
Hogg, R. 4
human resource issues: career paths 138–41; disciplinary system 71; local boys for local jobs 2, 71–2, 112, 169, 170–1; number of personnel 68–9;

police academy (Akpol) 28, *45*, 68, 70–1, 83, 141–2; promotion 46, 71, 81, 83, 84, 94, 138–41, *142*, 171–2; recruitment 44, *45*, 70–2, 94, 137–41, *139*, *153*; University (PTIK) *45*, 70–1, 142–3; women police 72–3; *see also* leadership of Polri
Hunter, Wendy 12–13

Iing Syam Arifin 117
Indarto 109
independence of police 6–8, **6**, 67–75; *see also* politicization
Indonesian Communist Party (PKI) 22, 26, 27, 28, 29
Indonesian Democratic Party of Struggle (PDIP) 55, 81, 108, 109
Indonesian Police Officers' Union (P3RI) 21
Indonesian Police Watch (IPW) 93–4
Intelkam (Security Intelligence Unit) 21, 111
intelligence units 21, 111
IPW (Indonesian Police Watch) 93–4
Irwasum (General Supervision Inspectorate) 73
Islamic police 143
Islamic preachers 112

Jakarta Stock Exchange bombing 56–7
Japanese occupation 19–20, 21
Japanese police model 19, 20

Kalmanowiecki, Laura 9–11
Kamdagri (internal security) 2, 35, 42
Kiayi (Islamic preachers) 112
kickbacks 95, 137–41, *139*, *142*, 153, 154, 171
Kodim (military district command) 109, 110, 116–21, 165, 166, 173
Kominda (local intelligence community) 111
Kompolnas (National Police Commission) 65n28, 73, 95
Kopkamtib (Command for Restoration of Security and Order) 36, 38
Korem (military sub-regional command) 109, 116–21, 165, 166, 173
KPK (Corruption Eradication Committee) 127, 128
KUHAP (Book of the Indonesian Code of Criminal Procedure) 37
Kunarto 39, *45*

Lantas (traffic unit) 153–4
leadership of Polri: clashes 26–9, 57–63, 68, 81–8; under Dutch rule 22; during Guided Democracy Era 26–9; during New Order Era 35–40; post-reform 81–8; recruitment pattern for 44–6, *45*; under Suharto 35–40; tensions within 26–9, 57–63, 68, 81–8; visible competition for 83
Legal Assistants for the Truth 82
Lemhanas (National Resilience Institute) 41
Linz, Juan J. 5
lobbying (for promotion) 140
local boys for local jobs 2, 71–2, 112, 169, 170–1
local government: and budget 116–21, 125–6, 150–1, 168–9, 171; and dekonsentrasi (semi-autonomy) 88, 92n47, 96, 112, 167–8, 169, 170–1; Forum of Local Leaders (Muspida) 109–10; and internal security 110–13; and kapolres 117, 124–5; and the military 109–10, 116–21, 165–7; and politicization of police 123–30; Polri's relations with 107–13, 116–21, 123–30, 150–1, 167–72; and post-disassociation police 107–10; 165–72; and role of the police 107–13; supports for Polri 116–21, 150–1; *see also individual districts and municipalities*

mafia participation (Parmin) 148–50, *149*
makelar kasus (case brokers) 93, 95, 97–9, 152–6, *152*, 172
Makmun Gunawan Sidik 126
Malari riots 36
Marenin, Otwin 4, 11, 12–13, 123
Markus *see* makelar kasus
Marsinah 39, 50n56
Megawati 40, 55, 81, 84–5, 86–7
Meliala, Adrianus 35, 158
menyangoni *see* kickbacks
military: Brimob 21, 22, 44, *45*, 72; disassociation from the police 8–14, *9*; disassociation from the Polri 41–6, 67–75, 109–10, 159–61; 173; and early Polri 1–3, 19–30, 36, 37, 38, 39, 46; Kodim (military district command) 109, 110, 116–21, 165, 166, 173; Korem (military sub-regional command) 109, 116–21, 165, 166, 173; and local government 109–10, 116–21, 165–7; and the police in developing countries 5–14, *13*; and Polres 109–10, 116–21, 165–6; post-disassociation relations with police 10–14, *13*; post-disassociation relations with Polri 44–6, 67–75, 162, 165–7, 173; and regime change 40–1
military model, and the police 20
minimum structure, rich implementation 72
Ministry of Internal Affairs 19, 20–1, 22, 24, 117
Ministry of Security and Defence Affairs 29, 41–2, 46
Mobile Brigade (Brimob) 21, 22, 44, *45*, 72
monitoring of Polri performance 73–4
Moon, Byongook 12
Muspida (Forum of Local Leaders) 109–10

Nasution, Gen A.H. 23
National Awakening Party (PKB) 55
National Police Commission (Kompolnas) 65n28, 73, 95
National Resilience Institute (Lemhanas) 41
Natsir, Prime Minister M. 24
Neighbourhoods Security System (Siskamling) 37
nepotism 83
Netherlands 19–23
Netherlands Indies Civil Administration (NICA) 20–1
New Order era 35–46, 93, 138, 159
NICA 20–1
Nield, Rachel 5
Nurhadi 143–4, 150

O'Connor, James 4
Officers' Honour Board (DKP) 61, 82, 89n15
ombudsman 73
open politicization 12–13
Dukop (Operational Support Fund) 94, 96, 148, 151
oversight of Polri 73–4, 95

P3RI (Police Officials' Union) 21
Pancasila 29
paradigm change 42–6, *43*
Parliamentary Era (1950–9) 24–5
Parman (friends participation) 148–50, *149*
Parmas (community participation) 148–50, *149*
Parmin (criminal or mafia participation) 148–50, *149*
participation schemes 67–8, 148–50, *149*

Index   191

PDIP (Indonesian Democratic Party of Struggle) 55, 81, 108, 109
personnel management *see* human resource issues
personnel, numbers 68–9, *69*
Petrus Affair 38
Pino 11
PKB (National Awakening Party) 55
PKI (Indonesian Communist Party) 22, 26, 27, 28, 29
Plan of Consolidation and Function (Rekonfu) 38
police (general): democratic policing 5–6; and democratic transition 8–10; in developing countries **6**, 6–14; and the government 13–14, *13*; independence of 6–8, **6**; and the military 5–14, **9**, *13*, 20; politicization of 12–13; post-disassociation role 10–14, *11*; professionalism 6–8, **6**, 10–11; role of in society 4–14, 42–4, *43*
police academy (Akpol) 28, *45*, 68, 70–1, 83, 141–2
Police Security Intelligence Unit (Intelkam) 21, 111
politicization of the police 6–8, 12–13, 26–9, 55–63, 85–6, 88, 162–4; by local government 123–30, 167
Polres (district police units): budget 116–21, 125–6, 147–56; corruption 137–45, 147–56; fixers and brokers 152–6; and internal conflict 137–45; and internal security 110–13; politicization of 123–30; relationship with local government 107–13, 116–21, 123–30; 150–1, 167–72; relationships with military 109–10, 116–21, 165–7; *see also individual districts and municipalities*
Polsek, types of 147
Polwan 72–3
Potholm, Christian P. 7, 10–11
Profession and Ethics Division (Propam) 71, 73
professionalism 6–8, **6**, 10–11, 13, 39, 42–4, *43*; process of professionalization 67–75
promotion 71, 94, 138–41, *142*, 171–2; Wanjakti (Police Promotion Board) 46, 81, 83, 84, 138
Propam (Profession and Ethics Division) 71, 73
protection business 102, 119, 149–50
PTIK (police university) *45*, 70–1, 142–3

public: expectation of post-disassociation Polri 160–2; monitoring of Polri 73–4
Purwokerto 21, 22

Radio Republik Indonesia (RRI) 62
recruitment 44, *45*, 70–2, 94, 137–41, *139, 153*
reformasi; defined 55
regeneration issues 46, 83, 85
Registered Security Guards (Satpam) 37, 69
Rekonfu (Plan of Consolidation and Function) 38
Reskrim (criminal investigation unit) 44, 45, 119, 153
rewards 71
RIS (United States of Indonesia 23–4
rivalries 55–63, 83, 96, 137–45, 164–6
Roesmanhadi 40, 41, 42, *43*, *45*, 56, 83
Rusdihardjo *45*, 56–7, 63n3, 83
RW police 111, 112

'salutation from the windows' 140
Sanoesi, Moch. 38, *45*
Sartono Mukadis 81
Satpam (Registered Security Guards) 37, 69
Satpol PP (municipal police) 110, 126
Security Intelligence Unit (Intelkam) 21, 111
security partnerships 111
semi-autonomy *see* dekonsentrasi
September 1965 Movement 28–9
Siskamling (Neighbourhoods Security System) 37
Sjahrir, Sutan 21, 22
Small Structure, Rich Functions policy 112
Soedjarwo, Anton 38
Soekanto, R.S. 21, 22, 23, 26–7, *43*, *45*
Soekarno Djojonegoro 26, 27, 28, *43*, *45*
Soemarto, Deputy Chief 22
Soetarto, Police Brigadier General 27, 28, 44
Soetjipto Danoekoesoemo 27–8
Soetjipto Joedodihardjo 28, 29, 44
Sofjan Jacoeb 41, 61, 81
Stepan, Alfred 5
stock exchange bombing 56–7
structure of Polri 72, 112
Struggle Programme 28
Suharto, Maj-Gen 29, 35–46
Suharto, Tommy 56–7
Sukarno 19–30, 43
Sukiman Wirjosandjojo 24
Sunaryo 109–10, 125
supervision of Polri 73–4, 95

surveillance inspectorates 73–4
Susno Duadji 150
Sutanto *43*, 44, *45*, 85, 86, 87–8, 90n31, *100*, 104n27
Syamsul Bahri 143–4

Takari Struggle Programme 44
Tanjung Priok tragedy 38
Tanner, Murray Scot 8
Tanuhandaru, Monica 138
Tasikmalaya District: budget 118, 128, 129, 147, *149*, 168, 170; community policing 111–12; corruption 128; 129, *142*, *152*, *153*, 154; description of 108; fixers and brokers *152*, *153*, 154; military and Polres 109, 119, 165–6; politicization 128, 129; promotion in 140, *142*
terrorism 71, 86, 87–8
trades in cases 129–30, 170
training: Akpol (police academy) 28, *45*, 68, 70–1, 83, 141–2; PTIK (police university) *45*, 70–1, 142–3

Travis, Jeremy 5
Trisakti Case 40, 41

United States of Indonesia (RIS) 23–4
University (PTIK) *45*, 70–1, 142–3

vertical mobility 26, 62, 144

Wahid, President 55–63, 75, 83, 85, 161, 164
Wanjakti (Police Promotion Board) 46, 81, 83, 84, 138
Wiatrowski 11
Widodo Budidarmo 36–7, *45*
Wilopo 24
Wiranto, General 42, 159
women police 72–3
Wowo Wibowo 127–8

Yogyakarta 21, 22–3
Yudhoyono, Susilo Bambang 85, 86, 90n31